A World Dream, the American Ideal -- For the Peasants, the People, the Planet

Daniel Lionberger

Published by Daniel Lionberger, 2020.

While every precaution has been taken in the preparation of this book, the publisher assumes no responsibility for errors or omissions, or for damages resulting from the use of the information contained herein.

A WORLD DREAM, THE AMERICAN IDEAL -- FOR THE PEASANTS, THE PEOPLE, THE PLANET

First edition. June 29, 2020.

Written by Daniel Lionberger.

Table of Contents

To my children and my children's children '...and beyond' (nod to Buzz Lightyear character from the 1995 movie, 'Toy Story').

While I dedicate this work to them, and all true Patriots to the American ideal, understand I remain ever dedicated to the continuance and furthering of the American democratic republic, and human development in general, and hope that they will always remain patriotic to the elusive American spirit, and cognizant of the need for bettering the planetary human and environmental condition, and its pursuit, ever striding towards their realization.

Foreword

By Hans Leuenberger

<u>Swiss Peasant War in 1653</u>

<u>and Governmental Suppression of Democratic Evolution</u>

Concerning Vindication of the Insurgents of 1653

Summary

The contents of this chapter is based on the article[1] "Niklaus Leuenberger, Predating Gandhi in 1653?" published in the February 2020 issue of the Swiss American Historical Society Review. The topic and the events are not specifically linked to Switzerland. Thus, the events could take place anywhere at any time in the history of mankind with a similar script.

The key players are the camp of privileged people supporting the ruling party to stay in power and their subjects being exploited, suffering from injustice, etc. The driving force of the ruling party is greed for power and money, promoting injustice, corruption and division. No individual person, no member of a family, no business, no congregation, no corporation, no syndicate, no party, no community, no country is immune to this strong driving force, being as powerful as a viral pandemic infection.

The latter was the case of the Swiss peasants in 1653 realizing that the rights of their ancestors had eroded since the time of the founders (peasants) of the Old Swiss Confederation[2], who swore the Oath of Rütli in 1291[3]. At the Landsgemeinde[4] in Huttwil, Swiss peasants, who felt that their rights were lost, wanted to renew and update the Oath of the peasants in 1653 (Oath of Huttwil[5]) without toppling the current regime of representatives of the Swiss nobility[6].

The Landsgemeinde[4] is the original form of the Swiss democratic system before Switzerland adopted and adapted, as the only European country, in 1848 the concept of the American Constitution of 1787[7]. This original form complies with the Swiss Federal Constitution[8] and attracts a lot of attention during the execution of such as in the Canton of Appenzell[4].

In historical times the revolt of the peasants of the Canton of Appenzell was supported by the peasants of the Canton of Schwyz during the Appenzell War[9], fighting for more democratic freedom from the bishop prince of St. Gall[10]. Thus, the peasants from Appenzell became free citizens of the Canton of Schwyz and part of the Old Swiss Confederation[2].

The referenced article[1], published as mentioned in the February, 2020 issue, was inspired by the book of Ilya Prigogine[11] and Isabelle Stringer's "Order out of Chaos". This book shows that the same laws which govern nature are also valid in social sciences. Thus, unfortunately, according to the second law of thermodynamics, an originally democratic system is also subject to an aging process and entropy that respectively increases chaos. Fortunately, according to the same authors, there also exists in an open thermodynamic system far from equilibrium the law which is responsible for the creation of life in the organic world and of beautiful crystals of a higher order in the inorganic world.

Thus, from time to time the democratic system needs to be reinvented. This was the goal of the movement of the peasants in 1653. Niklaus Leuenberger and his fellow patriots enormously contributed to the future democratic evolution of Switzerland! Niklaus Leuenberger was an eminent personality and leader. His high moral standards and the discipline of his army besieging the city of Bern with 15000 armed peasants are legendary[1,12] contrasting with the peasant revolt in 1477 (Saubannerzug[13], hog banner campaign) which prompted the treaty of Stans[14] of 1481 as a first step to limit the freedom of the peasants since the secret message of Brother Nicholas of Flüe [1,15] was not published in the treaty. Shown in the contribution below, this message led to a peaceful settlement of the revolt in 1477 without punishing the peasants.

The support of Nicholas of Flüe in 1481 was kept in mind as part of the peasant's Tellemlied[16] (patriotic song)in 1653. Niklaus Leuenberger and his fellow patriots succeeded by besieging Bern in that the peace treaty of Murifeld[17] was signed by representatives of the government of Bern and the peasants without any bloodshed. This treaty of 1653 contains modern elements, how to get out from an economic depression and that the peasants with a lower income need to pay less taxes which is today an important point in the program of the Social Democratic Party of Switzerland[18]. The Swiss peasant war ended in 1653 after the attempted assassination of the governor of Lucerne by killing a member of the state council of Lucerne. One of the three Tells[19], Kaspar Unternährer, was the only known assassin in the history of the old confederacy[1,19].

Switzerland kept in mind the events of 1653 when after World War II a separatist movement campaigned for a secession of the region of Jura from the canton of Bern. Fortunately, there was no internal military suppression of a democratic evolutionary process and a peaceful solution was found in 1979 by the creation of the Canton of Jura[20] in compliance with the Swiss Federal Constitution. Thus, a bloody conflict between Protestant settlers originating from the Canton of Bern and Catholic residents in the Jura region having some parallels to the troubles[21] in Northern Ireland could be avoided.

References

[1]Hans Leuenberger, Niklaus Leuenberger, predating Gandhi in 1653? SAHS Review, 56,1 2020,64-93.

[2]Old Swiss Confederacy, see https://en.wikipedia.org/wiki/Old_Swiss_Confederacy

[3]Oath of Rütli (Rütlischwur): Summary of Friedrich Schiller, appendix 1 & https://en.wikipedia.org/wiki/R%C3%BCtlischwur

[4]Landsgemeinde, see https://en.wikipedia.org/wiki/Landsgemeinde

[5]Oath of Huttwil, see text below and appendix 2

[6]Swiss nobility, see https://en.wikipedia.org/wiki/Swiss_nobility

[7]Constitution of the United States 1787, see https://en.wikipedia.org/wiki/Constitution_of_the_United_States

[8]Swiss Federal Constitution, see https://en.wikipedia.org/wiki/Swiss_Federal_Constitution

[9]Appenzell Wars, see https://en.wikipedia.org/wiki/Appenzell_Wars

[10]Prince Abbot of St. Gall, see https://en.wikipedia.org/wiki/Prince-abbot & Abbey St. Gall, see https://en.wikipedia.org/wiki/Abbey_of_Saint_Gall

[11] Ilya Prigogine and Isabelle Stringers, *Order out of Chaos*, Bantam Books, Inc., 666 Fifth Ave., New York, New York 10103.

[12] Swiss Peasant War, see https://en.wikipedia.org/wiki/Swiss_peasant_war_of_1653

[13] Saubannerzug, see https://en.wikipedia.org/wiki/Saubannerzug

[14] Treaty of Stans (Stanserverkommnis), see https://en.wikipedia.org/wiki/Stanser_Verkommnis

[15] Nicholas of Flüe, see https://en.wikipedia.org/wiki/Nicholas_of_Fl%C3%BCe

[16] Tellenlied 1653 (patriotic song of peasants) see appendix 3 & https://www.youtube.com/watch?v=Kzu5TXh6xko

[17]Treaty of Murifeld, see text and complete version of appendix 4

[18]Social Democratic Party of Switzerland, see https://en.wikipedia.org/wiki/Social_Democratic_Party_of_Switzerland

[19]William Tell (the three tells) see https://en.wikipedia.org/wiki/William_Tell

[20]Canton of Jura, see https://en.wikipedia.org/wiki/Canton_of_Jura

[21]The Troubles in Ireland, see https://en.wikipedia.org/wiki/The_Troubles#

The Peasant War

The peasant war of 1653 can be subdivided in the following phases:

• *The beginning of the rebellion in the Entlebuch valley, Canton Lucerne.*

• *The massive popular revolt under the leadership of Niklaus Leuenberger, chairman of the "League of Huttwil," as of the signing of the Oath of Huttwil [Bundesbrief] with the aim of a renewal of the Oath of Rütli of 1291 [author's remark] through to the conclusion of the Murifeld Peace Treaty.*

• *The willful and unilateral violation of the Murifeld Peace Treaty by the government in Bern following the jubilant withdrawal of the armed peasants as defined in the treaty.*

• *The abatement of the rebellion by the Bernese troops (Battle of Herzogenbuchsee) and the Federal Diets' troops (Battle of Wohlenschwil) under the pretense that the rebels had no right to gather in assembly as declared in the Treaty of Stans.*

• *The persecution, torturing and conviction of the ringleaders which culminated in the quartering of leader Niklaus Leuenberger and in the compilation of an extensive list of rebels to be convicted.*

• *The assassination of Lucerne councilman Kaspar Studer (†1653) and the end of the rebellion in Entlebuch.*

Better understanding will be gained through a brief explanation of the contents of the Federal Diet of Stans and singular aspects of the six phases of the peasant war. The focus of the text, however, is the impact of leader Niklaus Leuenberger, from his formulation of the Oath of Huttwil to his dismemberment by the executioner in Bern.

The Federal Diet of Stans

"Fasnacht" in Lucerne and the Secret Message from Nicholas of Flüe (1417-1487)

On Shrove Tuesday [*Fasnacht*, pre-Lenten carnival] in February 1477 [5] in the city of Lucerne some 2,000 men from central Switzerland resolved to procure the missing payments which had been promised them as compensation for their having fought in the Burgundian wars. These men formed a "hog-banner campaign" [*Saubannerzug*] and marched towards Geneva. Interestingly, this peasant revolt happened 200 years after the first revolt against the Habsburg Empire in the 13th century. This incident caused a crisis within the confederation of the eight cantons, the independent small states in the Old Swiss Confederacy. Delegates of the eight governments therefore met in December 1481 as a Federal Diet [*Tagsatzung*] in Stans.

According to the Lucerne chronicle, it was a message from Nicholas of Flüe which led to agreement, even though the specific contents remain unknown. It is conceivable that Nicholas of Flüe, who had served as a judge and a member of Obwalden's government [6], himself demanded that his message be treated as strictly confidential.

Council from the Wise Nicholas of Flüe

Nicholas of Flüe was consciously aware that the general public would not accept a banning of Fasnacht. It may therefore be assumed that Nicholas of Flüe counseled the eight cantons of the Old Swiss Confederacy to not ban Fasnacht but to listen to the criticism from the public in order to avoid such insurrection.

"Ausburger" as Burghers of Bern and Burgdorf

Burghers of the cities of Bern and Burgdorf who lived in rural areas were designated as "*Ausburger*" [i.e., non-residential burghers] and in case of war had the right to seek protection behind the surrounding walls of the town. Through their privileges as burghers, this group belonged to the upper class of wealthy free peasants and were assured security and legal assistance from Bern and Burgdorf in case of disputes with a neighboring lord.

This situation of the cities with wealthy free peasants was a "win-win" situation for both parties. Within the framework of the expansion of the territorial sovereignty of Bern [*Landeshoheit*] regarding Burgdorf and neighboring rural areas, the "*Ausburger*" and their descendants, free peasants, played an important role as allies, as the "fifth column" of Bern.

This upper class of free peasants residing on the environment of Bern represented the backbone of the rural economy owning farms, grain mills, smiths, taverns, tanneries etc. These free peasants kept alive the economy, also, during the period of decline of the lords who were often knights in the service of the Habsburg Empire. In this context, it has to be kept in mind that the lower jurisdiction is an integral part of the bailiwick of the lord as long as this bailiwick does not belong to the city of Bern.

Power Causes Greediness for More Power

With the decline of the feudal system, the patrician families in the cities started to purchase territories of the lords, i.e. its bailiwick with its lower jurisdiction, along with their serfs. At the same time the city started to purchase the freedom of the families of serfs of a lord living in a specific territory.

At the same time, a consolidation of all subjects followed – ransomed serfs were recognized as equals to free peasants. Through this consolidation, the hardest hit of all subjects was the "fifth column" of free peasants ("Ausburger"), burghers of Bern and Burgdorf and their descendants, who owned free farms within territories of a lord. All subjects residing in the territories purchased by Bern were obliged to pay a new feudal tax. These free peasants were opposed to paying this tax and felt cheated by the city of Bern. The discontent was fueled by the fact that they were obliged to prove that they were not serfs of the lord but descendants of free peasants. This was, too often, denied.

Concerning the Wording of the Diet of Stans

RE: The Federal Diet in Stans: It makes sense that the proceedings from Stans remain silent about the secret message of Nicholas of Flüe. It only included phrases which could be accepted by all parties: *the ban of forcible attacks; the security of cantons; the punishment of culprits; etc.* The presumed secret message from Nicholas of Flüe regarding the consultation of the subjects is clearly a step forward in the right direction. In the public awareness, Nicholas of Flüe was on their side. The William Tell Song [*Tellenlied*] of 1653, mentioning Nicholas of Flüe, supports this hypothesis.

The beginning of the Rebellion in Entlebuch and

the Magnitude of the Disturbances

The Entlebuch District Procession to Heiligkreuz

The pilgrimage procession to Heiligkreuz at the beginning of the rebellion is particularly significant. It was customary in times of crises and emergencies that Entlebuch's inhabitants sought comfort and consolidation through the veneration of the relics in the Heiligkreuz church. The fact that this pilgrimage took place on a Monday rather than a church feast day is especially noteworthy.

What were the reasons that caused Hans Emmenegger (1604-1653), the regional banneret [*Landespannermeister*] of the Entlebuch District, to support this pilgrimage on 10 February (Gregorian calendar), ten days before Fat Thursday? Did he want to soothe the enraged tempers of the peasants with this pilgrimage? Did Hans Emmenegger want to avoid having the Lucerne *Fasnacht* in 1653 get out of control to avoid a "hog-banner campaign" from being formed – as happened following the 15th century Burgundian wars- and to preclude the rage of the rural inhabitants from being discharged? Had he originally planned that at the beginning of the Lucerne *Fasnacht* on Fat Thursday – where according to Swabian-Allemannic tradition criticism of the authorities was unexceptional – the three Tells, carrying truncheons and wearing costumes as William Tell, Werner Stauffacher and Arnold von Melchtal would appear?

Based on the Lucerne government's stance on refusing the demands, which provoked the demonstration of peasants armed with truncheons on 6 February 1653, it appears that Hans Emmenegger arguably decided – with the consent of the clergy of the Entlebuch parishes – to undertake an Entlebuch District procession *on February 10th* to the Church of the Holy Cross [*Heiligkreuzkirche*] above the village of Hasle, Canton Lucerne.

On the other hand, no documents confirm that the three Tells wearing the costumes donated by Hans Emmenegger participated in the Lucerne *Fasnacht*. It, therefore, remains a mystery as to whether or not Hans Emmenegger originally planned to have the three Tells appear at the Lucerne *Fasnacht* of 1653 in their efforts to call the attention of the government authorities to their lost freedoms.

Refusal of the Oath Demanded of the Peasant Subjects (Untertaneneid)

On Fat Thursday, February 20th (Gregorian calendar), in front of the gates of Lucerne, the bailiff of the Rothenburg Bailiwick (Canton Lucerne) promised his peasant subjects – who felt that they had been treated unjustly – an improvement of their situation if they would take an oath bowing to the government authorities. The peasants, however, refused to swear the oath and, on that same evening, Kaspar Steiner (1614-1653) assured the Entlebuch peasants that they had the support of their fellow men from Rothenburg.

Meanwhile, the turmoils had spread further and even included the inhabitants of the little town of Willisau. That was the purpose why Lucerne's city mayor (*Schultheiss*), Knight Heinrich von Fleckenstein visited the town of Willisau on February 20th, the Saturday following the beginning of the Lucerne Fasnacht on Fat

Thursday. He reminded the local people in the little town that the city of Lucerne had provided them with diverse benefits in 1472 (five years prior to the turmoil of 1477!). But he was not able to calm the people in Willisau.

Swiss mercenaries such as Fleckenstein were much sought after and increased the incomes of the patricians in the cities.

Attempted Intervention from Mayor Waser in Zurich

The disturbances encompassed the Bernese region and further areas in Switzerland. Bern requested Johann Heinrich Waser (1600-1669), the mayor of Zurich, attempt an arbitration between the peasants and government authorities. In contrast to mayor Fleckenstein of Lucerne, Waser was able to gain the confidence of the peasant deputies. His proposal was ultimately accepted by the representatives of the attending bailiwicks. Niklaus Leuenberger was also one of the deputies. On 30 March 1653 in the Bern city hall, under threat of punishment, all of the representatives took a new oath of allegiance as a reminder that all subjects still had to swear an oath of loyalty.

Regional Assembly of the Peasants in Signau

The next day, hundreds of discontented peasants, *members of the Swiss Reformed Church,* from the entire Emmental and Aargau regions, *as well as Roman Catholic peasants* from the Entlebuch region and from Willisau, along with peasant farmers from the Solothurn bailiwicks, the Bernese Oberland and the communal dominion of Schwarzenburg were present in Signau. With a great majority, the representatives resolved to convene a new regional assembly with the goal – *as defined by the founders of the Swiss Confederation in 1291 (Oath of Rütli)* – to form an alliance for assistance when in need. Simultaneously, none of the peasants should swear the demanded oath of loyalty on the coming Sunday in the church.

The Assembly of Sumiswald

This new regional assembly with representatives from the farming community in the cantons of Bern, Lucerne, Solothurn, and Basel, along with the communal dominion, was held on 13/23 April in Sumiswald.

At the assembly in Sumiswald, Niklaus Leuenberger was elected as commanding leader (*Bundesobmann*) of the insurrection. Niklaus Leuenberger was a man of noble aspect and an excellent speaker.

This skill of logic could be acquired in the German Language Society of Jesus' school (Jesuitenschule) in the city of Fribourg, which was founded in 1582 by Peter Canisius (1521-1597). Inasmuch as lists of the names of students in Fribourg do not exist – as opposed to the Society of Jesus' school in Lucerne, where Kaspar Steiner had studied – the verification of Leuenberger's having studied there is difficult.

The Oath of Huttwil 1653

On 20/30 April the representatives of the peasants of the Confederation met under the leadership of Niklaus Leuenberger in the little town of Huttwil in order to take the Oath of Allegiance, the Oath of Huttwil 1653. The peasants chose the town Huttwil since it was their goal to renew the Oath of Rütli of 1291 for residents living in a town and/or a rural village of the Swiss Confederacy.

As an emblem of recognition banneret Emmenegger presented Niklaus Leuenberger with a magnificent red coat, a *Casaque*, which was to be worn on official occasions.

The Personality of Niklaus Leuenberger

Open Questions

- How was it possible for Niklaus Leuenberger as an alleged "weak personal leader" to be able to contain the sharpshooters in 1653 when his troops besieged the city of Bern?

- Was he a stupid peasant?

- Did he only believe in that which is good?

- Did he hope that with the successful signing of the Murifeld Peace Treaty in 1653 the conflict could be solved between the urban and rural population?

Figurative Portrayals of Niklaus Leuenberger

Fig. 1a shows Niklaus Leuenberger without a masculine headdress. The first thing that happened when a criminal was captured was for his beard to be cut off. Did the authorities have the intention of portraying the peasant leader as a penitent criminal and rebel in order to permanently insist that he had been forced against his will to take the office of the chief leader and halfheartedly support the peasant's concerns?

NICOLAUS LEUENBERG DE SCHONHOLTZ.
Bernas Rusticorum seductorum
per Helvetiam Dux.

Fig. 1a: Niklaus Leuenberger, the allegedly penitent revolutionist.

No portrayal of Niklaus Leuenberger, as a contemporary leader, exists that shows him after the Murifeld peace treaty had been signed. Those such as fig. 1b, below, were confiscated.

Fig. 1b: Contemporary Portrayal of Niklaus Leuenberger before he was captured.

The Leader's Personality as Seen in the Achievements of the Rebels

The following texts are an effort to gain a further description of the leader's personality based on the services rendered by the insurrectionists under the leadership of Niklaus Leuenberger.

The Federal Charter of Huttwil – a Remarkable Accomplishment of the Rebels

The text of the Oath of Huttwil, aimed at replacing the Oath of 1291 (Bundesbrief, author's note), as transcribed by André Holenstein (b 1959) [30] appears in the appendices. The Oath of Huttwil (Appendix 2) comprised seven articles, however, only articles 1, 2 and 5 will be mentioned in the following observations, to show the visionary views of initiators.

In the first, most important article, reference is made to the confederates' alliance, which was concluded several centuries earlier. This article not only includes the basic principle of mutual support when life, property and personal possessions are in danger, but also the principles that inequities are to be eliminated and not least that religious freedom is guaranteed, inasmuch as no difference is made between Reformed and Catholic peasants. This article simultaneously holds that all confederates are obligated to pay taxes to the authorities, and in so doing the authorities are not contested and should not be replaced by peasants.

The second article concerns the question of the dispensation of justice, in the case of new laws and unjust decrees being made: How are controversies with the authorities to be settled and how can inequities be avoided? It was the view of the responsible initiators that disputable issues could be resolved for all Swiss citizens – those in rural as well as urban regions (e.g., Huttwil, Willisau) – in accordance with a unified, legally binding arbitration process.

The third article is a supplement to the second article, in case the authorities should attempt to enforce unjust new decrees through the employment of local or foreign troops, the confederate allies commit themselves to disallow such actions and mutually assist one another.

In the fourth article a detailed definition of the third article is given, in case a fellow confederate should be aggrieved by measures taken by the authorities.

The fifth article states that the federal charter is to be renewed each decade. Simultaneously, an account of the effectiveness of the articles in the federal treaty is to be made. In so doing, it should be clarified whether complaints against authorities remain, by individual confederates, in order that they can be given assistance.

The sixth article concerns the relationship among the fellow confederates and how they should deal with traitors within their own ranks.

In the seventh article the fellow confederates commit themselves to not conclude a one-sided treaty with the authorities which contradicts the matters outlined in the Oath of Huttwil.

Commentary on the Freedom of Religion

Already mentioned, concerning the freedom of religion, no differences between Reformed and Catholic beliefs were made. That is a difference between the Treaty of Huttwil and the first version made by the public assembly in Sumiswald, where Catholic belief was given priority. It is reported that Niklaus Leuenberger's father, Hans, was an Anabaptist. Anabaptists were heavily persecuted. Therefore, many Anabaptists emigrated. Amongst others, descendants are living in the United States as Amish and as Mennonites.

Had the authorities in Bern and their fellow confederates at the assembly of the Federal Diet in Baden accepted the Treaty of Huttwil – to which the authorities had not objected – and showed strength for religious freedom as stated in article 1, Switzerland would have been spared from internal religious and fratricidal wars after 1648.

Accomplishments of the Oath of Huttwil 1653 (Summary)

In summary it can be stated that the articles as understood in our contemporary, positive perception are revolutionary in the positive sense of the word:

• It concerns the introduction of *freedom of religion*, of a *uniform dispensation of justice* and, in this context, of *political participation* on the level of the entire population of Switzerland.

• Following the Thirty Years' War, the Treaty of Huttwil corresponds thereby with a *modernized version of the Federal Charter of 1291 of the old confederates*, an Alliance which according to tradition was concluded at the time of William Tell.

• The Oath of Huttwil *does not challenge the authorities as an institution enabled to levy taxes (article 1)*.

• The right of *mutual support and self-defense in case the authorities should war against their own subjects, either with local and/or foreign soldiers (article 3)*.

Commentary

Article 1 would have enabled authorities at that time to enter into constructive dialogue with the rebels in order to become acquainted with their views, opinions and ideas, and examine them more closely. This alliance of the subjects, which does not question the authorities, conforms to a convergence of a parliamentary democracy, wherein the executive authorities are in permanent dialogue with the representatives of their subjects. In the Oath of Huttwil 1653 the question is raised concerning dispensation of justice. That question – in the sense of a further evolutionary, democratic development – finally leads to a general requirement of separation of powers between the authorities and the subjects' representatives, as well as to the additional establishment of an adjudication authority independent of the government.

Why did the rebels include article 3 in their oath? During the Thirty Years' War everything went well economically for the patricians in the city as well as the peasants. The patricians were able to earn considerable wealth through the intermediation of soldiers and the peasants were able to export agricultural goods to the warring countries. In Switzerland, an economic recession followed the peace treaty of 1648 and the soldiers enlisted by the patricians were out of work. The population was aware that in their mission soldiers were not only paid but were also officially allowed to increase their wealth through plundering. The fears of the population that the local patricians could wrongly use their soldiers for their own purposes is understandable.

Reasons for the Rejection of the Contents of the Oath of Huttwil by the Bernese Government

The events in England must have played an important role. King Charles I was executed on 30 January 1649. Cromwell fought against King Charles I, who wanted to transform England into an absolutist monarchy. Events in that country were importantly influenced by the draft of a constitution that included the postulates freedom of religion, equality before the law, general political participation and the end of prison punishment for debtors.

Can the Oath of Huttwil (1653) be interpreted as being a Swiss version of the Cromwellian and Miltonian Agreement of the People? As a person, Oliver Cromwell is controversial, however, the Cromwellian Republic, known as the "Commonwealth of England," was an important step towards England's democracy.

Commentary on the People's Assembly at Huttwil 1653

The Oath of Huttwil (1653) can be referred to as an important step on the way to Switzerland's democracy in the 19th century. Representatives of all social levels of the population participated in the assembly in Huttwil and no difference was made between Catholics, Protestants, registered citizens and residents without civic rights. Such residents were known as Hintersässen and held a residence permit (in the USA a green card) to live in the municipality but had no civic rights as the burghers had. In this context it must be understood that a Swiss citizen is primarily a citizen of a Swiss municipality, the place which appears in a Swiss passport as Heimatort (i.e., "municipality of origin," or "municipality of heritage"). Swiss citizens may have several "municipalities of origin." The oldest Heimatort denotes the municipality in which an ancestor of an individual first became a burgher. That place is of utmost importance in doing genealogical research.

The Siege of Bern under the Leadership of Niklaus Leuenberger

The siege of a city such as Bern is conditional upon an accurate general staff plan. Furthermore, it requires outstanding logistics in order to nourish some 16,000 armed peasants before the gates of the wealthy city of Bern. In this context the high level of discipline in the rebel's army is recognized without exception by all historians. No comparison can be made between the armed peasants under

Niklaus Leuenberger's leadership and the "hog-banner campaign" of the rebels in 1477. The high level of discipline impressed the authorities of the city of Bern without fail.

Did the Peasants' Leader Make Erratic Decisions or Follow a Plan?

Among other things Niklaus Leuenberger feared that **his plan not to attack, plunder and burn Bern** could be overruled by his own council of war. In order to avert such danger Niklaus Leuenberger recruited the following men for the council of war from his army camped at Murifeld: Hans Stampach, Daniel Ruch, Jakob Leuenberger, Joseph Kämpfer, Klaus Mey, Hans Kolb, Andres Leuenberger, Baschi Sommer, Alexander Leuenberger, Hans Frei, Melcher Hunziker, Bendicht Tschanz and Ulrich Krieg. Joseph Kämpfer from Kleinemmental was a neighbor of Jakob Leuenberger. Some insurgents, reportedly, were "hawks," some were "doves"—these men, hand-selected by Niklaus Leuenberger, seem to have been of calmer sense.

Was Niklaus Leuenberger Hungry for Power and Wealth?

Niklaus Leuenberger did not have the ambition to take power. He also did not want to gain wealth in a profitable military business like, for example, the Bernese patricians. Due to his noble stature and because of his appearance when mounted and wearing his red coat, Niklaus Leuenberger was often referred to in the vernacular as "king of the peasants" (*Bauernkönig*), a title which in the end brought him the harsh conviction of the maximum death penalty of being "quartered."

The Murifeld Peace Treaty of 1653 and the Rebel's Contribution of Achievement

A plausible and successful siege of Bern necessitated the occupation of strategic access roads, bridges and passes in order for the surrounded population of the city to realize the earnestness of their situation. This objective was achieved by the besieger, whereby should the siege of Bern be lifted, the rebels were guaranteed not only exemption from punishment but, also, orally agreed upon-reparation in the amount of 50,000 pounds in Bernese currency.

The Murifeld Peace Treaty of 1653 represents a compromise and is not a dictation from the peasants. The three documents had to be drawn up by representatives of the Bernese authorities and the rebels within a short period of time. It materialized on the basis of negotiations – without a drop of blood having been shed. The results represent an outstanding achievement of the participants. It came about only because during the siege of Bern, Niklaus Leuenberger and the peasants could bargain from a position of their strength.

The Peace of Murifeld

In confidence of the honesty of the Bernese authorities and compliance of the treaty, Niklaus Leuenberger announced the contents of the signed agreement to the rebels and ordered the armed insurgents to return home. The siege of Bern was rescinded.

On May 19th, the Feast of the Ascension of Christ (Holy Thursday), all sections of the troops were informed about the peace agreement and thousands of the rebels started with massed pipes and drums, flags and weapons, towards home, where work was waiting for them. On the same day dispatches were received stating that in the Sternenberg rural court jurisdiction at Neuenegg, insurgents had been arrested by authorities. Various bailiffs captured further rebels, contrary to contract on Friday, May 20th. Niklaus Leuenberger admonished the Bernese authorities to abide by the peace treaty. Contrary allegations resulted and the situation continued to become more acute, which on Saturday, May 22nd, caused Leuenberger to write a first official letter to the authorities in Bern because no improvement had taken place.

After dispatches arrived from the Aargau region concerning pillage and looting by Zurich insurgents, Niklaus Leuenberger is once again forced to proclaim military landsturm, a general mobilization, and writes to the authorities a last time on May 24th to observe the peace treaty because only then are the rebels willing to pay homage.

The Battle of Wohlenschwil

According to the Peace Treaty of Murifeld, the return journey of the armed peasants occurred on 19 May 1653. They responded to the peace treaty and withdrew from all of the important strategic points around the city of Bern. After some four days, it was an unbelievable accomplishment to convince the returning armed peasants that their situation was not futile and that they were competent to defend themselves. To maintain their validity, they had to be prepared on one hand to fight against possible attacks from General von Erlach's army in the west in case the Murifeld Peace Treaty was not observed. In the east, on the other hand, General Werdmüller's further advance had to be prevented.

It is impressive that with some 15,000 troops on 23 May / 2 June 1653 in Mägenschwil, Leuenberger and the peasant army were able to resist the penetration of Lenzburg by Major General Johann Rudolf Werdmüller with his cavalry, four cannons and 1,500 musketeers, a fourth of the well-armed Federal Diet troops. Lenzburg, namely, was war-weary and ready to surrender. The population had fear of pillage by the mercenary army of General Johann Rudolf Werdmüller, who fought on the side of the Swedes.

Leuenberger was concerned that his peasant army had no cannons at their disposal and were not as well armed. For fear of losing what they had gained and for the safety of his men, Niklaus Leuenberger wanted to better the peasants' situation, i.e. maintain the upper hand until all negative contingencies had been eliminated. Thus, he planned, covered by a thundershower on 24 May 1653, along with Schibi, a surprise attack on Zurich's artillery for improving his military position. However, Johann Rudolf Werdmüller's mercenary army cavalry also took advantage of the thunderstorm and broke through the lines. In addition, Johann Rudolf Werdmüller's mercenaries set fire to the villages of Wohlenschwil and Büblikon. Nevertheless, after this first standoff a cease-fire was agreed. Niklaus Leuenberger was aware that this pillaging would demoralize his troops. He was also aware that he could no longer negotiate from a position of strength as he had with the siege of Bern.

Niklaus Leuenberger was convinced that Generallissimo Johann Konrad Werdmüller did not know that the authorities in Bern had concluded a legally valid peace treaty with the insurgents. His only strength consisted in the fact that on his person he was carrying the legal peace treaty which he had concluded with Bern officials at Murifeld. He sent a copy of the Murifeld peace treaty to Generallissimo Werdmüller.

In the meantime, Schibi unsuccessfully attempted to convince Leuenberger to violate the cease-fire and make a surprise attack in the dark on the Zurich army.

On 25 May 1653 peace was declared at Mellingen.

Sigismund von Erlach's Vengeful Campaign against the Rural Population

On 27 May 1653 General Werdmüller received a writing from Niklaus Leuenberger in Herzogenbuchsee complaining of the violence being leveled on the rural citizenry and the need for mutual continued compliance with the peace treaty agreed upon at Mellingen.

In the meantime, Daniel Küpfer, the deputy of Niklaus Leuenberger, the Emmental's commanding officer, had mobilized about 5000 armed peasants at Herzogenbuchsee.

On 28 May 1653 Leuenberger received a puzzling reply from commanding Generallissimo Werdmüller. Thus, Niklaus Leuenberger instructed his troops that peace was at hand and that they should return to their homes. He left them with some question as to whether freedom and safety could be had by them all. At the same time, he had the premonition that his life would end soon.

Commentary

Indeed, Niklaus Leuenberger had the foreboding that the atrocities against the people committed by General von Erlach were actually directed towards him according to the principle of "Sippenhaft" ("collective punishment, i.e hostage taking in its absolute form"), – when the clan of an offender could be subject to revenge – and that his life was in danger. On the other hand, he trusted the commanding officer of the Federal Diet army, that based on the intervention from Zurich, the Bernese government would give in. He still believed in the good of mankind and that the Bernese authorities were interested in peace with the rural population. He, therefore, sent the soldiers home. Also, in part, because he knew the price that they would pay would be extreme.

Bernese authorities decided to renege on their agreements with the peasants, immediately after the abolishment of the siege of Bern. They attacked the peasants on their way back to their homes, families, and peacetime endeavors, now overdue. Was this decision agreed upon by all of the allies of the old confederacy? When was the decision among the members of the Bernese authorities unanimously decided – before, during, or after the Peace Treaty of Murifeld had been signed? Were the frightened Bernese authorities dealing, primarily, an action of punishment in order to prevent future revolts and to show the people "where God is seated"?

The Battle of Herzogenbuchsee

Thanks to the decision of Niklaus Leuenberger to send the 5000 armed rebels home, based on the peace treaties of Mellingen and Murifeld, greater carnage in the Battle of Herzogenbuchsee versus the mercenary army of General von Erlach was avoided. Although, among other reports from sources, some partisan and some independent, the chronicler Jost von Brechershäusern reported an uncalled-for attack on peasant insurgents on their way home, in Herzogenbuchsee by the troops of Sigismund von Erlach.

Jost von Brechershäusern was a wealthy peasant from Wynigen. Among other things, he also reported, in addition to the peasant war of 1653, about the First War of Villmergen in 1656. He was murdered in 1657 not far from his farm. The murder, however, was never clarified. Was this violence politically motivated, i.e. an early attempt to silence the press?

Commentary

With the Peace of Westphalia in 1648 and through the efforts of
Johann Rudolf Wettstein, the mayor of Basel, the old Confederacy
of Switzerland was officially recognized as being independent of the
Holy Roman Empire. As a result, there was no longer a possibility for
Confederacy members and their subjects to appeal to the emperor
as the final authority. It cannot be forgotten that the first treaty
of the Confederacy only came about inasmuch as the emperor was
the highest authority to guarantee special liberties to the original
cantonal states.

The Rebels' Punishment

The vengeance campaign of the authorities under the leadership of
General von Erlach can be seen in the sense of *Sippenhaft* tactics as
a part of the rebels' punishment. Those who betrayed an insurgent
received a reward.

Fig. 2: Torture of the leaders of the revolt.

Christian Schibi, Niklaus Leuenberger "confessed" while being tortured that the peasants had not urged, but instead forced him to accept the office as the head leader. He confessed nothing other than that. Perhaps he hoped for a reprieve owing to a passage recorded in the minutes of the examination proceedings: "As he [Leuenberger] adjourned from the last public assembly at Langenthal to his home town, Hobi, a man from Wynigen, called out "That [he] is our authority!'. Clearly, he [Leuenberger, on horse with his magnificent red coat] was very indignant [about that] and he hit him with the [walking] pole."

Commentary

The official representatives of the Reformed and Catholic churches supported the government authorities in the peasant war. Niklaus

Leuenberger's appeal for clemency was not accepted and his death warrant – "quartering" (i.e., dismemberment) – conformed with that of regicide, that punishment reserved for attempts to murder a monarch. Evidence in favor of whom they had labeled "the peasant king" was disregarded.

Executions of insurgents preceded the highest leaders' doomed legal proceedings and the displays of their body parts reportedly were particularly psychologically harsh on at least one of Niklaus Leuenberger's deputies.

The peasants were therefore clearly shown that participants in such a rebellious assembly had to reckon with the quartering of the body as the maximum death penalty.

The unity between the Bernese authorities and the church is supported by the fact that new governmental regulations were announced from the pulpit during Sunday church services. Furthermore, in addition to secular courts, a church "consistory court" (*Chorgericht*) existed in an ecclesiastical parish. Infringements were punished with monetary fines, whereby the bailiff, as the representative of the authorities, could mete out the fines and collect the fees. The pastor served as secretary and noted the monetary fines in the consistory court manual.

Niklaus Leuenberger, the Penitent Rebel, Exhibited in Bern

Niklaus Leuenberger, the most important prize of the peasant war, was portrayed to the public, in the city of Bern on 2/12 June 1653, as a penitent leader who had been appointed against his will. He was put in handcuffs and marched through the streets in a triumphal procession. Finally, he was put in irons in the so-called "killer's cell" in the Prison Tower.

The Conviction of Niklaus Leuenberger

On 6 September 1653 (Gregorian calendar) Niklaus Leuenberger's sentence was pronounced. The peasant leader was condemned for violating the authority which God had placed in the city leaders. He was also condemned to be beheaded, drawn and quartered, and to have his body parts mounted for display at the main square and the four gates of the city of Bern.

Commentary

The conviction of the leader of the peasant league did not take place until after the arrest, torture and questioning of Uli Galli and Hans Konrad Brenner. Both of them (not only) confirmed the leader's testimonies and confessions (in the examination minutes) but also provided closer and significant information concerning the (author's remark: so far unknown to the Bernese government) selfish intentions and plans of some hawkish chiefs of the revolt, in that they avowed that it had been agreed upon by them that upon capturing the city, it would be relinquished and plundered, the government council abolished and a new one installed, whereby Leuenberger and Daniel Küpfer be given the position of governing mayor (*Schultheiss*), Uli Galli that of treasurer, Michael Aeschlimann, called "*Bergmichel*," that of military ensign (*Venner*), and notary Konrad Brenner that of state and court scribe.

In point of fact, Niklaus Leuenberger's confession made no mention of the allegedly existing plans of his fellow campaigners (the hawks of the rebellion), no commensurate assignments of guilt and not even a clue that he said anything verifying plans to pillage Bern. He never betrayed his colleagues and their plan, even in order to enable a better stance for or to save himself.

The End of the Peasant War and the Assassination in Entlebuch on 19/29 September 1653

The peasant war started in Entlebuch where the three *peacefully demonstrating* peasants dressed in historical garments represented the three first confederates: Walter Fürst, Werner Stauffacher and Arnold von Melchtal. Following the legend of William Tell and symbolized as the "Three Tells," they wanted to call the attention of the Lucerne authorities to the lost liberties in the area of their bailiwick. As a result, Niklaus Leuenberger needed to give his full commitment in order to restrain those three hawks, when the siege of Bern took place with the 16000 men, from attacking the city with fellow hawks.

The peasant war ended in Entlebuch with the so-called "Tell's shot" by Kapar Unternährer (1621-1653) when he attempted to assassinate Lucerne's *Schultheiss* Ulrich Dulliker, who was wounded, and Lucerne councilman Kaspar Studer, who was killed. Kaspar Unternährer came from Schüpfheim, where he was born on 2 January 1621. Ueli Dahinden also participated in the assassination of 28 September 1653, and was killed on 8 October 1653 during his attempted seizure by Protestant troops.

Although the government troops were unsuccessful in their attempt to capture both men alive, they were subsequently tried in court. Kaspar Unternährer was beheaded, as was Ueli's corpse and both had their body parts displayed at key sites as a warning to the populace.

After regional military ensign Hans Emmenegger presented the "Three Tells" their costumes, Kaspar Unternährer internalized his role as William Tell and carried a crossbow in his right hand. The second "Tell," Ueli Dahinden, represented Werner Stauffacher. The Lucerne authorities were not certain if the identity of the third assassin was Hans Stadelmann or a peasant who was called, "long [tall] Zemp" and was known as the third "Tell." Hans Stadelmann was able to flee abroad, as many other insurgents of the peasant revolt. After being captured abroad he was betrayed by "long Zemp," who was therefore able to save his own skin. Hans Stadelmann was transferred to Lucerne in 1654 and beheaded on 5/15 July.

Kaspar Unternährer is the only known assassin in the history of the old confederacy.

Conclusions

Not one drop of blood was shed between the composition of the Treaty of Huttwil and the Murifeld Peace Treaty.

The peasant war was a war of the authorities against the peasants as a result of the unilateral termination of the Peace Treaty of Murifeld by the Bernese authorities in tune with the advice of "The Prince" of Niccolo Machiavelli's guidebook originally written with the intention of governance and not of tyranny, in order to gain a subsequently better military situation.

The fact that relatively few rebels lost their lives on the battlefield is clearly due to the outstanding merit, the humanity of Niklaus Leuenberger.

The Treaty of Huttwil and the Peace Treaty of Murifeld, which came about without the shedding of blood, are parallel milestones on the path of the old Confederacy towards democratization. They could only be reached from a position of strength and are comparable to the Glorious Revolution in England. The path of the Bernese patricians towards an aristocratic republic, however, continued. The erosion of democratic liberties was only stopped with the invasion of

Napoleonic troops in 1798. The law of 4 May 1798 spelled the end of the Swiss *Ancien Regime.*

A study of the events during the European revolutions in the 19th century and during the peasant war of 1653 presents a rich source for conflict research. In that conjunction diverse questions present themselves:

The questions of liberty- especially religious freedom- equality and fraternity, "forerunners" of the French Revolution, and about a more social tax system.

All were felt during the peasant movement in Niklaus Leuenberger's lifetime and addressed in the Oath of Huttwil and in the Peace treaty of Murifeld.

How can the questions be dealt with, concerning the deeper reasons for the government's revenge campaign against the peasants following the conclusion of the Peace Treaty of Murifeld, and the circumstances of some intimidated farmers acquiring a so-called "document of protection" (*Schutzbrief*) in order to be spared from looting by the government troops?

And, what about the question of councilman Studer's assassination as well as that concerning the legal judgment of the assassin of Kaspar Unternährer, who was one of the "Three Tells" and an exponent of the insurgent's hawks?

Nelson Mandela asked himself when the use of force could be justified and thereby differed from Mahatma Gandhi who completely renounced the use of force. Thus, Leuenberger may have had to think more in terms of Mandela rather than Gandhi as he began to suspect the authorities to be more capable of treachery than honor. This statement is the message of Urs Hostettler's book

"Der Rebell vom Eggiwil," published by Zytglogge Bern 1991. Urs Hostettler's documentary of the events in 1653 and of the life of Ueli Galli, shows the reality of life and the tension among the leadership of the peasants' movement.

Within the scope of the total abolition of the rebels at the end of the peasant war in Entlebuch, where the "Three Tells" were protected and hidden by the Catholic population, it became necessary for Protestant Bernese troops to be deployed. This fact created additional religious hatred. As a result, in the subsequent first religious war in 1656, 5000 Catholic soldiers from Central Switzerland under the leadership of Christoph Pfyffer won the battle of Villmergen against 9600 Bernese Protestant soldiers under the leadership of General Sigismund von Erlach. During this battle 600 Protestants and 200 Catholics were killed. Needless to say, the ecumenical Oath of Huttwil was lost between Protestants and Catholics. Thus, tensions between Christians also remained after the second religious war of Villmergen, where more than 3000 people were killed in 1712.

It is significant for church history that Nicholas of Flüe, who was later canonized by the church, was on the side of peasants at the time of the peasants' rebellion in 1477. However, in 1653 the church sided against the rebellious party. This positive position of the church towards the government never changed through the 19th century and is responsible for Martin Disteli's anticlerical parodies and the introduction of the article in the Federal Constitution of 1848 which forbade any activity of the Jesuits in church or state affairs.

Interestingly, however, the Catholic priests supported the rural procession to the Heiligkreuz Church at the beginning of the rebellion in Entlebuch. This *ecumenical unity* was *pioneer work* in

Swiss church history. As seen on the whole, however, the Reformed and Catholic churches supported the authorities. The churches and the theologians were responsible for the entire scope of human life before the secularization. Religion was not a private matter.

The Reformed pastor Michael Ringier was also on the side of the rebels in 1653: He referred to "murder," i.e, to a "crime" in his diary about the Battle of Herzogenbuchsee. In this respect the church betrayed their own values through their support of the authorities who induced a war against its subjects. The national and international rehabilitation of church history in the case of the crusades, the European peasant wars, the persecution of so-called "witches" and Anabaptists, and the wars in modern history, such as at the time of World War II, should be welcomed.

Expedient therefore to the Peasant War of 1653 and for justification of the title "Niklaus Leuenberger, the "Swiss Gandhi" of the 17th century?" are the following observations/quotations from Mahatma Gandhi:

• *An eye for an eye will only make the whole world blind.*

• *What a person wins with force can only be kept with force.*

• *Earth provides enough to satisfy every man's needs, but not every man's greed.*

• *Goodness can never arise from lies and violence.*

• *Be yourself the change which you desire for the world.*

• *Where love grows, life thrives; where hate emerges, ruin is a threat.*

• *There is no way to peace, peace is the way.*

•*If you are in the right, you can allow yourself to keep calm; and when you are in the wrong, you allow yourself to lose it.*

•*Power does not come from physical strength, but from unrelenting will.*

•*The weak cannot forgive. To forgive is a trait of strength.*

•*At first, they ignore you, then they laugh over you, then they fight you and, then, you win.*

Since the founding of the Confederacy, there is no historical precedent for the disproportionate punishment on the part of the authorities, if the treatment of Anabaptists and other dissidents in the 16th and 17th centuries is not taken into account.

The question concerning remuneration of the rebels who betrayed friends has not been discussed in this article. The Bonus-Malus-System and the issuing of documents of protection by the authorities is a further research domain.

The following questions come to mind, why is the history of the "victors" still, oppressively, being imposed on the populace and what can be done to bridge the ancient gulf?

- The Peasant War plays a very menial role in official Swiss historiography.

- The text of the Oath of Huttwil and/or the Peace Treaty of Murifeld not appear in any school textbook.

- As the ancient agreements were darkly swept aside, so is the truth of history being shaded, moved out of the light.

An answer is that the descendants of Swiss patrician families that hold public offices or are in diplomatic services have achieved outstanding accomplishments—now, in the sense of the statesman-like conduct of Nicholas of Flüe, the historic reparation of the rebels of 1653 should be initiated by these patrician families. Such an obliging gesture would enable the victims of the Peasant War and their descendants to cleanly rule off a dark chapter of Swiss history.

Appeal for Amnesty for the rebels in 1653

It is left to the readers and most especially the Swiss politicians whether the rebels of 1653 are worthy of an official rehabilitation and are recognized as the true heroes preparing the democratic system of Switzerland and its constitution in 1848 which is an adapted copy of the American Constitution of 1787.

Acknowledgments and References

The author thanks the work of Andreas Suter regarding the correct narrative of the Swiss peasant war in 1653 in his habilitation thesis, as well as in the Historic Dictionary of Switzerland (https://hls-dhs-dss.ch/de/articles/008909/2010-05-07/), the documentary of Urs Hostettler of the events in 1653 published in the book "Der Rebell vom Eggiwil," Zytglogge Bern 1991) and numerous persons cited in the book "Niklaus Leuenberger, the "Swiss Gandhi" of the 17th Century" self-published and available online, which contains 85 references, more details such as the detailed transcription of the relevant documents such as the Oath of Huttwil, the Peace-Treaty of Murifeld, the Song of William Tell, illustrations such as the mass execution of innocent rebels in Basel in 1653. This brutal event became a theme during the liberal uprising in Basel which led to the formation of the cantons Basel- Stadt (City) and Basel-Landschaft (rural part of the former Canton of Basel) and last but not least to the liberal constitution of the Swiss Federation of 1848.

Thanks to the liberal constitution Switzerland evolved to be a prosperous, peaceful country with a strong economy, a low unemployment rate, a highly developed health care system, a high standard of educational system that also teachers in primary classes are well paid, a highly social security network helping to avoid domestic terroristic attacks despite the fact that the density of weapons per resident is comparable to the United States. The constitution allows a cultural, religious, linguistic diversity which allow 4 official languages and a diversity of different political parties forming the government taking care that the diversity and the minorities are well represented.

The book, "Niklaus Leuenberger, the "Swiss Gandhi" of the 17th Century," shows, in addition, that thanks to computational science, artificial intelligence, all the sciences have a chance to converge for the benefit of mankind. In this context, the findings of Nobel Laureate Ilya Prigogine and the philosopher Isabelle Stengers (book: "Out of Chaos") play an important role since processes far from equilibrium in an open system with an influx of energy are present in the exact sciences (see publication "What is Life? In SWISS PHARMA 1-19, www.ifiip.ch/downloads) and can be modeled as well as in social sciences such as the history of mankind. Thus, in history the energy of such a process far from equilibrium can be used for a peaceful positive evolutionary process leading to a higher order of a democratic system, if this process is not suppressed as in case of the Swiss peasant war in 1653. On the other hand, the energy of a process far from equilibrium may lead also to a violent revolution such as the French Revolution of 1789, which did not lead quickly to a sustainable equilibrium. In this context, the book raises, also, the question, why has only Switzerland and no other European Country adopted and adapted the American Constitution of 1787?

The author of the book "Niklaus Leuenberger, the "Swiss Gandhi" of the 17th Century" appreciates the comments of Marc Tribilhorn, historian, writing in the NZZ (Neue Zuerich Zeitung) of April 4, 2018: "Switzerland does not suffer from too many historical narratives but of not enough and the wrong ones. Swiss History needs to be re-written from the perspective of unselfishness," i.e., not just to please the nation or its government. Thus, the author hopes with the book to contribute a small chapter of Swiss History without taking into account the nation's wish of complacency.

Last but not least the author thanks the great support of Paul-Anthon Nielson, bilingual American Swiss Genealogist and Historian for his support in the translation of the German version of the book. At the same time the author thanks Daniel Lionberger, an US citizen of ancestors who immigrated in the 18th century to Philadelphia, being a descendant of a brother of Niklaus Leuenberger, for proofreading the English version and for checking this condensed contribution to the SAHS Review. Daniel Lionberger is the author of the e-book "Dream View Two- The Kamikaze Candidate," an environmental and political thriller (https://books2read.com/b/DreamViewTwo), a printed version is also available online.

Appendix 1:

Summary of the **Oath of Rütli**, an approximate English translation of lines given in Friedrich Schiller's1804 play, "William Tell" from "Rütli Oath" in Wikipedia, https://en.wikipedia.org/wiki/R%C3%BCtlischwur:

> *We want to be a single People of brethren,*
>
> *Never to part in danger nor distress.*
>
> *We want to be free, as our fathers were,*
>
> *And rather die than live in slavery.*
>
> *We want to trust in the one highest God*
>
> *And never be afraid of human power.*

Appendix 2:

The Oath of Huttwil 1653

In the name of the Holy Trinity Father, Son and Holy Ghost, Amen.

Thus, we have sworn together in this

1st article

that we want to honor and maintain the first Swiss oath, which the age-old confederates together swore several hundred years ago, and help one another to dispose of injustice, protect and shelter with body, goods, chattels and blood, moreover that which belongs to the lords and authorities should remain theirs and be given to them, and that which belongs to us peasants and subjects should remain ours and be submitted to us, and this for everyone, regardless of their religion.

2nd article

We want to help one another to turn back all bad new treatises, but that in each place the subjects themselves should demand justice from their authorities, but if they want to dispute against their authorities, they should not however march up without the knowledge and volition of the other confederates with whom they swore the oath, in order that they can determine beforehand which party is right or wrong, and if our fellow confederates are in the right, we thereto then will help them, however if they are in the wrong, we then will turn away from them.

3rd article

Should the authorities want to direct or place external or local folk on our throats, we shall then help one another to turn them away and not suffer their presence, but should it also be necessary, everyone shall concededly help out one another.

4th article

If also just another person in urban or rural areas should move in due to the upsurge of such mongering of the authorities or other persons and cause harm to body or chattels or life, every man from all the places of our fellow confederates should help with their body, goods, chattels, and blood to conclude and redeem them, as though it had been individually encountered.

5th article

Every ten years, the oath to which we have sworn should be read aloud and renewed by our fellow confederates, and should it be that complaint is made about the authorities or others somewhere else, we want at all times to help them to retain their rights so that no new currency or undue complaints can further burden our progeny.

6th article

No one amongst us should be so impudent and impertinent as to speak against the oath or have a need to give counsel or do deeds which could be destructive or damaging to it, however he might be overlooked, such a person should be recognized as a perjurer and betrayer and be deservedly punished.

7th article

Also, no fellow confederates along with their authorities in any place should make comparisons or conclusions of this treaty until our remaining fellow confederates in all other places can agree to the resolution, and therefore that the resolution and peace should be ruled by all parties and likewise with one another.

Accomplishments of the Oath of Huttwil 1653 (summary):

•It concerns the introduction of *freedom of religion*, of a *uniform dispensation of justice* and, in this context, of *political participation* on the level of the entire population of Switzerland.

•Following the Thirty Years' War, the Treaty of Huttwil corresponds thereby with a *modernized version of the Federal Charter of 1291 of the old confederates*, an Alliance which according to tradition was concluded at the time of William Tell.

•The Oath of Huttwil *does not challenge the authorities as an institution enabled to levy taxes (article 1).*

•The right of *mutual support and self-defense in case the authorities should war against their own subjects, either with local and/or foreign soldiers (article 3).*

Appendix 3

The Entlebuch Tell Song 1653

Das Entlebucher Tellenlied von 1653

Als man zählt sechs-zehn-hun-dert und drei und fünf-zig Jahr,

er-eig-nen sich gross Wun-der; ist kund und of-fen-bar.

Ich sing es nie-mand z trat-zen; man soll mich recht ver-stohn: Von

we-gen gan-zen Bat-zen ist die-ser Krieg her-kon.

Translation by P.A. Nielson:

Verse 1

As one counts six hundred and fifty-three years,

Great wonder occurs; is obvious and proclaimed,

I sing it, not to defy anyone;

one should correctly understand me:

As if this war came about entirely because of coinage.

Verse 2

47

48

O God!

I have to complain about them,

the peasants' great lament:

It is, as I want to say,

really bright on that day.

Similar as in Tell's time,

it oscillates now again

The peasant should yield, give,

rather than to receive.

Verse 3

O, Tell!

I want to scream:

Wake up from your sleep!

The bailiffs want everything:

horses, cows, calves, sheep.

Each lord will live

like a young aristocrat;

all to them he must give,

the poor, condemned man.

Verse 4

A poor unwieldy peasant,

who doesn't want to go along,

Makes Entlebucher weapons

clubs that have iron studs upon.

Therefore, fellow men!

We stand abreast,

strong with firm intent!

Spurn lords' troops and strange guests!

Verse 5

Chase them from the country,

even with arms in hand,

To live in calm and peace

within our fatherland.

Remember Brother Klaus

and repeat early and late:

"Only clubs will lands delouse,

To bring that counsel's fate.

Source: Anderi Lieder, Bern 1979 (Zytglogge).

Appendix 4

The Murifeld Peace Treaty,

including: the Catalog of Demands, as published by Vock

(Translation by P.A. Nielson)

"Treaty of the City of Bern with Several of Its Subjects"

We, mayor, councilmen and burghers of the city of Bern, herewith proclaim: Inasmuch as subjects in the Emmental region including the Signau Bailiwick, as well as the Konolfingen Rural Court and the Steffisburg Free Court, as also those in our bailiwicks of Wangen, Aarwangen, Bipp, Aarburg and Lenzburg County, as well as the subjects of Burgdorf County, the subjects of Büren County, the subjects of Thun County, the subjects of Nidau County, Fraubrunnen Bailiwick, Landshut, as also Brienz and Frutigen Castellanies, concerning all kinds of general and specific complaints, grievances and demands, their regional customs, freedoms and demands, as also their subservient guiltiness towards us, their authority, met together and heard their reports, but also stated our own willingly inclined explanations and comments about the given, compliable, merciful situation not otherwise saturated, in that they finally came to our capital city with weapons in hand, intending to achieve their demands and requests by means of such force and organized through their manifold provocations, persistence and demands, upon which with a board from our midst we met with them, and once more with endurance and consideration heard all of their articles of complaints against us, and following such repeated misfeasance in their friendly manner in order that on our part from the beginning complete, versatile and practical amiableness and placidity the force of weapons was again brought forward and everything accruing through ruin and harm in the strife is protected, and after explaining all of their presented articles and we in turn stipulated conditions and reservations, the same also to be rebated in trust, and all those things gratefully saturated, we accept and promise towards our aforenamed subjects, as follows:

1. Firstly, our subjects in the named districts and places should and want at once following their homebound retreat and withdrawal, which with this compromise settlement should forthwith be fulfilled in order to meet the costs of all inflicted damage, and upon our initial demand take anew the oath of obeisance for our subjects, and agree to it as their forefathers did, without any supplements or reservations.

2. This oath of obeisance is completely contrary to the conjoined alliances because our protest against their correctness as also for our strongly declared invalidity and as accepted by them through these alliances, with the opinion that they completely renounce the bonds to which they swore based on our annulment through suzerainty and the alliances in the chancellery of one or another place to be declared void and null due to being an extraditable offense, and therefore each and all of our conventional authoritative prerogatives, glories, freedoms and justice, sovereignty, governance and esteem, regardless of the manner to which they are referred, concerning our authoritative stand and revenues, should remain as heretofore totally unweakened, the same as we in turn want to protect and hold, thereby granting our subjects all of their ancient rights, justice, good customs and practices as certified under seal, according to the old land agreements.

3. And we have approved that our subjects have the option of freely buying and selling salt.

4. At the same time, the approval of the free buying and selling of horses, cattle and other goods, and that every individual is free to take his grain to the most conveniently situated market place.

5. Nonetheless, it should remain within our governance and we should not be denied the right, for the good of the common man and depending on the course of time, to declare necessary authoritative objection to the sale and increase of grain prices as well as other foodstuffs.

6. However, to promote the sale of livestock, generally and without exception, we declare the export duty heretofore obtained to be rescinded.

7. Concerning the regional assemblies, which are demanded as in earlier times, it is our opinion that when something burdensome occurs to all of the dependents of a district, for which reason they meet together to counsel in assembly, our subjects should firstly and immediately present the matter to us with the expectation of receiving due relief. If they can be helped, then the situation should accordingly remain. If they cannot be helped, then six shall be chosen from every court in the district, as well as six from every municipality, or if they prefer, the men at the head of each household should meet, and if the cause requires and extends to nearby districts, then one, two or three from those districts should be appointed and admitted, in order that the matter being counseled and negotiated can thereupon be correctly presented to us.

8. We grant our permission for the Emmental region, as has been the practice for several years, to have a league leader as well as a banneret, both of whom, subject to their acceptance of swearing to us as their authority the oath of allegiance, to which we are entitled and is due us.

9. The coveted division of leased lands – earlier known as fiefs – in the Emmental region under the direction of a responsible agency, especially Trubschachen and Langnau, is definitely something which we cannot allow. Nonetheless, inasmuch as the largest and notable properties where it is not possible for a single heir to compensate or buy out the other heirs, we therefore want to allow that the respective bailiwick bailiff, as requested, can inspect the property and report the matter and

explain the desired division of such larger properties under the direction of a responsible landholder, inasmuch as we are of the opinion that the costs for the new land agreements resulting from such a division of leased lands are to be paid by the landholder.

10. Concerning the feudal tariffs, as also those of the bailiffs and ushers, as well as other common dominion rights, the same should only be singly obtained and paid for a property and leased land on which sundry houses are situated, and only 1 Batzen Bernese coinage should be collected from the poor for the landholders' "chicken" tax.

11. It is ruled that we should be paid 8 Crowns Bernese coinage annually for the "contract cheese" from Trub.

12. For the allocation of the seats of the common district jurors as well as that of the court usher, the bailiwick bailiff and the men at the head of each household within the court districts should meet together and make their recommendations for appointments, each one casting his vote, and those with the highest numbers are elected, albeit only after receiving our authoritative confirmation.

13. The large bulk mass shall not be more than that of two small or single masses. [author's commentary: A specific legal definition had to be made in order to prevent malpractice.]

14. We also find favor and want to be certain that throughout all of our German-speaking lands the local courts permanently regulate and maintain the same summer time.

15. The church accounts in all parishes are to be established and approved by the pastors and the members of the parish church council.

16. We allow and are not in opposition to normal obligations of debt security and similar promises be personally written, and additionally that schoolmasters and others be permitted to write about contractual matters which are not required to be certified under seal, providing that one is satisfied with such simple documents which are not legally binding.

17. In accordance with the wishes of our subjects, we want that riding and going to a mill in the Emmental districts can be freely selected and therefore no one is bound to go to a specific mill.

18. We want the administrative officers in the bailiwicks of Langnau, Trub and Lauperswil to be appointed from honest, solid persons designated by the municipalities, but further reserve the right to approve of their nominations and dismissals.

19. We permit the purchase of gun powder from the gun powder makers for all of our subjects for their own use but not for others, at the price which is to be paid to us.

20. Concerning the complaint against several of our bailiwick authorities about unjust monetary fines, on behalf of which at one time or another we have seriously investigated and appropriately dealt with, we repeat our declaration and opinion in this regard that such unlawful fines by these authorities will be repaid to the wrongfully fined persons.

21. Concerning the rules of escort in the department store along with the customs duty, we are of the understanding that fatigue (ending in weariness) is sought after, because our opinion has never been different than in old times and shall remain so.

22. Furthermore, concerning the estate inheritance tax on the allotted smaller lands [so-called "Schachen" and "Reisgrund" properties] for which no amount of inheritance tax has been recorded in the land agreement records, we have clarified this and herewith declare that instead of 5%, 2% and nothing more should be required and obtained.

23. Estate inheritance tax on mills and other properties for which however no specific amount has been recorded in the land agreement records, the inheritance tax shall continue to be definitely declared in the amount of 3½%; furthermore, that which is recorded in the land agreement records concerning other leased lands or properties [Hintersässengüter] belonging to municipality residents who, however, do not have legal rights of citizenship shall remain as in the past; all of these things with the difference and explanation that because of known and relinquished properties the inheritance tax shall not be credited higher than stipulated and obtained in accordance with the proportion and specific property value of the outstanding debt for the leasing of the property and not according to its value or earnings. We herewith want to emphatically mean and have understood that no inheritance tax should become due before the changes and possession have not really taken place.

24. Those who continue to borrow money on mortgage should do nothing other than to merely borrow money in cash, totally, without any deduction or giving away of the "Pfennwarte," and herewith the last regularity and deduction allowance on account of the insolvency regulations shall again be reversed; however should someone act against that, he should be held responsible for suitable replacement, providing that complaint is filed within a one-year period, albeit thereafter that person or his heirs can no longer be held accountable to make repayment. And because in the borrowing of money on mortgage it was never allowed to settle with "Pfennwarte," grain, wine, dairy and similar products instead of money in cash and therefore went against our authoritative regulations, therefore every person who has indulged in such things instead of paying with money in cash since the last permitted reductions in the insolvency regulations of 1647 in borrowing money on mortgage, the debtor thereby remains at fault to pay for the damages sustained and herewith the debtor settles with the lender or his heirs, but when settlement is not made the debtor can obtain legal assistance in order to come to an agreement with the creditor or his heirs, but if complaint is not made, endurance and calmness are necessary.

25. And in order that the debtor in these impoverished and financially difficult times can be better helped, we want the mortgage debt securities to be regulated by "eternal" interest rates, and that every individual shall be allowed and permitted to pay the capital and main property as well as the interest on three due dates with money in cash.

26. Hence, concerning the permission for the legal adviser in "Tröll" and other matters of justice we shall possibly suffer but let it be that the courts are made aware of said permission for the resident population to take advantage of such legal counsel and the respective bailiwick bailiff shall be relieved therefrom.

27. Thus, with regard to the bailiwick earnings and the alleged abolishment of engaging a messenger, every departing bailiwick bailiff during the period of his office and jurisdiction shall do it correctly and without additional costs either himself pay or obtain the funds from the usher's means to pay the messenger. That, however, which despite such practical efforts in the past year's income was not earned before the reductions, should thereafter fall under the established general regulations and realization for messengers.

28. That occasionally some minor matter requires inspection and further court justice or complete repeal can be avoided, we consent to allow the magistrate court jurors to act as justices of the peace.

29. Because permanent complaint has been made against the craftsmen's guilds in the rural regions and their abolishment is viewed as being beneficial, we therefore agree to the suspension of the same. Therefore, the guild charters shall be recalled inasmuch as the legal

complaints about agreements concerning increased earnings have been forfeited.

30. *Thus, concerning the permission to fish in the streams, we are not of the opinion that there where they have the right to fish and continue to do so, but as allowed in times long past, their request to catch fish for a meal in their small streams should not be refused.*

31. *All astute and perilous inductions and perpetrated velocity for recruiting mercenaries shall be noncommittal and invalid, therefore and to such an extent that when a man appears to have been also deliberately inducted, albeit without courageousness, he shall not be guilty for not having kept his word. We are thus of the opinion, that in such cases all excessive punishments shall be suppressed and such recruits not be cited before militia authorities.*

32. *We allow that money trade between individual parties, trade may be agreed upon, yet declare that on that account a court juror should be present in order to pay attention to important penal matters, and, if necessary, to duly file complaints about the same.*

33. *The initial measurement concerning the interest rate on property as supposed with the "small measure" is to be seen in the old land agreement records, which we therewith let stand because it was such in times long past.*

34. *The old regulations concerning the costs for courts of appeal brought us to the realization that such was dissatisfactory and that was the reason we had the new regulations published in the year 1648; therefore, the requested suspension of unnecessary costs for courts of appeal were instigated then and shall continue and remain valid.*

35. *As we also have already declared, the written mandate on carrying a sword has been suspended, and every man is therefore free to choose whether or not he wears a sword without having to worry about a*

penalty. [author's commentary: Every free male wears a sword as a sign of his freedom, e.g., as at the Appenzell regional assembly of the "Landsgemeinde⁴" This Swiss tradition corresponds to the second amendment of the Constitution of the United States.]

36. The things which differ concerning the registered complaints, grievances and obligations of fellow countrymen from one place or another shall be presented with all justifiable causes of complaint and considered for our equitable and conducive decision and remedial measure at another time, at the same time, however, all administered in accordance with old usages, rights and freedoms, and presented in all areas as recorded in the old land agreements, charters and documents with affixed seals, irrespective of more recent regulations.

37. Hereby is our ultimate, merciful opinion and covenant that we have allowed and permitted our above-cited beloved subjects in all of the stipulated manifold considerations, for which they can then be happy and for that reason express their continuing, equitable and everlasting gratitude, and owing a debt of obedience and fidelity shall apply themselves at all times to defend this, their lengthy, subservient allegiance and fealty towards us, their superior authorities, in that we shall protect, shelter and hold them. And with the consideration of these entire affairs, also, all that which has taken place in words and deeds in the continuing matter is forgotten and revoked, and no one will be punished on either body, privilege or property. [author's comment: "a general amnesty"] All these reputable and harmless matters, by the power of this agreement, which is herewith completed for our afore-cited subjects, and affixed with the privy seal. Given on 18 (28) May 1653.

Preface – Opinion: Swiss Peasants were the First Freedom Fighters for Modern Democracy & Why America Must Also Continue to Rebel

Probably not in vogue in this new century and millennium, old tales, residuals of ancient oral traditions, subliminally offering moral lessons for the young, were still popular in the medieval times over half a century past. One I was particularly enamored of was the tale of William Tell, a Swiss legend inspired by their history. Perhaps an old movie crafted from this story inspired me, as the Robin Hood stories and films that were among the old "swashbuckler" movies we could often find on one of the few, four or five, channels we had available on television. A hero who put others' interests ahead of his own, risking his life fighting to make things right for others, if not now, then for those following. I would like to recruit such heroes and heroines, now.

Paternal ancestors from Switzerland brought my family to America almost 300 years ago. From the same genes as a Swiss hero who was also inspired by the fable of William Tell, these landing forefathers were brave enough to fight the status quo of an oppressive, i.e., sick, society in Europe but knew that battle would probably outlive them and wanted their family and offspring to know a better way than they had been forced to. America offered that hope by the mid-18th century.

The hope that America offered then is still alive, but the flame is flickering as if the big, bad wolf is huffing and puffing to blow down a house built of straw or sticks. Sadly, in the last century, victims of fascism or other terror-inducing totalitarian regimes, refugees of rage and ruin, have come knocking at our door and we have slammed it in their faces, more than once. Fundamental fear has put a crucible in our path, again. The gateway to freedom was open to our ancestors but we will allow no more? Our house of hope was built of brick, the wolf will be denied.

American Presidents from Hoover to Eisenhower, Barack Obama to, maybe in the not so far future, Amy Klobuchar, are of Swiss descent. We will see. There is a possibility that one our greatest Progressive Presidents, before them, had that heritage, also, that he had clues of. Like him, to a lesser degree, President Obama righted the listing ship, but those same old pirates have lashed it to another, set on plundering it and submitting it to the flame of fanatic nationalism.

Do you recall the darkness perceived, the fear felt, when the Presidential election of the year 2000 was decided in highly questionable ways by the winner's (George W. Bush) brother's (Gov. Jeb Bush) state, Florida, and a Right-wing partisan Supreme Court? Did you have the feeling that the U.S. Constitution had become, just like that, so much toilet paper?

Sept. 11, 2001 may have removed that from many memories. Did the reports that the George W. Bush administration had been warned about a possible attack and turned the other cheek, looked the other way, cause the fiery pain of the questionable election results to flare up, again, like the two airliners' fuel on the flames? Was the Republican rush to war in Iraq, unilaterally, when the world was as wary of the claims of WMD's as were thinking Americans, making you recall the anti-war sentiments and songs of the war in Vietnam era. Did you paraphrase the "I Feel Like I'm Fixin' to Die Rag" of Country Joe McDonald and the Fish:

"...Hello oil, goodbye Saddam,

next step is in Iran."

...in your fear of the fabricated war, and its rapid privatization that was benefitting war-profiteers even in the White House and Capitol Hill circles?

Later, were you jumping up and down angry regarding the questions of election integrity in critical swing-states in the 2004 election, that allowed Bush and Cheney to continue draining the U.S. Treasury, ala Texas Politics 101? Read *Blood, Money, and Power* by Barr McClellan (the father of George W. Bush's press secretary and a member of the law firm that represented LBJ) for a primer on American Conservatism, Texas-style; I believe you will find it bears a ring of familiarity if not the déjà vu of a recalled nightmare.

Were you sure help was on the way, that the cavalry had arrived, when the Democrats achieved majorities in both houses of Congress in 2007, only to feel even further betrayed when no actions were taken against senior Executive Branch members or allies and their alleged violations of Constitutional law?

Did the election of Barack Obama as President of the United States in 2008, a gentleman with some Swiss ancestry (a heritage of a number of American Presidents), also with the credentials of being a Constitutional scholar and acting-professor, State and U.S Senator, feel like a breath of fresh air after suffering through waterboarding? Were you thinking of it as an assurance that the Dark Ages of America had been short-lived, indeed, and a Constitutional Renaissance would soon relieve us? In spite of the Republican obstructionism which invited rearing racism, did the reelection of POTUS #44 prevent you from seeing where America was headed? Did you not see the truth of what was going on until Mitch McConnell again pulled the Constitutional rug out from under us by disallowing the sitting President from placing his nominee, Merrick Garland, on the Supreme Court of the United States, not even considering his nomination in an unprecedented political move that surely prevented a Constitutionally authorized Supreme Court appointment? Only then, did you feel all hope of legitimate governance was vanished and that we were entering the Twilight Zone of totalitarianism?

In spite of the sun parting the dark clouds in 2008, giving us hope through 2016, those storm clouds were settling ever lower, from the steam rising from stewing and brewing authoritarians' ears as fear of another non-white, non-heterosexual, or non-male becoming America's leader created friction amongst their wildly oscillating brain cells.

Hillary Clinton's indubitable continuation of a Democratic Executive Branch would surely allow us a more Constitutional, i.e., less partisan-tool, SCOTUS. Hopefully, with a Progressive Congress, as well, American liberties and Barack Obama's economic gains would be saved. Maybe public healthcare would finally be realized, medical costs still draining a lot of American's potential. The scary specter of Donald Trump would surely be gone after November 8, 2016. Did you have that sense, too?

The "corp. d'état," aided by foreign money and actors, due to a Right-wing partisan SCOTUS aiding Conservatives in elections by its rulings in Citizens United vs FEC (aiding Conservatives by allowing endless corporate money, both domestic and foreign, in elections) and Shelby County vs Holder (crippling VRAA/ furthering disenfranchisement of Black voters) was accomplished by Nov. 9, 2016.

We (the so-called Resistance), fair and just-minded citizens of America, those interested in political and financial "law and order" (a favorite Conservative talking point regarding policing only the average voting American) above all else, have been struggling, since, to shine the light of truth and justice through the dusky storm clouds truly fallen upon the United States of America, threatening not only the People's view, but our voice, and our very vitality. Viva la vote!

The Republicans have long tried to spin the story against us by trying to put negative labels on those opposing them. Calling Progressives "Liberals," meaning it as a dirty word; now, making up ugly stories about "Antifa" members, as if they are the enemies of America, when it is they, the new GOP of the Extreme Right, the Fascists, who Americans must fear, and fight to the finish. Eat your spinach, y'all.

Please, relate to the observations of one member of the Resistance since the administration of George W. Bush and Dick Cheney. When, where, and how it will end, and if we must begin anew, we do not know, but people and the planet have suffered long enough at the hands of predators, pirates, privateers, and profiteers, too many of them politicians or the richly powerful allies or controllers of politicians.

Hopefully, you will relate to this review of humanity's current crisis, and the comparison to two possibly correlated struggles for democracy. One common person's perspective as compared to the news consistent with the chronology of his views—takes the reader from his family's fight, fatality from fascist-like forces, and subsequent flight in the 17th century to this millennium's birth complications and our struggles in the adolescence of the Twenty-first Century to procure or ensure freedom, justice, and human rights to where we must march.

In the current era, see the first major clue our Republic was in danger due to loss of election integrity, further assaults on our Constitution and its "Checks and Balances," to an outright coup d'état effort, in progress, by a corrupted Conservative Party and their American and foreign actors and enablers.

A large percentage of Americans, and global citizens, think that we are about to test, once more, if a government of the people, by the people, and for the people shall not perish from the earth. I certainly feel this way. The readers may see, if they follow through, why I ask permission to say, "please let another of Swiss heritage come to the fore, and the fray."

Chapter 1 - The American Dream

The Spanish settlements in Florida, and perhaps California, seem to have been more exploratory military excursions/outposts than actual colonizing attempts, though, if the indigenous peoples of the SW coast of the continent had worked the gold there, it probably would have been a different story, there. Wikipedia explains:

Florida was never more than a backwater region for Spain. In contrast with Mexico and Peru, there was no gold to be found. There was insufficient native population to set up the encomienda system of forced agricultural labor, and Spaniards did not set up plantations in Florida. The missions did supply St. Augustine with maize, and were required to send laborers to St. Augustine every year to work in the fields and perform other labor.[1]

And Roanoke Colony, which in the 16th century had the honor of being recognized as having the first English child, Virginia Dare, to be born in the New World, was a short-lived, abject failure. Although an interesting mystery, it will be precluded from consideration. Jamestown, which was James Fort, with almost 100% Englishmen for the first decade, being relabeled Jamestown in 1619, also will be considered an outpost rather than a colony, in its first decade, and should have served as a warning for men thinking of bringing their wife and children to this place. "American Beginnings" offers some grim numbers:

JAMESTOWN is justifiably called "the first permanent English settlement" in the New World—a hard-won designation. As historian Alan Taylor recounts, of the first 104 colonists who landed in April 1607, only thirty-eight survived the winter. Of the 10,000 who left

England for Jamestown in its first fifteen years, only twenty percent were still alive, and still in Jamestown, in 1622.[2]

8000 out of 10000 did not survive, or stick around, anyway, in a decade and a half there. A group seeking religious-freedom, beginning a trend that will be seen, seem to be the first colonists, or permanent settlement of families.

For the purpose of understanding why so many people chanced everything to come to the mostly unexplored continent of North America, let's first look to religious exiles, the Puritans per History.com:

One such faction was a group of separatist believers in the Yorkshire village of Scrooby, who, fearing for their safety, moved to Holland in 1608 and then, in 1620, to the place they called Plymouth in New England.[3]

Also, from Wikipedia:

Plymouth Colony was founded by a group of Puritan Separatists initially known as the Brownist Emigration, who came to be known as the Pilgrims. It was the second successful colony to be founded by the English in America after Jamestown in Virginia, and it was the first permanent English settlement in the New England region.[4]

We may be able to understand why men risked their lives for adventure and rumored riches. However, considering a James Fort/Jamestown attrition rate of 80%, and ripping their families' lives asunder in the old home, to take the awful chance of horrible hardships and premature deaths of their wives and children, what in hell drove them to that decision?

Consider what evils the church had planted in the minds of people in Europe against those who chose to think for themselves. Envision the horrible treatment religiously-independent people received, including torture and horrible, terrifying deaths. Reason determines that being stuffed aboard tiny ships on voyages that were often fatal of themselves, to the New World to seek and realize the "American Dream," where 8000 of 10000 had already failed if not died, was not immigrants' objective, at this point. More likely, their frightening journey was in hope of escaping the European nightmare they were living due to their passionate beliefs.

The Irish were early and numerous immigrants to the colonies. Did the Catholics persecute the Protestants more or the Protestants the Catholics in Great Britain and Ireland? The jury is still out, but from both and the English disdain for the Irish, in general, and their violent treatment of the "Irish" problem, the people of Ireland suffered mightily. The "Massacre of the Protestant Martyrs at the Bridge over the River Bann in Ireland," 1641, an engraving by Matthew Taylor, portrays Irish Catholics murdering:

...approximately one hundred Protestants from Loughgall Parish, County Armagh, at the bridge over the River Bann near Portadown, Ulster.

This atrocity occurred at the beginning of the Irish Rebellion of 1641. Having held the Protestants as prisoners and tortured them, the Catholics drove them "like hogs" to the bridge, where they were stripped naked and forced into the water below at swordspoint. Survivors of the plunge were shot.[5]

The church founded on Martin Luther's Reformation found the going tough in Europe, also. From Salzburg, many of the more fortunate Lutherans came to America whereas others were forced to freeze to death:

On October 31, 1731, the Catholic ruler of Salzburg, Austria, Archbishop Leopold von Firmian, issued an edict expelling as many as 20,000 Lutherans from his principality. Many propertyless Lutherans, given only eight days to leave their homes, froze to death as they drifted through the winter seeking sanctuary. The wealthier ones who were allowed three months to dispose of their property fared better. Some of these Salzburgers reached London, from whence they sailed to Georgia. [6]

The Reformers

Lutherans/Swiss Brethren/Anabaptists/Quakers/Mennonites/Amish

From the late 17th and into the 19th century, escape from religious persecution still figured predominately in immigration to North America. The Swiss Brethren, Anabaptist believers, many later melding into the Mennonite or Amish enclaves, accounted for a sizable percentage of emigrants from Europe per Wikipedia:

The Swiss Brethren are a branch of Anabaptism that started in Zürich, spread to nearby cities and towns, and then was exported to neighboring countries. Today's Swiss Mennonite Conference can be traced to the Swiss Brethren.

In 1525, Felix Manz, Conrad Grebel, George Blaurock and other radical evangelical reformers broke from Ulrich Zwingli and formed a new group because they felt reforms were not moving fast enough.

Rejection of infant baptism was a distinguishing belief of the Swiss Brethren. On the basis of Sola scriptura doctrine, the Swiss Brethren declared that since the Bible does not mention infant baptism, it should not be practiced by the church. This belief was subsequently rejected by Ulrich Zwingli. Consequently, there was a public dispute, in which the council affirmed Zwingli's position. This solidified the Swiss Brethren and resulted in their persecution by all other reformers as well as the Catholic Church.

Because of persecution by the authorities, many Swiss Brethren moved from Switzerland to neighboring countries. The Swiss Brethren became known as Mennonites after the division of 1693, a disagreement between groups led by Jacob Amman and Hans Reist. Many of the Mennonites in France, Southern Germany, the Netherlands and North America, as well as most Amish descend from the Swiss Brethren.[7]

The Anabaptists were a movement particular to Switzerland, born of the reformation, and, perhaps, the printing press, the social media of the time though relatively few could yet read, superseding, somewhat, the ancient bard system and the word of the church. The few literates able to read the scriptures, now, made their own determinations, and spread the "word" as they interpreted it. They firmly believed in the pacifism of Jesus, only becoming baptized when they could make that decision for themselves, as adults, and committing to following no orders except as they understood as the "word of God," the Bible.

The greatest landowners, and the Cantons of Switzerland, profited mightily from the conscripting of peasants to fight wars for other countries as mercenary soldiers. The Anabaptists threatened this source of income, mightily. The church was still powerful throughout Europe and they did not look kindly on the potential loss of income, either, or their age-old authority deteriorating, due to the Anabaptist movement.

All of this disturbed the State since much of the teaching was anarchistic: a social order in which the Church would be completely replaced by free Christian communities which would develop unmolested by pressures from the State. In addition to their unorthodox ideas on baptism, the Anabaptists believed in the innate purity and sinlessness of man. From this stemmed the Anabaptist opposition to military service, to the death penalty, and resort to violence; officials of the government should be guided by the Sermon on the Mount. To its teachings, government should literally adhere, and even interest and tithes should be abolished.[8]

This was a threat to the status quo which the powerful elite did not look kindly upon:

Government responded with severe punishments. Their leaders were drowned in the Zurichsee, hung, or banned from the city.[9]

The Anabaptists even faced accusations of witchcraft, consorting with the devil:

...many alleged evidences of witchcraft. In Zurich, the Anabaptists suffered under such charges.[10]

The witch hunts, torture, inhumane executions, continued even until 1782, in Glarus.

The violence against the non-conformers had eased by the mid-18th century but other ways of dealing with the unsettling problem were found. About the same time that the Lutherans were being forcibly removed from their homes in Salzburg, Austria, Bernese authorities were paying emigrant agents for each Anabaptist they got to leave for America.

Bern welcomed the exodus of Anabaptists, and, in fact, paid the emigration agents for each Anabaptist they succeeded in moving out of the canton.[11]

Some of the same trained Swiss mercenary soldiers mentioned earlier were probably part of the German-Swiss influx to America. They came as members of the "German" Hessian companies that the British used to supplement their own forces to try to subdue the colonist rebellion in America. Though probably neither Anabaptist nor Mennonite, many of them probably stayed to join the Swiss and German farming communities already thriving in the now United States of America, in Pennsylvania, Virginia, and North Carolina, predominately, after the British capitulated.

The American Dream Reality

On top of America's seeming greater tolerance in the eighteenth and early nineteenth centuries, her new independence and grand charter of equality for all was a beck and call to many still facing the old prejudices of Europe. America slowly became less of a risk, a less chancy sanctuary as it grew. Potential immigrants often knew and corresponded with friends and family in the United States and had a better idea of what to expect, and knew they had people to help them find their way in a new life, there. People began coming to America not only to escape a certain worse fate, but to realize their minds' "rumblings" of a better life. Not only safety and security, but personal solvency and an estate of some value reportedly could be gained in this new, and new kind of, country. The American Dream, after a long and painful labor, had finally been delivered.

The struggles of American expansion.

Near-anarchy on the frontier with a lack of ready law enforcement was a possible reality for pioneers. People were being conned out of their savings with fake property transactions, robbery, etc. Equality for all was suspect from our slave-owning founding fathers to those of old-school European descent with Holy Roman Empire mentalities where the Irish, the Reformers, and others, were suspect and, possibly, unwelcome neighbors. Not all of the colonists had been part of independent religious groups, or had broken off from their parents' ways, and feared or frowned on any "unlike" them.

European prejudices and bigotry had found their way across the Atlantic. The very first settlers soon assumed "god-given" superiority over the indigenous peoples of the new continents, killing them or using them for forced labor. As early as 1619 English colonists began bringing captured African people in as slaves. Perhaps not the religious reformer immigrants, but some of America's earliest settlers had already sowed the seeds of racial inequality, animosity, and hatred. Where was this born?

We know the Spanish treated the indigenous peoples of South and Central America even more horrifically. Now, the British, too had a record, though their inhumane treatment of Irish and Scots was well known. Perhaps the Roman Empire had left this pattern imprinted on all they had conquered.

We need to rededicate our country to the Statue of Liberty's promise:

The New Colossus

by Emma Lazarus (1849–1887)

Not like the brazen giant of Greek fame,

With conquering limbs astride from land to land;

Here at our sea-washed, sunset gates shall stand

A mighty woman with a torch, whose flame

Is the imprisoned lightning, and her name

Mother of Exiles. From her beacon-hand

Glows world-wide welcome; her mild eyes command

The air-bridged harbor that twin cities frame.

"Keep, ancient lands, your storied pomp!" cries she

With silent lips. "Give me your tired, your poor,

Your huddled masses yearning to breathe free,

The wretched refuse of your teeming shore.

Send these, the homeless, tempest-tost to me,

I lift my lamp beside the golden door!"[12]

Today, conditions in countries on both sides of the globe are such that many are still risking not only their life and limbs, but those of their loved ones. People are seeking sanctuary, at least, and a decent life at best, or, in another man's words, "life, liberty, and the pursuit of happiness," of course, from the Declaration of Independence. Crossing the Mediterranean from Africa to Europe, often in tiny storm-tossed overcrowded crafts, many lose their lives in the pursuit of saving them.

Thousands, every year, make the trek from deadly violence of southern Central American countries, across a thousand miles or so of hostile conditions of arid Mexico. They pray to make it to the United States for safety and sanctuary for themselves or their families, at the minimum, and hopes of peaceful, industrious lives, at best. They risk this, now, to have their children ripped from their arms and imprisoned in conditions more horrible than the worst county jail, and they are then forced back to survive the best they can, or, too typically, not.

Our nationalistic police forces are still killing Black people, time after time. On the average, three people a day are killed by the police in America. Not all of this mean number are darker skinned, but who would be surprised if two out of three were not. Too often police are seemingly killing people simply for the audacity of also trying to realize the promise, the charter, of America—"life, liberty, and the pursuit of happiness'. That is the American Dream, since Thomas Jefferson penned those words for the Declaration of Independence. Regrettably, this seems to be considered mainly for white people, then, and, even more inexcusably, now, as, en masse, we have no excuse for being that ignorant.

The author can only hope that the reason his ancestor and most of this ancestor's siblings sold their Virginia farms and moved to Illinois, in the 1830's, during the heat of the abolition fight, was as a commitment to the opposition of slavery. One of their brothers, or nephews, who stayed to run his plantation, as a "Gentleman" according to the 1850 U.S. Census, owned slaves, and had a son who was a lieutenant in the Confederate Army. The author believes that this relative was the exception to the rule of the family descended from pacifist Anabaptists and agitators for personal freedom and human rights.

The "American Dream" was not fully developed by the mid-1730's when the author's immigrant ancestors arrived. They surely had hopes of forgetting the emotional and societal pain the "land barons," the conservative wealth-holders in Bern, had burdened the family with eighty years before in the aftermath of the Swiss Peasant War of 1653. Or, maybe they were escaping the persecution they still felt because of their Anabaptist ties. It could be that the family's "rebel" label from the revolt and/or their Anabaptist history made them one of the undesirables the "aristocrats" of Bern would pay to have removed to the New World. It could have been as simple as peer pressure.

Whichever was the reason for their arrival in America, in 1735, Hans Leuenberger (Leyenberger on passenger list), Hans Ulrich L., Peter L., and the wife/mother and daughters/sisters undoubtedly carried their hopes with them and prayed to have left their fears behind. But, is this probably not true of most who must find and make a new home? Life, Liberty, and the Pursuit of Happiness would not become a recognized goal of immigrants to America for several decades, but they knew the truths that everyone should intrinsically understand, that equality must impact all others as it impacts them, in their hearts and their minds, was what they were lacking. *"Will we find a better life in America?"*

Chapter 2 - The Leuenberger in Lionberger

Anabaptists in the Leuenberger family had probably already brought a lot of negative attention to the family in the Emmenthal region, east of Bern. Putting the leader of a revolt against the aristocracy of the city, Niklaus Leuenberger, under even more excruciating disdain from the authorities. He was horrifically tortured and executed and drawn and quartered, twice made an example of. The author's ancestors were probably doubly pained by remorse and the feeling of shame leveled on them by some in the community.

By the latter part of the seventeenth century the persecution against the Anabaptists had subsided but still could bring suspicion, harassment, and "bad luck," to put it mildly. Perhaps the extra burden of the horrific execution of kin Niklaus Leuenberger after the peaceful siege of Bern and the supposed settlement of their grievances was, finally, too much to bear. Or, perhaps, they were also a part of the Reformers, the religious believers steadfast against the religious status quo, in Switzerland, as their recent ancestor Hans Leuenberger of Ruderswil, per Hans Minder's research:

Hans Leuenberger born 4.7.1586 in Lauperswil, died around 1638, married. on 24.9.1610 in Rüderswil with Elsabeth Moser, born about 1590...[13]

Hans was the first known Anabaptist in the family, but the movement first became a problem for the city patriarchs in 1525, so, it's possible that the family had already decided that they were old enough to make their own religious decisions, in some previous generation but it was safer to be open about it by the seventeenth century, though, it would still create "problems'. Hans Minder gave this information to this author's sister, the direct descendants will be shown in bold:

- **Ulrich** Leuenberger, born 24.11.1611 in Lauperswil, died before 1631 in Rüderswil, married to Barbara Lüthi, born in 1610

- **Ulrich** Leuenberger, b. 15.1.1643, married on 23.4.1670 in Rüderswil Margareth Oberli.[14]

Ulrich Jr., above, may have been the family member that joined the Anabaptist exodus out of the Bern/Emmenthal area. His and his wife Margreth's death records seem to be missing from Ruderswil, their date and place of death are not given. Family oral tradition tells of our ancestors coming to America from the Alsace-Lorraine region in what is now part of France.

In the last half of the twentieth century this family has expanded their knowledge to realize they are of Swiss descent and the old tradition that tells of French descent is still argued by some family members. They are undoubtedly correct in the statement that the ancestors came to America by way of Alsace, but they were not, generationally, "of" that region. Close, but no cigar. The family's Swiss ancestors undoubtedly were part of the migration of persecuted Anabaptists out of the Bern area, in their case, and into Alsace where there was a pocket of religious tolerance.

Below excerpt, very probably relates some "whys" and "whens" of some Leuenbergers' move from around Bern to Alsace (predominately German culturally):

The Thirty Years War (1618-1648) had been one of the worst periods in the history of Alsace and other parts of Southern Germany. It caused large numbers of the population (mainly in the countryside) to die or to flee away, because the land was successively invaded and devastated by many armies (Imperials, Swedes, French, etc.). After 1648 and until the mid-18th century, numerous immigrants arrived from Switzerland, Germany, Austria, Lorraine, Savoy and other areas. Between 1671-1711 Anabaptist refugees came from Switzerland, notably from Bern. Strasbourg became a main center of the early Anabaptist movement.[15]

In a few decades, or less, they would be part of the Anabaptist/ Mennonite movement to America.

Early American immigrant Leuenbergers were associated with Pennsylvania Mennonites. A large Mennonite enclave grew out of Alsace and came to America, many Anabaptists and Quakers were near to the Mennonites, as well. William Penn was given Pennsylvania to pay off the royal debt that he was owed. A Quaker, himself, he opened up Pennsylvania to fellow Reformers.

Persecuted in England for his Quaker faith, Penn came to America in 1682 and established Pennsylvania as a place where people could enjoy freedom of religion. The colony became a haven for minority religious sects from Germany, Holland, Scandinavia, and Great Britain. Penn obtained the land from King Charles II as payment for a debt owed to his father.[16]

If Penn's quintessential Quaker country had become the model for the entire country, with kind, trusting treatment and interaction with the indigenous peoples, the American Ideal wouldn't have got stuck in neutral, where it has easily been bumped into reverse. At least he had his "country" in first gear from where it is easier to progress, slowly, but steadily over tough inclines and rough terrain:

In Pennsylvania Penn hoped to provide a refuge for Quakers and other persecuted people and to build an ideal Christian commonwealth. "There may be room there, though not here" he wrote to a friend in America, "for such a holy experiment.[17]

Penn wrote a plan for conscientious governing of his province, "The Frame of Government," that some say was a precursor to American Democracy and the Constitution.

As proprietor, Penn seized the opportunity to create a government that would embody his Quaker-Whig ideas. In 1682 he drew up a Frame of Government for the colony that would, he said, leave himself and his successors "no power of doing mischief, that the will of one man may not hinder the good of a whole country."[18]

There are communities of Mennonites in Alsace and Pennsylvania, still, in addition to the other places they have migrated to. Members of later generations of Reformers in American were drawn to the Baptist religion. Some report that there is no connection between the German Baptists and the English Baptists, however, they both sprang up as part of the "reformer" movement. Whether it was an outgrowth of the Anabaptist movement, in the Netherlands where the Mennonites sprang from Anabaptists, or just another of the several Reformer religions, they had something in common. It may be that the same melting-pot theory of the growing colonies was soon applied to these various religions of similar roots.

German Baptists are not related to the English Baptist movement and were inspired by European Anabaptists. Upon moving to the United States, they associated with Mennonites and Quakers.[19]

From Pennsylvania where William Penn had given them room and security to develop, they seem to have remained in communities together from Pennsylvania to Virginia, and to Kentucky, Indiana, and Illinois, among others, but descendants of Anabaptist and Quaker families were later found in the Baptist church, which may have become the popular American version of reformation religion in America.

Ulrich and Margreth's son Hans and his wife, Elisabeth, seem to have been the lead immigrants of the family. Their ship's list[20] and manifesto[21], figures 1 and 2, respectively, document their arrival in 1735:

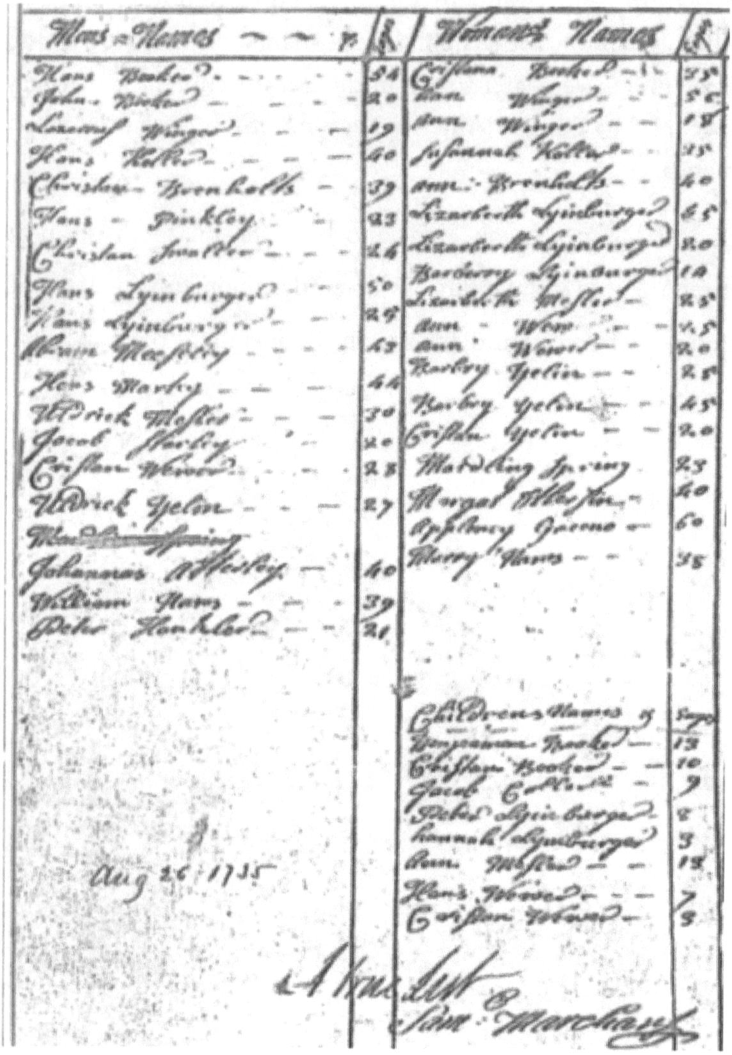

Fig. 1: Passenger list of the ship, Oliver, showing the men, women, and children aboard, respectively, when it landed in Philadelphia in 1735.

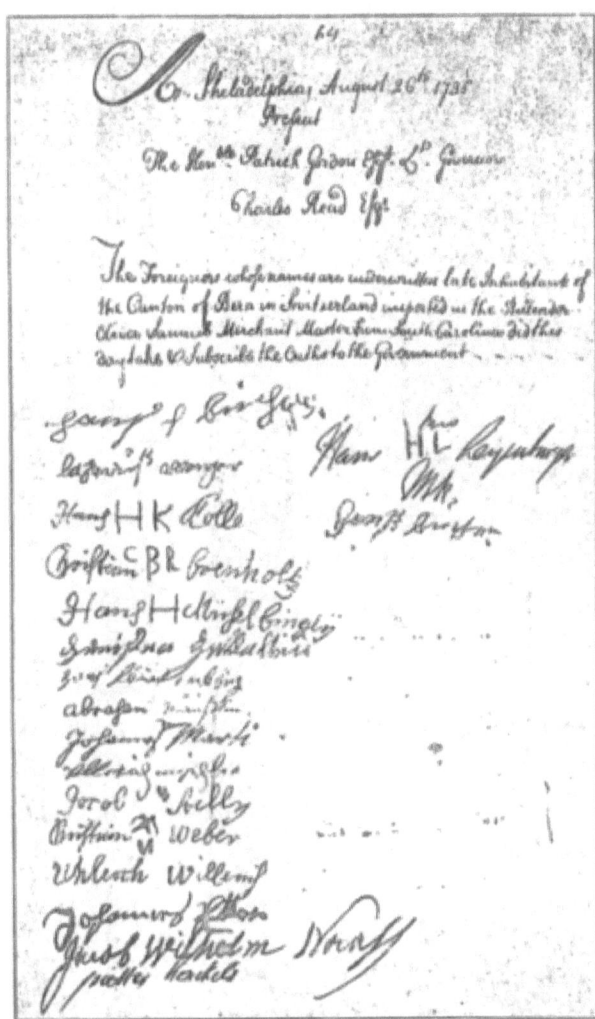

Fig. 2: Manifesto in the city of Philadelphia, from the ship, the Oliver, showing the Bernese men who swore the oath to King George III in 1735.

The younger Hans (John) and Peter "Lyinberger" above appear to be those brothers reported ahead to have gained a land grant in Virginia from the crown. This Hans (John) Jr. may not be the John that owned the land in Frederick County, in the pre-Shenandoah County configuration of the Shenandoah valley counties that is mentioned in the 1759 Virginia census document shown in the following "The Leuenberger in Lincoln?" chapter because it appears that he had already "bought the farm," if you will pardon the idiom. It will be shown that the third John, son of immigrant Hans Jr., is that man, as documented by land records and Hans' and John's wills.

After most of a century and several generations in the beautiful Virginia valley of Shenandoah, Abraham and most of his siblings packed up their wagons and headed for Illinois from approximately 1820-1850, Abraham and his immediate family in 1837.

After half a century in Illinois, with several family members, spanning three generations, already laid to rest in Hancock County, Illinois, there came another migration of family. Some of Abraham's branch stayed in Illinois but a few homesteaded and fiddled around in Nebraska. From there they split, some going "next door," back to the east in Missouri, and Abraham's grandson Albert taking his family to the Pacific Northwest. According to his son Glen's family history, "Al" had longed yearned to go to the "paradise" of Oregon he had heard so much about.

Fig. 3: "Dad" is Albert with two brothers, "Will" & "Ike," before moving to Nebraska with his older brother, Thomas, where those two fiddlers were popular at barn dances.

In Oregon, in the latter 20th century, the battle with southern cousins over the family's descent from French or Swiss ancestors began. Decades, a century, or millennium later, some have resolved the issue, leaving others to ask, Swiss heritage, okay, but where did the French-Alpine goats come from in figures 4 and 5?

Fig. 4 & 5: French-Alpine dairy goats on the Lionberger farm near Portland, Oregon from family photos. The author recalls helping with the "barn-raising" as young "chief-assistant."

An endnote on the Leuenberger/Lionberger descendance—the author being the youngest or the only boy, or both, always got stuck with the clean-up detail, concerning the goat pens and, also, rabbit hutches. It was much like the job of the crew with the wagon at the end of the Zurich Street Parade or the Burgdorf Kinder parade, following the goats, cows, and horses.

The foreword, that provides more European history of the family of the Swiss peasant leader Niklaus Leuenberger, was written by Hans Leuenberger, author of the article, "Niklaus Leuenberger, Predating Gandhi in 1653?" in the Swiss American Historical Society Review, February 2020,[22] and the book, *Niklaus Leuenberger, the "Swiss Gandhi" of the 17th century?: The Swiss Peasants' War 1653*.[23]

Chapter 3 - The Leuenberger in Lincoln?

Documents Reveal & Circumstances Hint of Kinship

German-speaking Swiss were among the so-called German or Dutch-German (although there were Dutch among the earliest immigrants to Pennsylvania, to label them all as Dutch was possibly a mistaken interpretation of Deutsche) immigrants, as described by many American histories. To a large degree this American heritage is unknown as, sadly, too much of our history is glossed over, at best. Numbers of them, in keeping with good company perhaps, also traveled the Great Wagon Road to the south and west, creating more like communities along the way. More on such sites in Virginia, ahead, including what would become West Virginia and Kentucky, also in the Midwest.

Shenandoah's social order was shaped from the very start of its occupation by Europeans through a large population of Swiss and other Germanic language immigrants or their descendants. So, the valley is to this day somewhat culturally anachronistic or disparate from the rest of the state.

Perhaps due to Reformed religions' objections to slavery, among other possible reasons, the Germanic settlers of the valley owned fewer slaves. Consequently, the area has never had a large African-American population. The earliest European settlers of the Shenandoah Valley, of Germanic roots, settled mostly in the northern portions of the valley, and the Scotch-Irish who mostly settled in the southern portions of the valley. This is not to say that these northern Virginians did not reap financial benefits from a slave-labor based economy.

Glen Lionberger's family history gives us this brief hint of the immigrant brothers John (Hans) and Peter Lionberger in Virginia:

In 1749 John and Peter Lionberger bought eleven hundred acres of land in Virginia, near Luray in the Shenandoah Valley.[24]

Glen's information was precisely right. A Luray, Virginia's "Page News and Courier" 1950 news story's 1970 reprint, fig. 6, relates that "John and Peter Lineberger" were among the 1st recipients of an Augusta County, Virginia land grant from Thomas Lord Fairfax.

One Of The First Land Grants From The Crown

(PN&C Issue of March 2, 1950)

The following is a copy of one of the first if not the first grants of land given in what is now Page County, then Augusta County, to John and Peter Lionberger in 1749.

The grant extended from a big oak tree south of Luray to Marksville and west to the present Eastside Highway.

Taken from the book, "A Family of Five Republics," belonging to (the late) Mrs. H. R. McKay, and written by Paul M. and Walter F. Lineberger.

The original grant as recorded in Richmond reads as follows:

"THE RIGHT HONORABLE THOMAS LORD FAIRFAX, Baron of Cameron in that part of Great Britain called Scotland, Proprietor of the Northern Neck of Virginia: To all to whom this present writing shall come sends Greeting.

Know Ye that for good Causes for and in Consideration of the Composition to Me Paid and for the annual Rent hereafter reserved I have given granted and confirmed and by these Presents for Me my Heirs and Assigns do give grant and confirm unto John and Peter Lionberger of Augusta County a certain Tract of Waste and ungranted Land in the said County upon the Little Hawks Bill and Bounded as by a Survey thereof made by Mr. John Baylis as Followeth:

BEGINNING at three Pines on the side of a small Rising and Running thence So. 17 degrees Wt. Four hundred and Sixty Six Poles and an Half to a Pine, thence So. 73 degrees Et. 18 Poles to a Pine on a Hill side; thence So. 17 degrees Wt. Three hundred and Fifty Six Poles to a Pine in a Valley; thence So. 73 degrees Wt. One hundred and Forty Poles to Peter Ruffner's Corner a white oak and Pine on the East Side of the Little Hawks Bill, to the beginning containing One Thousand One Hundred Acres.

Together with all rights Members and Appurtenances thereunto belonging Royal Mines Excepted and a full third Part of all Lead Copper Tin, Coals from Mines and Iron Ore that shall be found thereon.

To have and to hold One thousand One hundred Acres of Land Together with all Rights Members and Appurtenances belonging or in any Wise appertaining Except before Excepted to them and the said John and Peter Lineberger their Heirs and Assigns therefore Yielding and Paying to Me my Heirs or Assigns or to my certain Attorney or Attorneys Agent or Agents or to the certain Attorney or Attorneys of my Heirs or Assigns Proprietors of the said Northern Neck Yearly and every Year on the First Day of St. Michael the Archangel, the Fee Rent of One Shilling Sterling Money for every Fifty Acres in proportionably for a Greater or Lesser Quantity; Provided that if the said John and Peter Lineberger their Heirs or Assigns shall not Pay the above reserved Annual Rent so that the same or any part thereof shall be behind or unpaid by the space of two whole Years after the same shall become Due it Lawfully Demanded That then is shall and may be Lawful for Me my Heirs or Assigns Proprietors as aforesaid my or their certain Attorney or Attorneys Agent or Agents into the above granted Premises to Reenter and hold the same so as if the grant had never Passed.

Given at my Office in the County of Fairfax within my said Proprietary Under my Hand and Seal dated this ninteenth day of September in the Twenty third Year of the Reign of our Soverign Lord George the Second by the Grace of God of Great Britain France and Ireland King Defender of the Faith, &c. A. Dni. One thousand seven Hundred and Forty Nine.

John and Peter Lineberger's deed for 1100 Acres of Land in Augusta County).

Fairfax
Land Office
Richmond, Virginia,

I hereby certify that the foregoing is a true copy from the records of this Office. Witness my hand and seal of office, this 12th day of August, 1922.

John W. Richardson
Register for the Land Office

EDITOR'S NOTE—The foregoing is reprinted here with the identical punctuation and capital letters as it appeared in the Page News and Courier March 2, 1950.

Fig. 6: Lineberger/Lionberger land grant from George II story in the Page News and Courier, Page County, Virginia, 1970.[25]

To those that know the language of surveyors, the article informs most closely about the location of the Lionbergers' Virginia land-holdings. This site is somewhat southwest of the city of Luray in Page County, Virginia.

The Pages News and Courier article is supported in "Early Settlers on the Shenandoah River (South Branch), Augusta County, VA," see fig. 7. This was the John (Hans Jr.) and Peter, b. 1710 and 1726 in Rüderswil, respectively, who arrived with their parents and sisters in Philadelphia in 1735, as seen in Table 3:

- **John Baylis** of Prince William Co., 4 Jan. 1749 - 5 March 1749; 400 acres on branches of the Hawksbill; adj. Andrew Yougham. CC - Jacob Overbaker & Andrew Yougham. Pilot - Jno. Lyenberger/Lienbarger. Surv. George Hume. [Abstracts of Virginia's Northern Neck Warrants & Surveys, Orange & Augusta Counties, with Tithables, Delinquents, Petitioners, 1730-1754, Volume One, Peggy Smomo Joyner, pg. 19].

- **Samuell Beam**, 20 Nov. 1748 - 15 Dec. 1749; 170 acres on the east of the Hawksbill; adj. Samuel Beams own line. John Lyenberger. Petter Ruffner. CC - Micall Koffman & Petter Ruffner. Surv. George Hume. [Abstracts of Virginia's Northern Neck Warrants & Surveys, Orange & Augusta Counties, with Tithables, Delinquents, Petitioners, 1730-1754, Volume One, Peggy Smomo Joyner, pg. 19].

* * *

- G-325: John & Peter Lienbarger of Augusta County, 1,100 acres in said County. Surv. Mr. John Baylis. On Little Hawks Bill, adj. Peter Rufner. 19 Sept. 1749. [Virginia Northern Neck Land Grants, 1742-1775, Vol. 2, Gertrude E. Gray, pg. 39].

Fig. 7: John and Peter Lienberger listed in "Early Settlers on the Shenandoah River."[26]

It has been shown that Lionberger surname predecessors were residents of northern Virginia from at least 1749. The proximity of the Virginian Leuenberger-Lionbergers to the Lincolns, as in Pennsylvania, however, cannot be documented for nearly twenty years after that. The first known Lincoln to the Shenandoah Valley was John Lincoln, who joined in the train of people "en rut" on the Great Wagon Road to settle lands to the south, in 1768.

The Papers of Abraham Lincoln report that his great-grandfather John moved to Virginia in 1768:

In 1765, John sold the last of his land in Pennsylvania and shortly thereafter moved to Virginia, in 1768 purchasing six hundred acres on the west side of Linville Creek, a few miles north of Harrisonburg in what became Rockingham County. He lived there for the remainder of his life.[27]

The county of Leuenberger-descended families' residences in Virginia is shown to have also changed names several times. From the original land grant in Augusta County, the property became part of Frederick County, then Dunmore County which became Shenandoah County, as mentioned, see county history brief, below, before finally becoming Page County. Whether the county of residence changed via county reorganization or the family's purchase of acreage in adjacent counties is unknown but the former is believed to be the correct answer.

Frederick County was formed in 1738 (government established 1743) from Orange County. Part of Augusta County was added later.

Frederick County was created from Orange County in 1738, and was officially organized in 1743. The Virginia Assembly named the new county for Frederick Louis, Prince of Wales (1707–1751), the eldest son of King George II of Great Britain. At that time, "Old Frederick County" encompassed all or part of four counties in present-day Virginia and five in present-day West Virginia, see the following three extracts:

•*Hampshire (West Virginia), created 1754*

•*Dunmore, created 1772 and renamed Shenandoah in 1778*

•*Berkeley (West Virginia), created 1772*

•*Hardy (West Virginia), created 1786*

•*Jefferson (West Virginia), created 1801*

•*Morgan (West Virginia), created 1820*

•*Page, created 1831*

•*Clarke, created 1836*

•*Warren, created 1836[28]*

Shenandoah County was named for the Shenandoah River, which passed through the county. Shenandoah is an Indian word meaning beautiful daughter of the stars. The county was named Dunmore when it was formed from Frederick County in 1772 and named for John Murray, fourth earl of Dunmore and governor of Virginia from 1771 to 1775. Lord Dunmore's actions at the outbreak of the American Revolution made him so unpopular with Virginians that the General Assembly changed the county's name to Shanando (now Shenandoah) in 1778.[29]

Page County is located in the Commonwealth of Virginia. As of the 2020 census, the population was 23,709. Its county seat is Luray. Page County was formed in 1831 from Shenandoah and Rockingham counties and was named for John Page, Governor of Virginia from 1802 to 1805.[30]

Page County was formed from a western portion of Shenandoah County (including Luray) and eastern portion of Rockingham County, where Abraham Lincoln's father was born before his family moved to Kentucky. Lionbergers' farms in the Shenandoah Valley SW of Luray from 1749 through 1840 (at least one until 1860 or later) were about eighteen to twenty miles as-the-crow-flies from John and Abraham Lincoln's Rockingham County properties where they lived from 1768, see the Bing.com map in fig. 8 with approx. locations of both families' properties. Amazingly, this is about the same distance determined to separate the two families in Lancaster County, then becoming Berks County, in Pennsylvania:

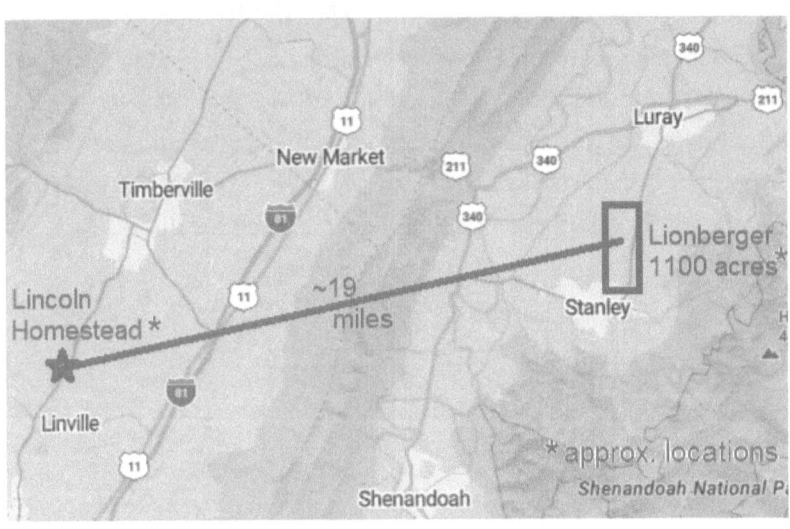

Fig. 8: Distance, "as the crow flies," between the Leuenberger-descended Lionbergers' and President Lincoln's ancestors, plus contemporary uncles/cousins. (map from Bing.com [31] and author added Lincoln/Leuenberger distance diagram.)

In 1782, Abraham took his family, including President Lincoln's father, Thomas, to live in Kentucky:

Thomas Lincoln, Abraham Lincoln's father, was born January 6, 1778, to Bathsheba and Abraham Lincoln, near Linville in Rockingham County, Virginia. Thomas was the fourth of five Josiah, and Mary. Thomas had a younger sister named Nancy. During the early 1780's the family moved to Kentucky in Jefferson County. Native Americans killed Thomas' father, Abraham, in an attack in May 1786.[32]

Census records of 1820 (fig. 9) and 1830 (fig. 10) respectively show Abraham Lionberger as property owner in Shenandoah County with its seat in Strasbourg. The arable land along Hawksbill Creek is about five miles SW of Luray, as the crow flies. Luray and Lionberger properties became part of Page County in 1831, about the time that the first of the Lionberger siblings began leaving for Illinois.

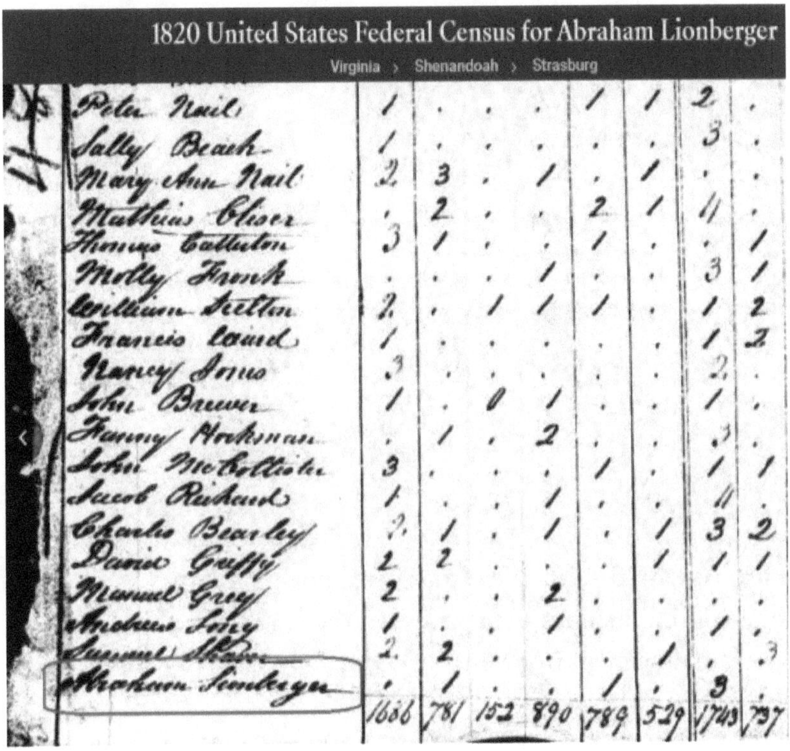

Fig. 9: 1820 U.S. Census from Shenandoah County, VA.[33] Abraham and his brothers wouldn't get their property inheritance until youngest brother Jacob, b. 1801, came of age. Abraham may have acquired some land, before that. Document copied from Ancestry.com.

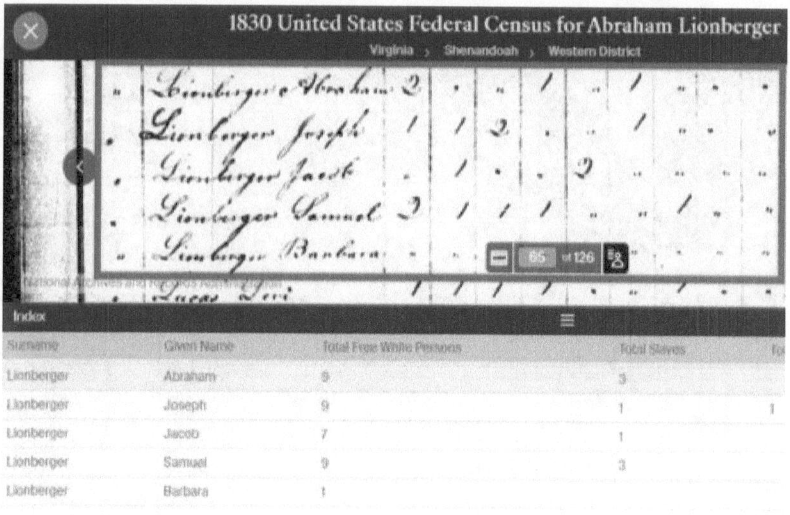

1830 United States Federal Census for Abraham Lionberger

Virginia › Shenandoah › Western District

Index

Surname	Given Name	Total Free White Persons	Total Slaves	To[illegible]
Lionberger	Abraham	9	3	
Lionberger	Joseph	9	1	1
Lionberger	Jacob	7	1	
Lionberger	Samuel	9	3	
Lionberger	Barbara	1		

Fig. 10: 1830 U.S. Census, Shenandoah County, Virginia[34] showing Lionbergers with property there, sadly, real and human. Copy of document from Ancestry.com.

Generations of this Swiss-immigrant Leuenberger family (by various anglicized spellings, as seen) were in Virginia for close to a century, from about 1748 to the mid-1830's before some moved to the Midwest. Others remained in the South and there are some there still according to census and other records and directories, and, of course, Google. The direct lineage of the author's Leuenberger-Lionberger family is continued in bold letters:

***Hans (John) Ulrich Leuenberger**, 1710, Ruderswil, Bern, CH - 1756, Hawksbill, Shenandoah, VA and wife Barbara Bär/Baer, 1711, Ratlisberg, Zurich, CH.)) They had the following children: **John,** David, Peter, Elizabeth, Magdalene, Mary, Barbara and Anna.*

***John** Lionberger, 1746–1815, Hawksbill, Shenandoah, VA and wife Barbara Hershberger, 1760, Woodstock, Shenandoah, VA. - 1845,*

*Page, VA. Children: Samuel, **Abraham**, Joseph, Jacob, Silas, Mary, Leah, Magdalene, Christina, and Rebecca.*

Abraham Lionberger, *1790, Hawksbill, Shenandoah, VA - 1868, Hancock Co., IL and wife Anna Jane Koontz, 1795, Page, VA - 1850, Harmony, Hancock, Ill. Abraham married Anna Jane Koontz on Dec. 7, 1815. They had the following children: Barbara, Elizabeth, Jane, Amanda, Isaac, Isabel, **Thomas J.**, Ambrose, Rebecca Ann, Mary Catherine, and Margaret Frances.[35]*

Fig. 11: Thomas J. Lionberger, b. 1825, mentioned above, moved to Illinois with family in 1837. Only known photo of author's Virginia ancestors, from family photo collection.

Glen Lionberger's family history has his great-grandfather purchasing a farm about 13 miles from the Lincolns of Linville, Virginia:

Abraham inherited from his father (John) the farm on the Hawksbill in Page Co., Virginia, where they lived until 1832, when they sold the farm with the full intention of going west. For some unknown reason they changed their plans and bought a farm in Rockingham Co., Virginia, about three miles east and across the river from McGaheysville, and about 30 miles from the Natural Bridge. This farm was purchased from John Yancy and four years later sold to Wm. Yancy. [36]

The accuracy of Glen's family history is borne out, again, this time by Rockingham County records, replete with Lincolns as grantees and grantors, and family name misspellings of Abraham's surname from Linebaugh to Lineberger as Lionberger was in use on his father's will:

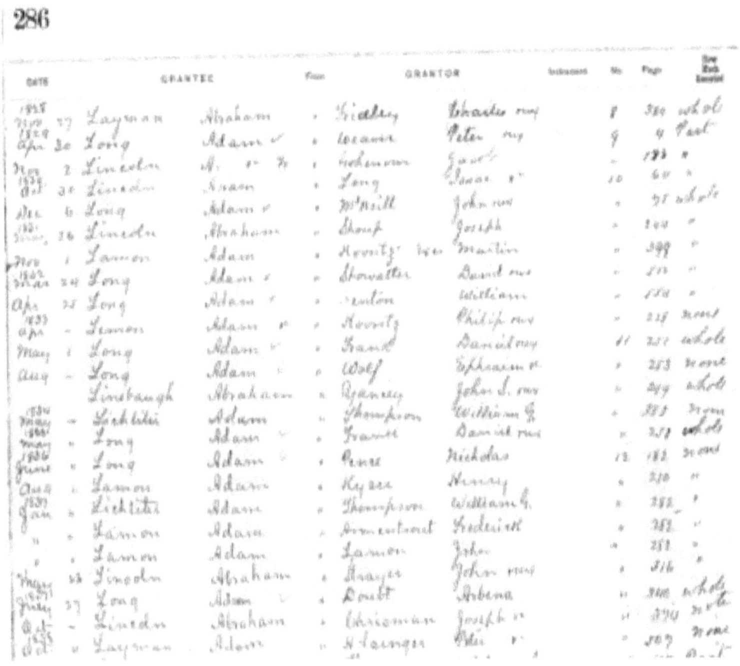

286

DATE	GRANTEE		Form	GRANTOR		Instrument	No.	Page	Sew Each Executed
1828 Nov 27	Layman	Abraham	"	Fridley	Charles		8	380	whole
1829 Apr 30	Long	Adam	"	Weaver	Peter		9	9	Part
Nov 2	Lincoln	A.	"	Johnson	Jacob		"	193	"
1830 Oct 31	Lincoln	Isaac	"	Long	Isaac		10	64	"
Dec 6	Long	Adam	"	McNeill	John		"	75	whole
1831 Jan 16	Lincoln	Abraham	"	Shoup	Joseph		"	144	"
Nov 1	Lamon	Adam	"	Koontz	Martin		"	399	"
1832 Mar 24	Long	Adam	"	Showalter	David		"	513	"
Apr 25	Long	Adam	"	Fenton	William		"	558	"
1833 Apr –	Lamon	Adam	"	Koontz	Philip		"	218	none
May 1	Long	Adam	"	Rand	Daniel		11	251	whole
Aug –	Long	Adam	"	Wolf	Ephraim		"	253	none
	Linebaugh	Abraham	"	Ramsey	John S.		"	249	whole
1834 May –	Lichliter	Adam	"	Thompson	William G.		"	381	none
1835 May "	Long	Adam	"	Francis	Daniel		"	351	whole
1836 June "	Long	Adam	"	Pence	Nicholas		12	182	none
Aug "	Lamon	Adam	"	Kyser	Henry		"	310	"
1837 Jan "	Lichliter	Adam	"	Thompson	William G.		"	282	"
" "	Lamon	Adam	"	Armentrout	Frederick		"	282	"
" "	Lamon	Adam	"	Lamon	John		"	251	"
May 23	Lincoln	Abraham	"	Harper	John		"	316	"
1837 July 27	Long	Adam	"	Doubt	Arbena		"	300	whole
Oct –	Lincoln	Abraham	"	Chrisman	Joseph		"	390	none
1838 Oct "	Layman	Adam	"	Hoffinger	Peter		"	509	none

Fig. 12: Rockingham County nineteenth century record of grantors and grantees. See grantee Abraham Linebaugh, 13th from the top [37].

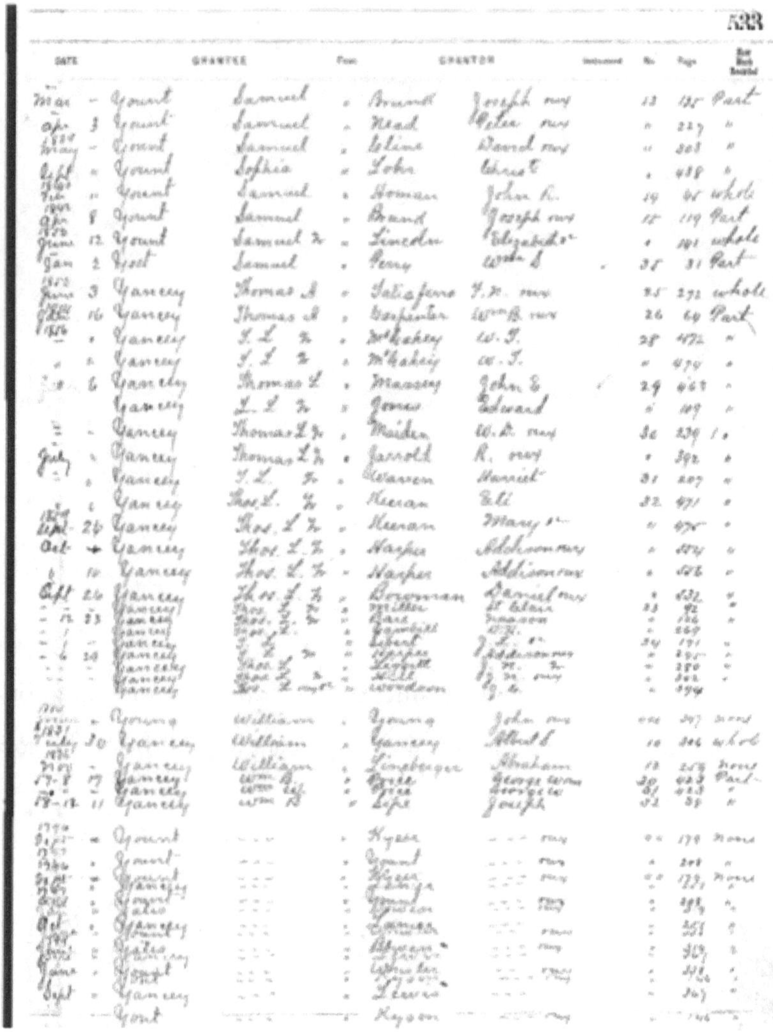

533

DATE	GRANTEE		GRANTOR		No.	Page	

(handwritten ledger of grantors and grantees — largely illegible)

Fig. 13: Rockingham County nineteenth century record of grantors and grantees. Abraham is listed as grantor Abraham Lineberger in this instance[38].

Amongst the close community amongst Leuenberger descendants and President Lincoln's extended family there was at least one inter-family relationship even closer. The two families are shown to have even shared quarters and more, see fig. 14, in northern Virginia. This 1850 Census[39] reveals yet another Abram (Abraham) Lincoln, albeit younger than his more famous cousin, living with a John Lionberger's family:

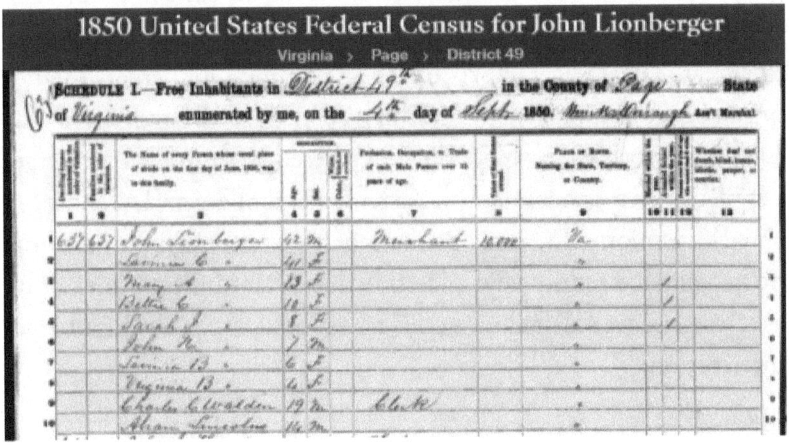
1850 United States Federal Census for John Lionberger

Virginia › Page › District 49

SCHEDULE I.—Free Inhabitants in District 49 in the County of Page State of Virginia enumerated by me, on the 4th day of Sept. 1850.

Fig. 14: Lionberger household with another Abraham Lincoln in residence shown on an 1850 U.S. Federal Census, Page County, VA. Document copied from Ancestry.com.

The records reveal that this was due to a marital and genetic relationship between the two families. The young man, a 2nd cousin of President Lincoln, was one of the effectively orphaned children of a Lincoln and Lionberger marriage. His father, Jacob Lincoln, Jr. (a nephew of Capt. Abraham Lincoln), died mysteriously on a trip to Ohio according to one report and in a community barn-raising accident in another, and his poor mother had to be placed in a mental institution. From what is known of asylums and mental hospitals of that era, the father may have been the luckier one. The younger of their nine children were taken in by another relative, but this Abraham, being old enough to help with farming, i.e., "earn his keep," was placed with relative John Lionberger.

Below is genealogy, fig. 15, showing the connection between the Leuenberger-descended Lionberger family of Virginia to the grandfather and great-grandfather of Abraham Lincoln, Abraham and Mordecai Lincoln, respectively. This info is available thanks to the great genealogical efforts of the late Elaine Lionberger. She not only collected family data for thirty years, the old-fashioned way (sans the worldwide web), but engineered a national Lionberger newsletter and annual national extended Lionberger (Leuenberger, et al) reunion. In one of her newsletters, Elaine gave the now-expanded family new ancestral and other kinship information as it was discovered, including this news about a Lincoln-Lionberger intersection:

```
Children of MORDECAI LINCOLN:

JOHN LINCOLN, born 3 May 1716, Monmouth county, New Jersey; died November 1788.
     Married: REBECCA.FLOWERS, 1720-1806, dau of ENOCH & REBECCA FLOWERS.
          Children:
               ABRAHAM LINCOLN  1744-1786/8
               ISAAC LINCOLN     1750-1816
               JACOB LINCOLN     1751-1822, married DORCAS ROBINSON, both died Virginia.
                    their children were:
                    JACOB LINCOLN Jr. married NANCY LIONBERGER, widow of JOSEPH ROADS.
                              (Nancy had 2 ROADS/RHODES CHILdren, and 9 LINCOLN children)
                    ELIZABETH LINCOLN
                    JOHN LINCOLN 1773-1818 married MARY YARNELL
                    ABRAHAM LINCOLN 1799-1851
                    MARY LINCOLN HARMON 1802-1874
                    DAVID LINCOLN 1781-1840
```

Fig. 15: Genealogy of Abraham Lincoln's great-grandfather Mordecai[40] by Elaine Lionberger. (Record is property of author's family).

The following records validate Elaine's shared information concerning a Lincoln-Lionberger relationship. Fig. 16-17 are three more official complementary documents from U.S. Census and Pennsylvania Mennonite records, as found on Ancestry.com:

Lionberger, Nancy in tree "Daniel Lionberger family tree"   Lincoln, Jacob in tree "Daniel Lionberger family tree"

Name:	Nancy Lionberger		Name:	Jacob Lincoln
Gender:	Female		Gender:	Male
Spouse Name:	Joseph Rodes		Spouse Name:	Nancy Roads
Spouse Gender:	Male		Spouse Gender:	Female
Marriage Date:	21 Nov 1812		Marriage Date:	29 Oct 1821
County:	Shenandoah		County:	Shenandoah
State:	Virginia		State:	Virginia

Fig. 16: Widow Nancy Lionberger Roads[41] wed Abraham Lincoln's 2nd Cousin, Jacob Lincoln[42]. Documents accessed on Ancestry.com.

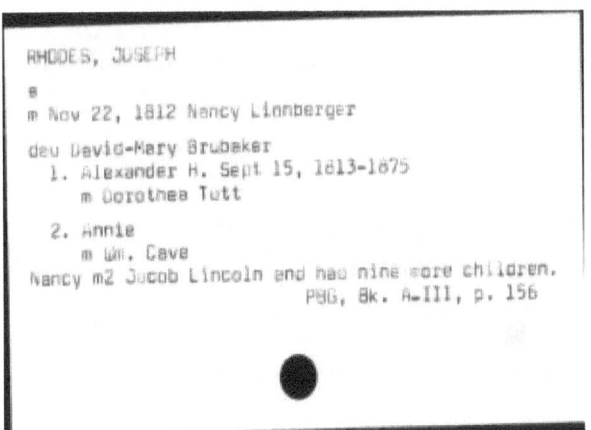

Fig. 17: Lancaster Co., PA, U.S. Mennonite Vital Records, 1750-2014[43]. File found on Ancestry.com.

Abraham would have inherited property from his father about 1820-1822, when his youngest brother came of age. He planted and harvested for about a decade in Page County before deciding to move elsewhere, if Glen's rendition is correct. U.S. Censuses provided support Glen's telling of it. Abraham's mother survived until 1835 or 1836; that may have "stayed his hand" in moving to join siblings in Illinois, until 1837.

Glen Lionberger reported that his great-grandfather and grandfather, Abraham and Thomas J. Lionberger, respectively, and their immediate family lived near Luray, Virginia. In his family history written in the mid-twentieth century[44], he wrote that their farm was on Hawksbill Creek, which is also referred to as Little Hawksbill Creek and Hawksbill Run in various family wills and histories. This was validated by newspaper article and another source, shown previously.

Subsequent to moving to Illinois in 1837, Abraham Lionberger sold his Virginia property. His father's and mother's wills had each given him a percentage of his father's land. His father's will authorized 20% of the property to him in 1815 and his mother's will an additional 5% in 1836. With the profit from that, he moved to Illinois with his wife Anna and son Thomas and bought 500 acres in Hancock County, according to Glen Lionberger's family history which is supported by U.S. Censuses of the time and county.

The reason why the bulk of the family left the beautiful, verdant, and vibrant Virginia valley of the Shenandoah of the early nineteenth century can only be speculated upon. The slave issue of that time that may have been the agent of change that caused them to uproot most of the family. The abolition debate, to put it mildly, was well heated by 1837. The *Wikipedia* article, "Abolitionism in the United States," said pro-slavers were in the minority, "In 1830 most Americans were, at least in principle, opposed to slavery."[45]

The partial family migration may have been a split caused by the question of slavery, although most of the Lionbergers that moved to Illinois were shown to own one to three slaves prior to moving to Illinois on an 1830 US Federal Census document from Ancestry.com, as previously mentioned and shown in fig. 10. It is not known where the family stood on the issue, but they chose to move from a slave state to a free state, see Virginia and Illinois on map in fig. 18, in the midst of the political and social uproar over abolition.

Fig. 18: Free v slave states in 1837. [46]

If not slavery, or in addition to slavery, perhaps the split in the Baptist church may have caused a schism in the Lionberger family. The Baptist church had at least some family members among its congregation. One major division between "Old School" and "New

School" Baptists is recorded to have occurred in 1832, coincidentally when Abraham Lionberger is said to have first sold his farm with the intent of moving. A later rift in the Baptist church, in 1845, was related to the heated arguments over slavery, cementing their differences as the Northern Baptist (Old School/Primitive) and Southern Baptist (New School) denominations.

Glen Lionberger's family history says that these ancestors were Baptist, even noting what churches they belonged to in Virginia and, then, in Illinois. The Baptist question could have drove them asunder, though, slavery may have played into that, as well, as related by Jewel Spangler in her article, "Baptists in Colonial Virginia," in Encyclopedia Virginia:

Early Baptists were routinely subject to verbal and physical abuse as well. While the learned offered pointed written critiques of Baptist belief and practice, anyone could heckle at open-air meetings. Sometimes criticism turned to violence.

Dozens of ministers were attacked by local mobs in the formative period of Baptist expansion. Early congregations also gathered at their own risk, as when the well-bred men of Culpeper County galloped their horses through a crowd that had formed to hear the Reverend James Ireland preach from his cell while incarcerated for disturbing the peace over the winter of 1769–1770. The reasons for such opposition ranged widely, from a critique of adult baptism and other practices related to biblical literalness to concern that the fast promotion of uneducated preachers inappropriately elevated men who could be socially dangerous in leadership roles.

Historians have long debated the nature of Baptist dissent. Some treat it as a cultural challenge to the hierarchal secular order constructed by Virginia's planter class, highlighting the "republicanism" of Baptist church government; the relative empowerment of women, slaves, and "plainfolk" in congregations; antislavery attitudes; and the like. Others have read nearly the same evidence as indicative of the social conservatism and proslavery of early Baptists.[47]

The Baptists were a major part of the early settlements in Virginia. Leuenbergers, now spelled Lionberger or sometimes Leonberger from one record to the next, belonged to the "Old School Baptist Church" in Luray, Virginia[48], when they lived in what became Page County, as recorded by their great-grandson which will be quoted, later.

President Abraham Lincoln's grandparents were also known to be Baptists, drifting there from their reported earlier Quaker convictions. So, both families were born into Reformed religious perspectives. The Lincolns are even recorded as having helped build a Baptist church in Linville, Virginia, where Pres. Lincoln's father was born.

John and Rebecca Lincoln, who migrated from Freehold, New Jersey, to Virginia, were Baptists. They assisted in building the Linville Creek Baptist Church on their own farm. Lincoln's grandfather, Abraham Lincoln, was a member of this congregation before relocating to what would become Kentucky:

When he located in Kentucky in 1782 he also gave land upon which to build a church, which was called Long Run Baptist Church.[49]

Honest Abe's parents were historically affiliated with a Baptist church, also, in Kentucky.

On the other side of President Lincoln's family, the Hanks lived about sixty miles "as the crow flies," from Leuenberger-descended families' plantations when his mother Nancy was born in Hampshire

County, Virginia (now Mineral County, West Virginia) in a cabin
on Mike's Run, a tributary of Patterson Creek:

*Nancy Hanks was born to Lucy Hanks in what was at that time part of
Hampshire County, Virginia. Today, the same location is in Antioch in
Mineral County, West Virginia. She was born in a log cabin on the Doll
farm near Mike's Run at the base of Knobly Mountain near Antioch,
West Virginia, and baptized in the Broad Run Baptist Church there,
which still retains the baptismal record.*[50]

It has been shown that the Leuenberger and Lincoln families lived
in areas largely populated by people of Germanic heritage. The
"German" community (as in Pennsylvania, this adjective/noun was
used for all people with a Germanic mother tongue) was thick in
the Hank's neighborhood, as well, just north of the county of
Leuenberger-Lionbergers' landholdings when Nancy was born in
1784:

*Germans were among our very earliest settlers. They arrived in what is
now West Virginia in the 1720s, along the Potomac River. They called
their settlement Mecklenburg (now Shepherdstown), having come from
Mecklenburg, Germany. The town was incorporated in 1762.*

*Soon other Germans came. Among them were Jacob Reger, John
Minear, and Johann Dahle. Reger settled in Hampshire County, but
he and his family later moved to what is today north-central West
Virginia, eventually settling farms in the Tygart, West Fork, and
Buckhannon river valleys. Some of them settled along a tributary of
Hackers Creek in what in 1816 became Lewis County. Near its
headwaters a small community named Berlin was established. Minear
settled in present Tucker County and erected the first sawmill west of the
Alleghenies. Dahle, a Hessian deserter from the British army during the*

American Revolution, settled in Pendleton County around 1781, and some of his descendants settled in what is today known as Dolly (from Dahle) Sods.

By 1748, according to a Moravian missionary to the region of the South Branch of the Potomac and Patterson Creek, there were so many Germans along those streams "that in order to reach the people a minister should be fluent in both German and English." In 1762, about 30 percent of the population of Jefferson and Berkeley counties was German, and the centers of the German population were Shepherdstown and Martinsburg.[51]

The area where the Hanks family sojourned at least long enough for Lucy Hanks to conceive and deliver a daughter of, by Abraham Lincoln's own testimony, a Virginia planter was densely populated with Germanic people, Anabaptist-descended and others. From Shepherdstown to Helvetia and south through the Shenandoah Valley the haplogroups of the persecuted who fled to the Palatinate were plenty. Among these were the Anabaptists and their offshoots the Amish and Mennonites, also, Moravians were among these communities. Those who had ventured farther into the wilderness from the Swiss contingents of the "Dutch" (or, Deutsche) of Pennsylvania, the Swiss labor camps/communities in North Carolina, and the "Hessians" (aka "German" mercenaries) of the French-Indian War and the American Revolutionary War were not inconsequential.

We have seen that people from Germanic cultural centers were at the fore in the forays into the wilderness. They were among the "Delta Force" intended to open areas west of the Shenandoah Valley, as well. The "Transylvania Colony" which would become Kentucky was among these. However, dark strategy with prejudice at its roots might lay behind this migration pattern. It might explain the "attraction" (read cheap government land offers) of those considered less-Anglican, such as Germanic and Celtic (read, those labeled as Irish) peoples, to unimproved Pennsylvania and then to undeveloped and dangerous Virginia territory. Western Carolina University's "German Settlers in the Appalachians" describes the seeming Anglo-oriented politics or bigoted business of sending German-speaking immigrants along with Scots and Irish to the frontier, to build a "buffer zone":

The fertile Shenandoah Valley between the Blue Ridge and Allegheny Mountains attracted settlers looking for good land to farm. The earliest German settler in the valley was Adam Miller (also spelled Muller and Mueller) who arrived between 1726 and 1727. In 1727 German settlers established New Mecklenburg which was incorporated in 1762 as Shepherdstown. The now famous historic town of Harper's Ferry was established at the Great Falls, the junction of the Shenandoah and Potomac Rivers, by a German Robert Harper in 1734.

In the early 18th century, increased French activity in the Ohio country prompted

Virginia's government to take actions to defend the Old Dominion's western claims. Therefore, in 1730 Virginia's laws were changed to grant land speculators a thousand acres for each family they could settle west of the Blue Ridge, a law intended to create buffer settlements, of primarily Scots-Irish and Germans, in the mountains to protect older settlements in the Piedmont and Tidewater regions. German Jost Hite established one of these buffer communities, the Opequon settlement, in 1731.

Recently arrived immigrants from Germany finding less land available than they had hoped for in Pennsylvania, along with second and third generation settlers, gladly took up the offer of cheap and fertile land in the Shenandoah Valley. Large numbers of Germans from Pennsylvania swept into the valley before and during the American Revolution. After the Revolution, Germans pushed into the Southern slope of the valley below Lexington. This protected and profitable valley became a predominantly German area before the 19th century.[52]

Both the Lincolns and the Hanks were "in the thick of it" as far as German culture was concerned:

The Shenandoah Valley region of Virginia and parts of West Virginia is home to a long-established German-American community dating to the 17th century. The earliest German settlers to Shenandoah, sometimes known as the Shenandoah Deitsch or the Valley Dutch, were Pennsylvania Dutch migrants who traveled from southeastern Pennsylvania. These German settlers traveled southward along what became known as the Great Wagon Road. They were descendants of German, Swiss, and Alsatian Protestants who began settling in Pennsylvania during the late 1600s. Among them were German Palatines who had fled the Rhineland-Palatinate region of southwestern Germany due to religious and political persecution during repeated invasions by French troops.[53]

Following Leuenberger descendants' pursuit of fertile grounds for individualism as plotted on fig. 19, from "German Americans[54]," a map from *Wikipedia* shows "German" (Dutch, et al) settlements; diagram and labels from the author, show where the famous Lincoln family crossed or shared roads with Leuenberger descendants and other Swiss-German immigrants and their descendants for more than a century in America:

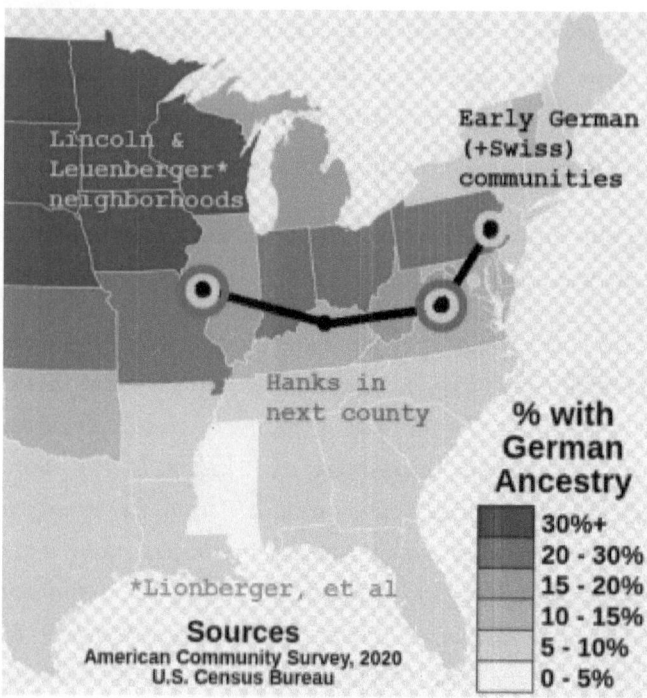

Fig. 19: Current U.S. Germanic ancestry percentages with diagram and labels of subject families' parallel paths added by the author. Original map from American Community Survey, 2020. U.S. Census Bureau.

There are descendants of both families in Pennsylvania, Virginia, and Illinois communities, yet, along with many other states. Along with the continued migrations of descendants of the Leuenberger family, members of President Abraham Lincoln's family have been shown to have moved serially with the Leuenberger-Lionbergers, geographically if not always chronologically. Documents have shown members of both families in close or neighboring community and even intimate contact in these three states. One marriage between the two families has been documented: Nancy Lionberger (the

Widow Rodes/Roades/Rhodes) to a first cousin (once removed) of the sixteenth president. An orphan of this marriage, a second cousin of President Abraham Lincoln, was shown to be documented as a member of a Leuenberger-descendant Lionberger household in Page County, Virginia.

The sixteenth president of the United States and the Leuenberger progeny of Northern Virginia may have more than one relation in common. Abraham Lincoln, the president assassinated for remaining loyal to the ideals of the American Constitution, may relate to Niklaus Leuenberger, a precedential leader executed for trying to ensure adherence to the promises of their government's earlier pacts with the people, in more than one way.

The American-immigrants' ancestral relative, the 1653 Bernese rebels' leader Niklaus Leuenberger was a proven literate and fluent Germanic-language orator. He was educated, well-respected, and judicially-placed, although the source of his knowledge is not known. Abraham Lincoln appeared to follow in Niklaus Leuenberger's footsteps as a highly successful autodidactic student in general and of the law, more specifically. Were the two men's similarities an absolute coincidence or was a more relative factor involved? Their means, mentalities, missions, morals, and mortal ends make them seem to practically have been carbon-copies. See them in parallel in fig. 20.

Fig. 20: Abraham Lincoln and Niklaus Leuenberger seem to be cut from the same cloth.

Was Niklaus influenced by the radical Anabaptist view of reformation? This could have led the "popularly-elected" leader of the rural rebels to the conclusion that he had an official and moral duty to convince the government at that time to return to the ideals/pacts/laws of the fathers. The story of Jesus' efforts to restore the Promised Land to the Law of Moses as portrayed in the scriptures, against an earlier alliance of church and aristocratic state, could have spoken to him.

To some eyes, Pres. Lincoln shared the physical appearance of many from the Leuenbergers' paternal haplogroup or its close relations. However, assumed distant kin of President Lincoln gave their evidence that his paternal heritage could be R1b:

Two descendants of Samuel Lincoln have submitted their Y-DNA for analysis. Although the allele values have not been revealed, the data shows that the two anonymous individuals match at 36 of 37 markers. One is listed as belonging to Haplogroup R1b1, and the other is R1b2.
[55]

If his paternal descent from Samuel Lincoln of Hingham, Mass. is fact, Abe would have also had a R1b Hg. There are a number of different Lincoln descendant lineages in America, of various YDNA haplogroups. A few of them are shown by a Bob Lincoln on his Lincoln-Family site, see fig. 21:

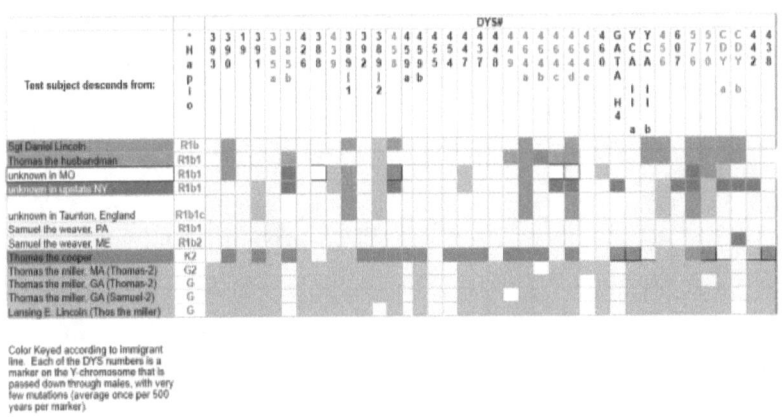

Fig. 21: Anonymous genetic results of male Lincolns[56] on Bob Lincoln's Genealogy Web Pages link.

Abraham's spoken doubts about his father's and Hanks' contributions to his physiological nature, his intelligence and honesty supporting, should tell all the sleuths that Nancy Hank, likely through genetic contributions from her mystery father, was the source of Abe's physical and mental differences with Thomas, i.e., his better qualities. The probability of being more like one's father or mother is entirely random:

For many DNA tests the sex of the person being tested is irrelevant. This is because of the 23 pairs of chromosomes that make up our DNA, only one pair determines sex. The chromosomes that determine sex are X and Y. Those born genetically male have one X chromosome inherited from their mother, and one Y chromosome inherited from their father. Those born female have two X chromosomes: one inherited from their mother, and one from their father.

Our remaining 22 chromosomes have nothing to do with determining sex, and are randomly inherited from both our mother and father. These contain the information that determine things like eye color, skin color, hair texture, and so on.[57]

The last paragraph, above, is the key one. Realistically, then, many of Abraham Lincoln's physical and cerebral features were randomly inherited from his enigmatic maternal grandfather if Pres. Lincoln's profession of his debt to his maternal grandfather for his best qualities is accepted.

Male descendants of Samuel Lincoln might claim another haplogroup, but, indirectly, the multiple generations that Abraham Lincoln's forbears, both Lincoln and Hanks, spent in or near German/Swiss communities in Pennsylvania and Virginia (including what is now West Virginia) increased the probability that some of their genetic heritage could be found in his chromosomes. More directly, at least a few of the farmers of Anabaptist or Mennonite descent in the Shenandoah Valley were genetically related to "The King of the Peasants," if not directly than at least through some Last Common Ancestor.

If Pres. Lincoln's paternal heritage is deemed beyond question, "there is more than one way to skin a cat," as the famous rail-splitter may well have borrowed from contemporary humorist Seba Smith.[58] Regarding Nancy Hanks' enigmatic paternity—before the tales and arguments of old concerning Abraham Lincoln's maternal heritage, i.e., his mother's father, are voiced. William Barton long-ago thoroughly subdued these in his book, *The Paternity of Abraham Lincoln*. Besides disassembling the many other claims of Nancy Hanks' paternity, he states a statement from one of Lincoln's closest associates:

We give in Mr. Hernden's own words what Mr. Lincoln told him about his mother. Mr. Hernden says (Chapter I, page3):

"It was about 1850, when he and I were driving in his one-horse buggy to the court in Menard County, Illinois. The suit we were going to try was one in which we were likely, whether directly or collaterally, to touch upon the subject of hereditary traits. During the ride he spoke for the first time in my hearing of his mother, dwelling on her characteristics, and mentioning or enumerating what qualities he inherited from her. He said among other things that she was the illegitimate daughter of Lucy Hanks, and a well-bred Virginia farmer or planter; and he argued that from this last source came his power of analysis, his logic, his mental activity, his ambition and all the qualities that distinguished him from the other members and descendants of the Hanks family. His theory in discussing the matter of hereditary traits had been, that for certain reasons illegitimate children are oftentimes sturdier and brighter than those born in lawful wedlock; and in his case he believed that his better nature and finer qualities came from this broadminded unknown Virginian."[59]

Honest Abe's own candid testimony, simply put, condemned the alternative stories and offered for posterity the realization that his unnamed maternal grandfather was a "gentleman" Virginia planter.

The sixteenth American president's biological maternal grandfather may well have been one of the many of Swiss or German genetic heritage in northern Virginia which included what is now W. Virginia, at that time, that shared a common ancestor with Niklaus Leuenberger, democratic leader of the Swiss peasants of Bern. Nancy Hanks, b. Feb 5, 1784, would have been conceived in April or May 1783. Lucy Hanks' father, Joseph, located in Richmond County, Virginia in 1779, see fig. 22, moved in or near Germanic communities of northern Virginia ~1780. The earliest record found of this is from 1782, see fig. 23.

Joseph Hanks
in the Virginia, U.S., Compiled Census and Census Substitutes Index, 1607-1890

Detail	Source
Name	Joseph Hanks
State	VA
County	Richmond County
Township	No Township Listed
Year	1779
Record Type	Rent Role
Page	NPN
Database	VA Early Census Index

Fig. 22: Joseph Hanks' 1779 Richmond County, Virginia location from Virginia census records from Ancestry.com[60].

Joseph Hanks
in the Virginia, U.S., Compiled Census
and Census Substitutes Index, 1607-1890

Detail	Source
Name	Joseph Hanks
State	VA
County	Hampshire County
Township	06 00
Year	1782
Record Type	Continental Census
Page	26
Database	VA Early Census Index

Fig. 23: Joseph Hanks' 1782 Hampshire County, Virginia location. about 1780, before daughter Lucy's pregnancy and bearing of Nancy Hanks, Pres. Lincoln's mother. [61]

The genes that Pres. Abraham Lincoln credits for his better qualities, which he concluded could not have come from his father, might have come from a Swiss-colony, "Pennsylvania Dutch," or "Hessian" (all three groups including more or less Swiss among their demographics) descendant farmer along the Shenandoah and Potomac Rivers or their tributaries. The amount of genetic material our "Honest Abe" might have shared with Niklaus Leuenberger, the Swiss peasant leader of 1653, cannot be known except through a DNA comparison which, sadly, cannot be. The two men seem built according to the same genetic blueprint. The two were each determined to become educated men, both were dedicated to putting their countries back on the ideal and just path blazed by their forefathers... for the people... and each paid the ultimate price. Their respective relatives were in close or neighboring community for generations.

There exists a possibility of more than an inherent link but an inherited one between these two incomparable men, through a possible Swiss-American relation in eighteenth century Pennsylvania or Virginia. A Leuenberger and Lincoln relationship or a Hanks and Lionberger one, respectively, is tantalizing to the writer, and perhaps to other descendants of the many Swiss immigrants who sought freedom in America.

The Swiss peasants and their more-or-less popularly-elected leader, Niklaus Leuenberger, were demanding the Swiss precedent of the American Dream. They had fought for these ideals several times before. Gains towards democracy were made but were subsequently lost or forgotten over time. In the agrarian people's minds, progress must be made or recovered. The reason that an "American Dream" supplanted many Swiss' hopes for a more ideal existence in their ancient home, especially within the Anabaptist population, was that the struggle for fair and just treatment had been too costly, for too long, for too many. America became the best hope for thousands of people. Amazingly, it still is today, although obstacles and oppression are creating the need for a new charismatic and courageous leader for the common people of this country.

Attempts to shackle the "American Dream" with the Anglo-Saxon Dream have been ever evident, to those who look, since Europeans first took the beaches on would become America. It still has a dampening effect on democracy, today, ever denying the majority achievement of the egalitarian ideals of the often and loudly trumpeted charter of the United States. Crucible after crucible has flamed anew from current bellows to be doused before the steel of new resolve can be tempered, constitutional crises come and gone but neither resolved nor forgotten. Colin Kidd offers a look at Sarah Churchwell's thoughts on this in his survey of her book, *Behold, America*, which ties the American Dream to America First nationalism rampant, again, in the twenty-first century:

The expression "American dream" also bears responsibility for some unattractive outcomes. But back in the early 20th century when the phrase first crept into common currency, the American dream was conceived in terms of social and economic equality, not of the opportunities open to individuals to rise from rags to riches. It functioned as a "corrective, not as an incentive," transmitting "moral disquiet" about the dangers of runaway capitalist excess. The rise of a plutocrat class founded on vast concentrations of wealth was deemed to be un-American, because it threatened the cherished American dream of equality and social justice. Over the course of the 20th century, however, the notion was turned inside out, becoming instead the anaesthetizing fantasy which douses socialist aspiration in the underclass.[62]

One of the American people's crucibles that was definitely such a crisis, the insurrection of the southern states, a.k.a., the "War Between the States" was set off by the southern minority of the wealthy and powerful slaveowners' fear that Abraham Lincoln's and many other citizens' "American Dream" of the United States finally realizing the ideal of the founding fathers, as written into the Constitution, that all of mankind should have equal rights:

In February 1861, en route to his first inauguration as president, he stopped in Trenton, New Jersey, and told the state senate: "I am exceedingly anxious that this Union, the Constitution, and the liberties of the people shall be perpetuated in accordance with the original idea for which that struggle was made."[63]

* * *

Lincoln believed that during his fractious times, looking back to the Founding could provide guidance on how to perpetuate American self-government. He did this most famously in his Gettysburg Address. That speech begins at the nation's beginning: "Four score and seven years ago our fathers brought forth, on this continent, a new nation, conceived in Liberty, and dedicated to the proposition that all men are created equal." If you do the math, you find that he takes his audience back not to the Constitution, but to the . . . Declaration of Independence. Not to the body but to the soul of the nation. If America stood for anything, it was liberty and equality.[64]

The groundwork he established to ensure the correction of the "American Flaw" was doomed with his assassination. It still progressed well until "the Reconstruction" was all but razed by Rutherford B. Hayes in an agreement with Southern politicians for his interest in political expediency.

In what had to be much a shared frame of mind, Niklaus Leuenberger and Abraham Lincoln each saw and fought to overturn the fatal flaw of their respective governments' failure to allow the contracted (paid for with their peoples' blood) charter to persevere. Niklaus Leuenberger led the demands to resurrect the promise of what can possibly be termed the "Swiss Dream." The common people of the Bern canton wanted the governing elite to live up to the agreements, the ideals of the fathers, the Oath of Ruetli and the Oath of Huttwil. Abraham's dream was to uphold the U.S. Constitution, the ideals of the founding fathers of American democracy. Both men would hold the chartered interest of the people as being the foremost responsibility of their country, and themselves.

If Niklaus Leuenberger had led with as great a resolve as Abraham Lincoln, without the moral dilemma that Anabaptist belief may have caused him, the Swiss people may have sooner triumphed, i.e., realized the ideals that their forefathers also fought for. After the Bern government's treacherous betrayal of an honorably-gained agreement, almost two-hundred years passed before they achieved a democratic constitution:

It is left to the readers and most especially the Swiss politicians whether the rebels of 1653 are worthy of an official vindication and are recognized as the true heros preparing the democratic system of Switzerland and its constitution in 1848 which is an adapted copy of the American Constitution of 1787.[65]

Whether the remarkable similarities of Niklaus Leuenberger and Abraham Lincoln had a more biological, cultural, or merely coincidental humanitarian relationship cannot be known. For the better part, the descended Leuenbergers' "American Dream" surely has the same roots as the ideals and beliefs of both of these men and the people and their predecessors that they faithfully and loyally acted as agents of. An American dream now is to build belief in what has, undoubtedly, always been mankind's common vision—egalitarian and just culture—and hope it perseveres in the progeny of America's immigrants, indentured, enslaved, and indigenous, i.e., all of us, for posterity.

Chapter 4 - The Supernova Event of Abraham Lincoln

The effect that Niklaus Leuenberger's sacrifice may have made towards a more democratic society, following on the heels of England's strike against a strict monarchy and a move towards a more parliamentary form of government, as Dr. Leuenberger described in the previous chapter, possibly reached America as from the wings of a butterfly.

A desire for freedom and contempt for injustice was possibly engraved in the hearts of the Anabaptists driven from Switzerland to the neighboring Alsace-Lorraine region of France. Mentioned earlier, they later migrated to the British colonies of America with the Mennonites, as some Leuenbergers (and later anglicized spellings of that name) are documented (the author's ancestors among them), perhaps to achieve the "American Dream," e.g., the personal, religious freedom that was denied to them in Europe. Are we in danger of losing what our forefathers died for on this and other continents?

Consider the possibility of a relationship beyond a philosophical one, between Niklaus Leuenberger and the American President Abraham Lincoln, who also sacrificed his life for freedom's ideals in the furthering of a democratic republic. Recall that Chapter 3 offers a new perspective on Abraham Lincoln's maternal grandfather—a relationship, documented and speculated (due to a good number of circumstantial points) to folks who could claim Niklaus Leuenberger, Leader of the Swiss Peasant War of 1653, as an ancestral relative, if not a more direct one.

Lincoln was one of the Progressive personalities that helped create the Republican party which was birthed opposed to Conservative

Pro-slavery forces. The pro-slavery forces were not only in the Party of Democrats, which was dominant in the South, but some in Lincoln's own Whig Party. The time for a more Progressive Party was upon the nation as Abe's law partner, Wm. H. Herndon, describes it:

The Whig party, having accomplished its mission in the political world, was now on the eve of a great break-up. Lincoln realized this and, though proverbially slow in his movements, prepared to find a firm footing when the great rush of waters should come and the maddening freshet sweep former landmarks out of sight.[66]

Herndon expanded on that:

The stump speech which Thomas H. Benton charged that Douglas had "injected into the belly of the bill" contains all there was of Popular Sovereignty—"It being the true intent and meaning of this act not to legislate slavery into any Territory or State nor to exclude it therefrom, but to leave the people thereof perfectly free to form and regulate their domestic institutions in their own way, subject only to the Constitution of the United States," an argument which, using Lincoln's words, amounts to this: "That if any one man chooses to enslave another no third man shall be allowed to object." The widespread feeling the passage of this law aroused everywhere over the Union is a matter of general history. It stirred up in New England the latent hostility to the aggression of slavery; it stimulated to extraordinary endeavors the derided Abolitionists, arming them with new weapons; it sounded the death-knell of the gallant old Whig party; it drove together strange, discordant elements in readiness to fight a common enemy; it brought to the forefront a leader in the person of Lincoln.[67]

The warriors, young and old, removed their armor from the walls, and began preparations for the impending conflict. Lincoln had made a few speeches in aid of Scott during the campaign of 1852, but they were efforts entirely unworthy of the man. Now, however, a live issue was presented to him. No one realized this sooner than he. In the office discussions he grew bolder in his utterances. He insisted that the social and political difference between slavery and freedom was becoming more marked; that one must overcome the other; and that postponing the struggle between them would only make it the more deadly in the end. "The day of compromise," he still contended, "has passed. These two great ideas have been kept apart only by the most artful means. They are like two wild beasts in sight of each other, but chained and held apart. Some day these deadly antagonists will one or the other break their bonds, and then the question will be settled."[68]

Herndon had this to say about the Republican Party's beginning:

If he approved or disapproved my course I asked him to write or telegraph me at once. In a brief time came his answer: "All right; go ahead. Will meet you—radicals and all." Stuart subsided, and the conservative spirits who hovered around Springfield no longer held control of the political fortunes of Abraham Lincoln. The Republican party came into existence in Illinois as a party at Bloomington, May 29, 1856. The State convention of all opponents of anti-Nebraska legislation, referred to in a foregoing paragraph, had been set for that day. Judd, Yates, Trumbull, Swett, and Davis were there; so also was Lovejoy, who, like Otis of colonial fame, was a flame of fire. The firm of Lincoln and Herndon was represented by both members in person.[69]

William Herdon gave the exact time of the birth of the Party of Lincoln, "The Republican party came into existence in Illinois as a party at Bloomington, May 29, 1856."[70] Here is how he describes Lincoln's speech at that event:

In referring to this speech some years ago I used the following rather graphic language: "I have heard or read all of Mr. Lincoln's great speeches, and I give it as my opinion that the Bloomington speech was the grand effort of his life. Heretofore he had simply argued the slavery question on grounds of policy,—the statesman's grounds,—never reaching the question of the radical and the eternal right. Now he was newly baptized and freshly born; he had the fervor of a new convert; the smothered flame broke out; enthusiasm unusual to him blazed up; his eyes were aglow with an inspiration; he felt justice; his heart was alive to the right; his sympathies, remarkably deep for him, burst forth, and he stood before the throne of the eternal Right. His speech was full of fire and energy and force; it was logic; it was pathos; it was enthusiasm; it was justice, equity, truth, and right set ablaze by the divine fires of a soul maddened by the wrong; it was hard, heavy, knotty, gnarly, backed with wrath. I attempted for about fifteen minutes as was usual with me then to take notes, but at the end of that time I threw pen and paper away and lived only in the inspiration of the hour. If Mr. Lincoln was six feet, four inches high usually, at Bloomington that day he was seven feet, and inspired at that. From that day to the day of his death he stood firm in the right. He felt his great cross, had his great idea, nursed it, kept it, taught it to others, in his fidelity bore witness of it to his death, and finally sealed it with his precious blood." The foregoing paragraph, used by me in a lecture in 1866, may to the average reader seem somewhat vivid in description, besides inclining to extravagance in imagery, yet although more than twenty years have passed since it was written I have never seen the need of altering a single sentence. I still adhere to the substantial truthfulness of the scene as described. Unfortunately Lincoln's speech was never written out nor printed, and we are obliged to depend for its reproduction upon personal recollection. [71]

Herndon seems to be correct in that the speech is unavailable, however, excerpts of these speeches made by Abraham Lincoln about two and three months later may cover some of his same points:

From a Speech at Galena, Illinois... July 23, 1856

Do you say that such restriction of slavery would be unconstitutional, and that some of the States would not submit to its enforcement? I grant you that an unconstitutional act is not a law; but I do not ask and will not take your construction of the Constitution. The Supreme Court of the United States is the tribunal to decide such a question, and we will submit to its decisions; and if you do also, there will be an end of the matter. Will you? If not, who are the disunionists—you or we?[72]

...and:

Speech at Kalamazoo, Michigan August 27, 1856

This is one of Lincoln's clearest cut arguments against letting slavery spread into the new territories. Lincoln takes especial care to define abolitionism and the relationship of the new Republican party to it.

Aug. 27, 1856

"Under the Constitution of the United States another Presidential contest approached us. All over this land—that portion at least, of which I know much—the people are assembling to consider the proper course to be adopted by them. One of the first considerations is to learn what the people differ about. If we ascertain what we differ about, we shall be better able to decide. The question of slavery, at the present day, should be not only the greatest question, but very nearly the sole question. Our opponents, however, prefer that this should not be the case."[73]

Abraham Lincoln took the office of President of the United States knowing full well that the question of slavery was going to be the biggest issue he would have to face as Executive and Commander-in-Chief of the country. He may well have known it was on the way to becoming the greatest crisis this country had ever known. He knew, without a doubt, though, that the question had to be faced, and answered, firmly and without a quaver, if the United States of America was to survive.

President Lincoln chose able men to assist him in running the country and the war, many of whom who did not agree with him, but he took advice from them, gave orders, and stood fast upon his decisions. A later president who surrounded himself with unqualified "yes" men, took advice from almost nobody except his "controllers," who Tweeted orders and later denied most of them, and rather than trying to keep the country united, tried to divide it—he is the most negative-image of Lincoln that one could imagine. Herndon's description of Lincoln as President immediately brings to mind that the exact opposite of that applies to those currently in power in Washington, DC:

When we first went to Washington many thought Mr. Lincoln was weak, but he rose grandly with the circumstances. I told him once of the assertion I had heard coming from the friends of Seward, that the latter was the power behind the throne; that he could rule him. He replied, "I may not rule myself, but certainly Seward shall not. The only ruler I have is my conscience—following God in it—and these men will have to learn that yet."

The Secretary of State, whose ten years in the Senate had acquainted him with our relations to foreign powers, may have been lulled into the innocent belief that the Executive would have no fixed or definite views on international questions. So also of the other Cabinet officers; but alas for their fancied security! It was the old story of the sleeping lion. Old politicians, eying him with some distrust and want of confidence, prepared themselves to control his administration, not only as a matter of right, but believing that he would be compelled to rely upon them for support. A brief experience taught them he was not the man they bargained for.[74]

Herdon's description of Lincoln's prosecution of the war, his patience with Generals and staff but ability to remove and replace men when they proved themselves incapable again makes one realize the opposite in the White House, now, who fires the capable and replaces them with incapable sycophants:

The long-expected upheaval had come, and as the torrent of fire broke forth the people in the agony of despair looking aloft cried out, "Is our leader equal to the task?" That he was the man for the hour is now the calm, unbiassed judgment of all mankind. The splendid victories early in 1862 in the southwest, which gave the Union cause great advance toward the entire redemption of Kentucky, Tennessee, and Missouri from the presence of rebel armies and the prevalence of rebel influence, were counterbalanced by the dilatory movements and inactive policy of McClellan, who had been appointed in November of the preceding year to succeed the venerable Scott. The forbearance of Lincoln in dealing with McClellan was only in keeping with his well-known spirit of kindness; but, when the time came and circumstances warranted it, the soldier-statesman found that the President not only comprehended the scope of the war, but was determined to be commander-in-chief of the army and navy himself. When it pleased him to place McClellan again at the head of affairs, over the protest of such a willful and indomitable spirit as Stanton, he displayed elements of rare leadership and evidence of uncommon capacity. His confidence in the ability and power of Grant, when the press and many of the people had turned against the hero of Vicksburg, was but another proof of his sagacity and sound judgment.[75]

The rebellion of the Southern States was fomented, for the greatest part, by supposed "aristocrats" of the plantations, most of their politicians of that mix, much of their wealth wrapped up in the enslavement of darker skinned people from Africa. How they got all of the poor white people of the South to put their lives on the line for something they had little to no stake in, is a great mystery, to this author. They knew they would not be in the majority when it came to a vote, so rather than live by the rules of democracy upon which this nation was founded, the great landowners of the South would rather destroy it. The war that left so many Americans dead was 100% on the heads and hands of the proprietors of the largest estates of the South, a list that included most if not all of their politicians. Abraham asked this question at the end of his first inaugural address as provided in the collection by Stern:

"In your hand, my dissatisfied fellow countrymen, and not in mine, is the momentous issue of civil war. The Government will not assail you. You can have no conflict without being yourselves the aggressors. You have no oath registered in Heaven to destroy the Government, while I shall have the most solemn one to "preserve, protect and defend it." You can forbear the assault upon it, I cannot shrink from the defense of it. With you, and not with me, is the solemn question of "Shall it be peace or a sword?"[76]

Much like the Conservatives of today, and every day before, the ones in hereditary positions of power, and to a lesser degree some who have assumed a position of power by another route, would continue to profit off of people, no matter what the cost to the country. Raising the old question, what came first, wealth or the loss of humanity? One of Lincoln's speeches reveals that he knew right from wrong and that the battle came down to precisely that:

"Developments during the past ten years had led Lincoln to make this decision, fateful as it was. He had seen compromise after compromise with the slaveholding interests fail as they greedily reached out for more territory and for more privileges. He had no intention of attempting to prohibit slavery in the states where it already existed, but he was determined to arrest its spread. And he was convinced that slavery itself was wrong, an evil thing that had no right to exist in a civilized world, although for expediency's sake he was willing to let it stand as it was. Yet in the basic moral issue he was as inflexibly convinced as he was in the matter of confining slavery to its already established borders. This was the real issue—"the issue that will continue in this country when these poor tongues of Judge Douglas and myself shall be silent. It is the eternal struggle between these two principles—right and wrong—throughout the world."[77]

Abraham Lincoln had strong feelings of his impending mortal end, from this great conflict, yet he pushed on. He achieved victory as a war president, ensuring the continuity of the United States of America, in its most costly war in terms of human lives, ever.

"He held most firmly to the doctrine of fatalism all his life. His wife, after his death, told me what I already knew, that "his only philosophy was, what is to be will be, and no prayers of ours can reverse the decree." He always contended that he was doomed to a sad fate, and he repeatedly said to me when we were alone in our office: "I am sure I shall meet with some terrible end." In proof of his strong leaning towards fatalism he once quoted the case of Brutus and Caesar, arguing that the former was forced by laws and conditions over which he had no control to kill the latter, and, vice versâ, that the latter was specially created to be disposed of by the former. This superstitious view of life ran through his being like the thin blue vein through the whitest marble, giving the eye rest from the weariness of continued unvarying color."[78]

The would-be aristocrats, self-described men of honor, i.e., Southern honor, the charlatan chivalric order they envisioned of themselves, would forever bring dishonor on their States. First, they brought upon America a selfish war that would not only come close to ending the country, because they didn't like the democratic outcome, but would waste so many young lives. Secondly, they would further violate American law with the continued forcing of their will on Black men and women, aided by politically pressuring the premature end to the "Reconstruction" that protected the newly freed citizens from being prevented from realizing the country's charter, "Life, Liberty, and the Pursuit of Happiness." Third, they have been attempting to deny the voice of the majority, from seceding from the Union, to disenfranchising Black voters, to diabolical efforts to this day. Behavior to deny a democratic outcome that they disagree with by controlling the vote of the entire electorate by whatever method they can manage to maintain their unconscionable, unconstitutional, unethical, unwanted power over people has been their modus operandi for far, far too long. Evidence of it rose immediately after the holocaustic war against the Southern insurrection:

Following Lincoln's assassination in April 1865, Andrew Johnson became president and inaugurated the period of Presidential Reconstruction (1865–67). Johnson offered a pardon to all Southern whites except Confederate leaders and wealthy planters (although most of these subsequently received individual pardons), restoring their political rights and all property except slaves. He also outlined how new state governments would be created. Apart from the requirement that they abolish slavery, repudiate secession, and abrogate the Confederate debt, these governments were granted a free hand in managing their affairs. They responded by enacting the Black codes, laws that required African Americans to sign yearly labour contracts and in other ways sought to limit the freedmen's economic options and reestablish plantation discipline. African Americans strongly resisted the implementation of these measures, and they seriously undermined Northern support for Johnson's policies.[79]

Between Andrew Johnson's, a Southerner, and Rutherford B. Hayes' self-serving political dealings, the protections intended for the newly freed people were weakened and then eliminated just when they were becoming successful and politically active, causing horrific treatment of these people and their descendants, to this day.

Hayes, a Republican, lost the popular vote in 1876 but assumed the presidency after considerable controversy and negotiation. The Electoral College gave him a one-vote edge over his Democratic opponent, but Democrats challenged the decision on grounds that some states submitted two sets of returns.

Facing the possibility the country would be left without a president, both parties considered taking the office by force.

But in the end, the Republicans struck a secret deal with Southern Democrats in Congress, who agreed not to dispute the Hayes victory in exchange for a promise to end Reconstruction and withdraw federal troops from the South.

Hayes made good on the deal. He swiftly ended Reconstruction and pulled federal troops out of the last two occupied states, South Carolina and Louisiana.

"Instead of withdrawing, he should have sent additional troops out there," Clay said. "An 1871 report to Congress says that in nine counties in South Carolina, there were 35 lynchings, 262 black men and women

were severely beaten, and over 100 homes were burned. The Ku Klux Klan was already riding roughshod."[80]

The 16th President of the United States was indubitably its rescuer and, maybe, the first true Executive "of the people." He is certainly the man who gave the government to the people, "if we can keep it." "Hear" this validation by Mr. Henry Wilson, the 18th Vice President of the U. S. during the U. S. Grant administration, of Herndon's evaluation of Abraham Lincoln:

Two years after Mr. Lincoln's death, Mr. Wilson wrote me as follows: "I have just finished reading your letter dated December 21, 1860, in answer to a letter of mine asking you to give me your opinion of the President just elected. In this letter to me you say of Mr. Lincoln what more than four years of observation confirmed. After stating that you had been his law partner for over eighteen years and his most intimate and bosom friend all that time you say, "I know him better than he does himself. I know this seems a little strong, but I risk the assertion. Lincoln is a man of heart—aye, as gentle as a woman's and as tender—but he has a will strong as iron. He therefore loves all mankind, hates slavery and every form of despotism. Put these together—love for the slave, and a determination, a will, that justice, strong and unyielding, shall be done when he has the right to act, and you can form your own conclusion. Lincoln will fail here, namely, if a question of political economy—if any question comes up which is doubtful, questionable, which no man can demonstrate, then his friends can rule him; but when on justice, right, liberty, the Government, the Constitution, and the Union, then you may all stand aside: he will rule then, and no man can move him—no set of men can do it. There is no fail here. This is Lincoln, and you mark my prediction. You and I must keep the people right; God will keep Lincoln right." These words of yours made a deep impression upon my mind, and I came to love and trust him even before I saw him. After an acquaintance of more than four years

I found that your idea of him was in all respects correct—that he was the loving, tender, firm, and just man you represented him to be; while upon some questions in which moral elements did not so clearly enter he was perhaps too easily influenced by others. Mr. Lincoln was a genuine democrat in feelings, sentiments, and actions.[81]

From where cometh the next great liberator? And, when?

Chapter 5 - March of Martyrs, Must We?

All American's ancestors have had the "dream" of providing safety and security fotheir family when they made the decision to emigrate to the "New World". Some were "sold a bill of sale" as the powers-that-be wished to be done with people they considered distasteful, or dangerous to the status quo. Others knew that their beliefs put them and theirs in mortal danger, at worst, and in a hard place to exist, at best, and hoped that the heard of tolerance and opportunity in America was true.

Having only American history to judge by, growing up, and the fact that his forebears survived and that he has realized a comfortable and, usually, enjoyable life, the author believed that the "American Ideal" was something the entire world should shoot for. He found out, when a teenager, due to the hue and cry for civil rights and the atrocities being performed against those striving for it, and an unpopular war serving only those in power, that the "American Ideal" was a severely tarnished silver mantelpiece. It has since received additional dings and dents, yet we, Americans, keep holding it aloft, proudly displaying it as our greatest heirloom. Now, our political circumstances have been so far degraded, that heirloom is in great danger of being melted down to profit the few holding power. This is our latest crucible.

This book was intended to be something of a whip to spur more people to vote against the "land baron" mentality that is and will move us farther from the American ideal, as imperfectly as it was initiated. We have been playing "catch up," ever since, against Conservatives' unethical recruiting and offensive lines. A friend, and relative, who graciously contributed to this work, enticed this author to add an apple or carrot, positive motivation, to "dangle" before readers.

In the author's opinion, history has always seen a war of "progressives" vs "conservatives," and the conservatives, because they are more apt to make and control the "laws" (and break as they see fit, being in control) have the upper hand, as they almost always have. He believes it is the progressives who are most guided by this "dream," the so-called American Ideal, and have always been trying to make progress toward that goal while the "others" only provide obstacles and obstructions, as if they are under siege rather than being offered membership in the human family.

Another crucible is on the fire. We must control the heat, use our bellows to soften, make malleable, rather than reduce it to molten ore, to re-forge our softened "mantelpiece" to something even bigger and better. On proud display, we must continually polish it until it to reflect only the light, the truth.

Dawn of Neo-Dark Ages

One American's Observations

The author suspects that he had plenty to say about the Presidential election of the year 2000, though he seems to have lost that memory. Bush and Cheney's failure to protect America from the terrorist attack which brought the World Trade Center buildings down and cost us ~3000 lives, the shutting out of our allies for unilateral actions in the Middle East, Conservatives' war-profiteering, among other unanswered-for acts against the demands of the American majority, if not the U.S. Constitution surely had this writer furiously tapping on keys. However, like so many abused peaceful protestors now, in all fifty American states, decrying the murder of George Floyd, specifically, and Black Americans, in general, at the hands of criminal cops, this one's past computers and too many files have fallen by the wayside. The first term of POTUS #43, George W. Bush, will lack coverage, here, the author's irate reactions to his taking of the Presidency in y2000 and his unimaginable first term remain unrecovered.

The earliest non-poetic or lyrical political writings of the author's desperate creation that he has found concern the War in Iraq that George W. Bush was so partial to and the dirty secrets about it revealed in May, 2005 by the British press.

Downing Street Memo (Wikipedia):

The Downing Street memo, sometimes described by critics of the Iraq War as the smoking gun memo, is the note of a 23 July 2002 secret meeting of senior British government, defence, and intelligence figures discussing the build-up to the war, which included direct reference to classified United States policy of the time. The name refers to 10 Downing Street, the residence of the British prime minister.[82]

Let's get to the memo:

Is there anything important in the Downing Street memo? This is the now-notorious secret transcript of a British ministerial meeting on July 23, 2002—obtained and published by the Sunday Times *of London just this past May Day—which seems to suggest that, nine months before the war in Iraq got started, the Bush administration a) knew Saddam Hussein didn't pose a threat; b) decided to overthrow him by force anyway; and c) was "fixing" intelligence to sell the impending invasion to a duped American public.*

Many critics see the memo as the ultimate proof of Bush's duplicity—and, given that no U.S. newspaper picked up the story for two weeks (and then buried it deep inside), as further evidence of the mainstream media's cravenness. Others, and not just Bush apologists, see the affair as overblown and the document's contents as no big deal. [83]

Wikipedia has been borrowed from to refresh our memories, and Slate, which, possibly, from its date and the date of creation of the author's letter, might have been what fired up this citizen to write his subsequent thoughts of June 16, 2005:

Discussing the Downing Street Memo

Evidence of the Bush Administrations' illicit war-mongering has again surfaced, to be once more ignored by the Republicans and the right-wing American press. The Downing Street Memo cannot and must not be ignored. Now is our opportunity to get the American ostriches hiding their collective heads in the dark recesses to finally see the light.

Please, every concerned citizen, help take this fight wherever it must lead. Our liberties, our democracy, our esteem in the eyes of our international allies and enemies depends on our system of checks and balances working as our forefathers intended. The misuse and abuse of government power has to be stopped and prosecuted to the full extent of the law to ensure that the American ideal will shine its light upon the entire world.

The Shot That Was Heard Around the Water Cooler

March of 2006 brought hope to Progressive voters distraught about the shameful, if not charlatan, shenanigans of the Bush and Cheney GOP. Some Democrats were finally taking steps to restore, or instill, "Law and Order" to the Bush II presidency.

In an exclusive interview on "This Week with George Stephanopoulos," Democratic Sen. Russ Feingold called on the Senate to publicly admonish President Bush for approving domestic wiretaps on American citizens without first seeking a legally required court order.

"This conduct is right in the strike zone of the concept of high crimes and misdemeanors," said Feingold, D-Wis., a three-term senator and potential presidential contender.

He said Bush had, "openly and almost thumbing his nose at the American people," continued the NSA domestic wiretap program.[84]

This voter was moved to thank those moving in the right direction, and implore others to do the same when he wrote the following on Apr. 1, 2006:

Sen. Russell Feingold's (D-Wisconsin) Censure Resolution

The censure resolution has attracted only two co-sponsors, Democratic Senators Tom Harkin of Iowa and Barbara Boxer of California. The Senate's other 41 Democrats have distanced themselves, many saying they want to, first, see the results of a Senate Intelligence Committee investigation of the matter.

Privately, Democrats in the House and Senate have said that embracing a censure resolution before the facts are known would damage their credibility this election year. Once more, this writer put down his thoughts about the sorry situation, and, this time, sent them to his senator:

Dear Senator Wyden:

Please stand up to the partisan power pandering continuing to weaken our democracy. You must lend your full support to Senators Feingold, Harkin, and Boxer to try to make our system of checks and balances continue to work.

Waiting for the Senate Intelligence Committee to verify the facts is like waiting for the White House to admit to wrongdoing.

The fact that Bush violated American law in ways much greater than Nixon's Administration is inarguable.

Please, please, please—get on your soapbox and preach to the choir, very loudly, for they have fallen asleep and our nation's security is threatened more by scofflaws in office than any external red herrings that the Republicans would have us fishing for.

Thank you very much for believing in and protecting the U. S. Constitution. Make our system work, it is our only hope.

To his representative:

Dear Senator Boxer:

Thank you, so much, for your support and sponsorship of Senator Feingold's censure resolution. I so hope that most democratic senators will follow suit and that the miracle of some Republican senators making the ethical decision will occur. Please find, below, the letter I am endeavoring to send to all of the D. senators, alphabetically, you surmise, correctly, that I have a long way to go.

And to all the rest on Capitol Hill:

To all Senators:

I sent this message to my senator, Ron Wyden, of Oregon, I hope that you will take it to your heart, also, as it came from mine.

Please stand up to the partisan power pandering continuing to weaken our democracy. You must lend your full support to Senators Feingold, Harkin, and Boxer to try to make our system of checks and balances continue to work. Waiting for the Senate Intelligence Committee to verify the facts is like waiting for the White House to admit to wrongdoing. The fact that Bush violated American law in ways much greater than Nixon's Administration is inarguable.

Please, please, please—get on your soapbox and preach to the choir, very loudly, for they have fallen asleep and our nation's security is threatened more by scofflaws in office than any external red herrings that the Republicans would have us fishing for.

Thank you very much for believing in and protecting the U. S. Constitution. Make our system work, it is our only hope.

Too often, the GOP seems to vote against the desires of the majority of Americans. Not sure when this began, the tendency to ignore the electorate's desires and vote against them, representing Corporate America or the Religious Right, but here is one instance of the many. George W. Bush's ceding to the Religious Right is suspected in this case, among others:

President Bush issued the first veto of his 5½-year presidency on Wednesday, rejecting legislation that would ease limits on federal funding for embryonic stem-cell research.

Later Wednesday, the House failed to override Mr. Bush's veto...[85]

This guy got on his social media soapbox the day he read the above article, on July 22, 2006. When science is working for the good of people or the planet, the religious radicals find something wrong with it; when science is put to work to find better ways to kill people, they seem to be silent—this writer could not:

Where Does George Get Off?

When will George W. Bush cease giving the finger to the American public? This last insult, putting the override vote on the floor of the

House as soon as he possibly could after vetoing the Stem Cell Bill, ignoring the desire of the great majority of American voters, can only be seen as that symbolic gesture. Where does that man get off doing this to the greater American electorate? HERE—is where he should get off. Let's give him and Dick the old heave-ho; they should not be allowed to take advantage of this country, ever again. How many times must we "turn the other cheek" before the religious right figures out that this man is, in fact, a wolf in sheep's clothing, wearing his Sunday suit as a mantle of invisibility, preventing them from really seeing him. The television character, Earl Hickey ("My Name is Earl") practices "Christian acts," a.k.a., "the golden rule," or, empathy, more than George W. Bush.

John Bolton, a career Conservative sycophant finding niches in many Republican administrations, is not very popular, even within his own Party. Bush, again, ignored the desires of the American public to place Bolton in the United Nations. This was just another "dirty trick" which have increasingly become S.O.P. for the G.O.P. Bolton is one of the recurring nightmares Right-wing administrations continue to give us. We have seen him float to the top, once again, in the Trump government. Fred Kaplan wrote this about Bolton:

Bolton, of course, has been U.N. ambassador since August, but the Senate had never confirmed him. Last summer, the committee sent his nomination to the floor without recommendation. (Republicans on the panel outrank Democrats 10-8, but, in a big surprise, Sen. George Voinovich, R-Ohio, came out against him, spawning a 9-9 tie.) On the Senate floor, Democrats pulled a filibuster. Republicans could not rally the 60 votes needed for cloture. So, Bolton seemed doomed—until, during the July 4 holidays, Bush shoved him into office with a "recess appointment."[86]

This one's July 30, 2006 reaction to the news was by now a reflex, it seems:

Revoltin' Bolton

The Bush Administration has continually ignored the desires of the American public and forced its way on us. We are tired of being victims of these men's desires. Yes, we are angry, very angry, as victims often are.

Bolton's original placement was forced on America, the veto of the Stem Cell Act was other example of Bush ignoring Americans' cries of "No, No, NO!" Do not be an accomplice to this Administration's latest affront of the vast majority of U.S. voters. Refuse to ignore their victims' pleas, as has been so many times in the last five years. Honest and responsible representation is gravely needed, now. The respect of the world for our country has fallen so low, we need to put someone that we all respect and trust in that position. Bolton is the antithesis of that.

Listen to the voice of America.

Something else the Bush and Cheney White House failed to hear the public on was the dilemma they had instigated in Iraq. The Iraq Study Group co-chairs sent this letter to James A. Baker, III, et al, in his position as Secretary of State for George W. Bush:

There is no magic formula to solve the problems of Iraq. However, there are actions that can be taken to improve the situation and protect American interests. Many Americans are dissatisfied, not just with the situation in Iraq but with the state of our political debate regarding Iraq. Our political leaders must build a bipartisan approach to bring a responsible conclusion to what is now a lengthy and costly war. Our country deserves a debate that prizes substance over rhetoric, and a policy that is adequately funded and sustainable. The President and

Congress must work together. Our leaders must be candid and forthright with the American people in order to win their support. No one can guarantee that any course of action in Iraq at this point will stop sectarian warfare, growing violence, or a slide toward chaos. If current trends continue, the potential consequences are severe. Because of the role and responsibility of the United States in Iraq, and the commitments our government has made, the United States has special obligations. Our country must address as best it can Iraq's many problems.[87]

This writer's immediate reaction to the news was to get his feelings off of his chest, the modus operandi everyone should develop, particularly in letters to our representatives. This is the resultant letter from this constituent on Dec. 9, 2006, from the news of that week:

Letter to Congress—I Saw the News, Today

I saw the news, today, and I am, again, angry as I have been about the usurping of our government for more than five years. The Iraq Study Groups' report, though so-called "bi-partisan," and Bush's response to it just smack too much of same old "white-washing" of Bush's culpability and "rubber-stamping" of his policy in Iraq.

Bush's touting of the Group's finding that the situation in Iraq, left unchecked, is "...a threat to the global economy..." is another clue, albeit politi-speak or Orwellian doublespeak, that control of the second largest oil reserve in the world is our continued primary goal of this war, as true patriots have been saying all along. To allow unchecked production of this great supply will cause serious reduction in the price of oil and petroleum. Economically speaking, the only one this will hurt is "Big Oil". Our current administration's partners, and controllers, will not allow this.

I have heard or read no mention of the best and wisest course of action that the United States could take at this juncture, this junction in our "go it alone" road to "success" in Iraq. That is, we should admit that our plan, our policy, counter to the United Nations' recommendations and the world's opinion, was seriously and fatally flawed. We must humbly admit that we were wrong and petition and persuade and agree to let the U.N. make any further decisions about appropriate actions in the "building" of Iraq's "democracy." We, for all intents, alone, just continue to stumble along, blindly, down the path of i.e.d.'s, snipers, and suicide bombers.

We need to do an immediate "about—face!" and George W. Bush should personally address the U.N. General Assembly, offer his apology for ignoring and disregarding their findings, and ask for their assistance in trying to resolve the hell our policy has wrought in Iraq. This is, in fact, the only way for us to ultimately save what's left of our face and begin to regain some semblance of World respect as a reborn member of that community.

Please, as a representative of caring and sharing people who long for world peace and an "eternally" sacrosanct environment for our descendants, do whatever you can to help the U.S. Congress understand the importance of getting the entire world, via the United Nations, involved in achieving peace in the Middle East, and simultaneously and systematically disengaging ourselves.

Millions in the U.S. and throughout the world condemned the Bush-Cheney government for taking armed actions against Iraq in spite of the U.N.'s suggestions against such aggression. America's near-unilateral attack (the British joined the U.S. in warfare against Iraq) on the forces and country ruled by Saddam Hussein alienated us from many allies and raised much angst in American voters. Many were outspoken in rebuke of this American President and his administration's moves and motives. See following article and letter:

What were the contentious issues in the sanctions debate?

• *U.N. authority. Some Security Council members, including war opponents France, Russia, and Germany, wanted the United Nations to play a leading role in Iraq in order to balance U.S. authority. The amended resolution raises the profile of the United Nations in Iraq and allows a U.N. special representative to work with the United States and Britain to set up new Iraqi institutions. But the United Nations still does not have legal authority over Iraqi reconstruction, and how much influence it will have on U.S. policy remains unclear.*[88]

Letter dated 14 November 2006 from the Permanent Representative of Iraq to the United Nations addressed to the President of the Security Council:

I have the honour to enclose herewith a letter from Nuri Kamel al-Maliki, Prime Minister of the Republic of Iraq, dated 11 November 2006, regarding the Security Council review of the mandate of the multinational force and the arrangements for the Development Fund for Iraq and the International Advisory and Monitoring Board (see annex). I would appreciate it if the present letter and its annex could be circulated as a document of the Security Council.[89]

The author had this to say about the situation in Iraq on Jan. 7, 2007:

A Win-Win Solution

Our involvement, though still partially in place, can no longer be suspect when the U.N. is in control of assisting the new government of the people of Iraq, and perhaps tensions will ease off when they see that their government is really theirs, rather than a tool of an imperial country. The multi-national peacekeepers must try to help remove insurgents from other countries, while Iraqi's sort through the rubble and rebuild what is theirs.

I hear the arguments from both sides of the "fence"; start pulling the troops out (saving us from many more casualties) and let Iraq control their own destiny, or, bring in more troops to put down the insurgency thereby allowing the Iraq troops and police a more secure environment to establish their own control of.

The truth is that we were purposely and illegally conned into this war that is needlessly killing and maiming tens of thousands of our hard-working young people, not to mention the thousands of Iraqi citizens dying, also unacceptably, as "collateral damage". The truth that the American "war industry," i.e., arms manufacturers (making billions from overpriced and often unneeded weapons), the oil industry (profiting from the prevention of pumping oil from Iraq's great reserves) and, the newest vultures on the block, military services contractors (also overcharging and undersupplying), not to forget the great profiteering funeral business that, since it's virtual birth during the Civil War, have reaped their greatest profits during times of war. They, all, have much to lose by our withdrawal from Iraq. That has much to do with why many lobbyists and their U.S. Treasury-tethered puppet politicians are fighting so hard to continue or escalate our involvement in the Mid-East.

The crooked reasons for our involvement in this Middle East maelstrom are the main reasons that most honest Americans are so inclined to want to end our erroneous, if not felonious, participation. Overlooking our onerous official offerings for our Babylonian involvement, some believe we must continue the "good fight" until "success" has been accomplished, this view further persuaded by the pushing of the idea that we have to defeat the terrorists on their soil or they will surely have to be defeated on ours, the sophomoric view if we don't "win" we therefore "lose".

In spite of the criminal intent with which our officials authorized our invasion of Iraq, the fact remains that this mess, which we begat, is our responsibility to resolve. The problem, herein, is that we, because of our irresponsible reasoning for the war, our ill-advised unilateral approach to the alleged "problem," and our continued hemming and hawing about... everything... tells the American electorate, and the world, that the U.S. is not in the best interest of Iraq.

The answer? Admit that we did not and cannot administer the best assistance to Iraq, that we were wrong to spurn the greater opinion of the United Nations, and ask them for forgiveness and their assistance in Iraq. The U.N. should recognize the necessity of reduced U.S. involvement in Iraq and agree to send multinational peacekeeping forces to supplant the troops that we can begin to withdraw.

This course of action will begin to regain our lost global respect and will be welcomed by the Americans who believe that we have already lost too many thousands of Americans and too many billions of dollars in this ill-advised and fated course of action and appease those Americans who realize that it would be wrong to leave Iraq's new government alone in the crossfire that we allowed, if not created; this is a Win-Win solution. Only foreign financial interest in Iraq will loudly protest U.N. control. Iraq's restored agricultural, business and economic sectors will do the most to achieve stability in that country. The U.N. can better achieve that, since empirical entrepreneurs put a lock on Iraq's economy.

Let me repeat myself, lobbyists and their U.S. Treasury tendered, tenured, and tentacled puppet politicians were fighting hard to continue or escalate our involvement in the Mid-East. Sadly, this symbiotic predation of the taxpayers was around before this and the Greedy Oligarch Party of Trump has taken it "where no Con has gone before."

The Crusade of Dick & Dubya

"Christian" concerns in the Middle East have always had profiteers and losers. Dick and Dubya's debacle was no different. War profiteering has always been big-business, the first crusade of the twenty-first century was no different:

The number of U.S.-paid private contractors in Iraq now exceeds that of American combat troops, newly released figures show, raising fresh questions about the privatization of the war effort and the government's capacity to carry out military and rebuilding campaigns.

More than 180,000 civilians—including Americans, foreigners and Iraqis—are working in Iraq under U.S. contracts, according to State and Defense department figures obtained by the Los Angeles Times.

Including the recent troop buildup, 160,000 soldiers and a few thousand civilian government employees are stationed in Iraq.

The total number of private contractors, far higher than previously reported, shows how heavily the Bush administration has relied on corporations to carry out the occupation of Iraq—a mission criticized as being undermanned.[90]

Especially challenging for the Bush Jr. administration was Cheney's ties to the privatization of the military through his company, Halliburton:

In this phase, the evading of accountability takes center stage. The administration had bitten off in Iraq far more than it proved able to chew unilaterally, and to hold off the domestic political repercussions the administration had to relentlessly hide the full ongoing anticipated scale of the war's cost, now estimated by economists at as much as $2 *trillion.51 So, the administration dodged serious budgeting, including any discipline of military procurement costs by canceling superfluous high-tech weaponry, and by abuse of outside-the-budget annual "emergency" supplemental appropriations.52 The administration largely escaped serious congressional oversight until a Democratic majority took Congress in 2007. 53 Additionally, this phase was shaped by the belatedly revealed abuses of contractors like Halliburton, 54 long the monopoly logistics contractor 55 to the military in Iraq. 56[91]*

The author's outrage exploded, again, in ink-stained invective on July 26, 2007:

Save Us

Well-documented deceit by the executive branch is costing 99.9% of America's taxpayers over $20 billion a day. 0.01% of America is reaping this cash bonanza, and they are all Bush cronies and supporters. This milking of the treasury is Texas' dirty-politics tradition. The Texas oil-garchy is now cozenly and confidently doing the same to the Federal coffers. Restore the world's faith in U.S. democracy!

This article by Joseph Palermo from the month before may explain the outcry:

Here are four Articles of Impeachment as put forth by the Center for Constitutional Rights. Each of the four have substantial supporting documentation, which includes the Congressional Record, private correspondence from government officials, public statements by President Bush and other Administration officials, press accounts, and court documents. I have written below verbatim the Articles of Impeachment from a book by William Goodman, Legal Director of the Center for Constitutional Rights, entitled: "Articles of Impeachment

Against George W. Bush," (Hoboken, New Jersey: Melville House Publishing, 2006).[92]

Only one voice out of millions, the author's, is highlighted here, but these words on Aug. 03, 2007 are echoed from others:

Save Our System

S.O.S. We cannot trust the Neo-Con seeded Federal court system to protect mainstream Americans and their Constitutional rights. The Judicial Branch has proven time and again, beginning with the 2000 Presidential election, that they will be supportive of their party rather than the U. S. Constitution and the desire or demands of the majority of Americans. The only way to restore our democratic system and our trust, and the faith of the world, in it is to do what James Madison and our founding fathers allowed for in just such usurpation—impeach the wrongdoers. It is the only way to save our system.

Some in the press still told it like it was, when the political privateers were picking the pockets of the general public:

WASHINGTON – The war in Iraq could ultimately cost well over a trillion dollars—at least double what has already been spent—including the long-term costs of replacing damaged equipment, caring for wounded troops, and aiding the Iraqi government, according to a new government analysis.

The United States has already allocated more than $500 billion on the day-to-day combat operations of what are now 190,000 troops and a variety of reconstruction efforts.[93]

The polls may have sunk the GOP's ship of state for waving the Skull and Crossbones too boldly:

According to a recent CBS News poll, President Bush's approval rating has fallen to an all-time low of 34 percent. A July survey by the nonpartisan American Research Group found that 45 percent of respondents said they want Congress to begin impeachment proceedings, while 46 percent opposed the idea.[94]

This lone voice, though just one of a huge choir, sang out in solo again, to whomever would listen, about the greedy corruption of the GOP, on August 28, 2007:

Save Us, II

The executive branch's deceit is costing America's taxpayers over $300 million a day. One tenth of one percent of Americans, Bush's financiers, reap this cash crop. The war industry, fear as their marketing tool, is, in a very cozen way, draining Federal coffers. Owning judges—milking the treasury—must not become our tradition. U. S. troops, economy, and democracy, all standing on artificial legs, must be reinvested—but—no longer in Iraq, nor by profiteering at taxpayers' expense.

The criticism of MSM has been long and deserved, but their objective failure seems to just be getting worse:

It's hardly controversial to suggest that the mainstream media's performance in the lead-up to the Iraq War was a disaster. In retrospect, many journalists and pundits wish they had been more skeptical of the White House's claims about Iraq, particularly its allegations about weapons of mass destruction. At the same time, though, media apologists suggest that the press could not have done much better, since "everyone" was in agreement on the intelligence regarding Iraq's weapons threat. This was never the case. Critical journalists and analysts raised serious questions at the time about what the White House was saying. Often, however, their warnings were ignored by the bulk of the corporate press.[95]

The less-heard press, not MSM, seems to be the fourth estate for the least of American property owners, the last of our checks and balances not owned by the ultra-wealthy:

A new report by the progressive media watchdog group Fairness and Accuracy in Reporting shows the complicity of the capitalist media in selling the U.S. invasion of Iraq to a skeptical U.S. public.[96]

One voice yodeling from the precipice overlooking the chasm continued to make this claim on Aug. 28, 2007, but the noise of industry drowned out:

MSM MIA

Where is the press that so covered the breadth, and every breath, of the Clinton-Lewinsky interlude? Is it just a one-sided partisan tool? Scoff-laws, Constitutional violators, criminals—are running the U. S. Government. Into the ground, I might add.

Our Constitution, the backbone of our democracy and freedom, has been under attack, violated, yay, decimated since George W. Bush lost his first Presidential election in 2000 and the press, one of the greatest tools of our supposed free society, has been scared, at best, and compliant, at worst, to speak out about this Executive Administrations' atrocities. There have been dozens of them.

What, in the name of truth, justice, and the American way, has happened to the objective, nay, the objecting press that helped forge the liberties that we are now in danger of losing because of the now tight lips of the same once valiant voice. The "free" press is our last vestige of hope; in our time of greatest need, where is it?

Conservative corruption has infected corporate America, from manufacturing overpriced goods and services for the military, to political punditry and partisanship of the press, and politicians in much higher tax brackets than their government-pay should provide. On Counterpunch, another human who didn't just fall off the turnip truck lays it out, here:

Cheney personifies war profiteering. He slid through the revolving door connecting the public and private sectors of the defense establishment on two occasions in a career that has served his relentless quest for power and profits.

As Defense Secretary, Mr. Cheney commissioned a study for the U.S. Department of Defense by Brown and Root Services (now Kellogg, Brown and Root), a wholly-owned subsidiary of Halliburton. The study recommended that private firms like Halliburton take over logistical support programs for U.S. military operations around the world. Just two years after he was Secretary of Defense, Cheney stepped through the revolving door linking the Department of Defense with defense contractors and became CEO of Halliburton. Halliburton was the principal beneficiary of Cheney's privatization efforts for our military's logistical support and Cheney was paid $44 million for five year's work before he slipped back through the revolving door of war profiteering to become Vice-President of the United States. When asked about the money he received from Halliburton, Cheney said. "I tell you that the government had absolutely nothing to do with it."

Before the Iraq War began, Halliburton was 19th on the U.S. Army's list of top contractors and zoomed to number 1 in 2003. Cheney stated he had, "severed all my ties with the company, gotten rid of all my financial interests."[97]

Spurred by articles such as the one above, this citizen spoke up to with this thread on social media to promote a pledge to invest in democracy, on Aug. 28, 2007:

"Business As Usual" is Exhausting America

The American people are tired of being victimized by big business and their unethical friends in government. The trillion or so that this war is draining from the living expenses of the working class of the United States is predominately going to U. S. corporations and their partners in political positions of power. The only people gaining from this war is the military-industrial complex that has had the American government in its pocket since the end of WWII.

We must, somehow, find representatives of the electorate that have the fortitude, the insight, and the scruples to make the right choices in Congress; choices that won't milk blood and bucks from the American people, anymore. Where is the "...government of the people, by the people, and for the people..."? What happened to that government? Give it back to us—please. Fight for it, before we have to.

Start, by signing this pledge to fund only the exit from this vacuum tube that is delivering our deposits to George's and Dick's and friends' accounts. Draining the treasury for personal gain, with the help of the courts, is "business as usual" in Texas politics, how in the hell did we let it become s.o.p. of the G.O.P.? Oh, yeah, the "Conservatives". What—in the name of truth, justice, and the American way—are they conserving?

To a growing extent, American citizens must listen to non-mainstream and non-domestic press to hear what those in power don't want us to:

Petraeus has previously stressed that his testimony was his own and had not been shown to anyone in the White House or Pentagon amid suggestions from Democrats prior to the hearing that it would be politicized.

But in an editorial on Tuesday, the New York Times described the general's testimony as "another of the broken promises and false claims we have heard from Mr. Bush."[98]

Personal content from social media from Sept. 11, 2007 as a member of the choir repeating the refrain as heard from multiple sources, such as above article:

Petraeus Paints Surreal Portrait of "Surge"

White acrylic dabbed over lakes of red blood. Vital parts omitted from the picture. Numbers floating in some places and inverted in others. General Petraeus must have studied Picasso at West Point. His report is certainly a picture to obscure reality.

Obviously, he is one of the boys handpicked to replace the best of our military leaders that were early casualties of Bush's war on truth. Perhaps Petraeus fears that a "Brass bomb" has his name on it. Is he afraid of his military career ending or losing his post-military position in the war-profiteering industry?

Oh, for a million or more followers on Twitter.

This writer implored to the universe in general to use the brief Congressional control of both houses that the Democrats briefly held to make an example of the Bush administration for consideration by future executives in the White House. Pelosi and Harry Reid failed to secure and safeguard our Democracy by exposing the actors and exemplifying the cost of corruption for such. Ari Berman objectively covered one of Pelosi's arguments against in this part of a paragraph from an article he wrote for *The Nation*:

...Pelosi sketched her case against impeachment. "The question of impeachment is something that would divide the country," Pelosi said this morning during a wide-ranging discussion in the ornate Speaker's office. Her top priorities are ending the war in Iraq, expanding health care, creating jobs and preserving the environment. "I know what our

success can be on those issues. I don't know what our success can be on impeaching the president."[99]

It is not known whether this letter dated Sept. 14, 2007 ever made it to Madam Speaker's desk, but it is feared that its ripples or echoes may reach toes or ears of further alarmed citizens standing on dangerously shifting sands in the near future:

Letter to Pelosi

We, the American people, never should have allowed a family so connected to Nazi Germany to reign supreme in U. S. politics. However, the people, in general, do not hold the ultimate blame for these mistakes, our political leaders should have ensured that the voters knew the history of the Bush family and their failures in protecting the American public. Now, we are at a great crossroads in our history.

The best that we can hope for is that this will be called our darkest hour.The worst, if we don't restore our government's functionality, recover our system of checks and balances, renew our citizens' and allies' faith in our democracy? Theocracy, oil-garchy, or some mutant variation in between. If we haven't already, we will have certainly lost our ability to control our leaders. And we, as we already have lost it, will be unable to regain the global respect we once knew.

Please, with all due respect, admit your mistake in disregarding impeachment, and put it back on the table. And pound the hell out of our government with the gavel until it conforms to our founding fathers' design and the current constituency's desire and will not be warped again.

Give us our government back!

This writer was a little early with that call, our darkest hours' hard beginning was still ten years down the road. Though, the seeds of insurgency were being planted for decades, before.

——————————————————————————————————-

Fear of another Conservative president after the Dick and Dubya debacle, further cementing of Conservative-Christian control of our government, and increased devaluation of the U.S. Constitution wrung this cry from the author to any Progressive voters paying attention on social media as the next election loomed, Sept. 25, 2007:

Baseball, Mom, and Apple Pie

The electorate has been rejected, again, after again and again and again... When will the voter once more be recognized as the voice of America? The media has been editing the truth for too long. Now is the time for all Americans to step up and hit the ball, and our biggest hitters are in Congress If our Congressmen are content to throw the game then the last of our system of checks and balances is gone and our democracy is a total failure. We must hit every one of these pitches to win the big game. If we strike out... Mom and apple pie are next.

Breathing a sigh of relief after Barack Obama won the presidency in the election of November, 2007, but realizing that the GOP did not recognize or play by the rules of ethics as the Democrats did, some realized that it was imperative to make wayward politicians pay a penalty for disregarding their duty and violating their oath. In the heat of the moment, at that time, Dec. 14, 2007, perhaps this writer, on social media, was too vehement:

Guillotime

Until George W. Bush and his captains are condemned for mutilating our democracy and tens or hundreds of thousands of human beings, our government is in danger, our rights are in danger, and we are not "safe". Everybody has the responsibility, the duty, to condemn the actions of this president and vice president. If you fail to, you are part of the problem. If you try to prevent condemnation of this presidency, you are his abettor. The majority of Americans are crying for action to restore our government, our democracy, our constitution!

Too many times this administration has decried, "Let them eat bread!" or "Let them put moldy bread on their festering wounds!" while funneling America's treasury into the pockets of this country's wealthiest. A symbolic guillotine must be erected and the heads of this tainted and treasonous government severed to regain the trust of the American public and our global partners. If Dick Cheney must be the first to answer for his crimes against the United States of America, then so be it.

The best medicine to battle the cancer that has seriously infected all three branches of our government and the media is in your hands. The health of our government, nay, the existence of our democracy, depends on you to administer the cure. You really have no choice if you value your country, it sorely needs you to act, and act now.

However, in retrospect, ten years later...?

The end of the George W. Bush administration was no more constitutionally quirked than the body or the beginning. But, as then, the "Get Out of Jail Free" card effected by the Conservative partisan Supreme Court, and a split Congress or better, gave Republicans no pause to act in whatever way benefited them in power and pay-to-play schemes. The privatization of military support services and lack of controls on such was just the latest affront on American taxpayers:

Halliburton, the company with $2 billion in Iraq contracts, is accused of once again joining the U.S. government in covering up a terrible crime by some employees.[100]

Social media was this writer's favorite outlet for sharing the latest news to spur readers to more active resistance to Republicans reaping whatever they wanted with a partisan judges and SCOTUS and lame-duck Congress willing to cover their asses. Echoing the less-Conservative press on Dec. 16, 2007:

Halliburton Bad Behavior

This is what happens when our leaders are not held accountable for illegal or unethical actions. The rest of their organization quickly follows suit. This yet another of many black marks against the United States since Bush and Cheney took office. Our inability to control or correct this behavior is inexcusable and all means of putting an end to America's international indiscretions should be exercised, immediately.

Reuters added this postscript about Halliburton's "bad luck":

HOUSTON, Dec 19 (Reuters) - Major Pentagon contractor KBR Inc (KBR.N) and former parent Halliburton Co (HAL.N) are facing rising political heat from a lawsuit filed by a woman who says she was gang-raped by fellow employees of a KBR unit in Iraq.[101]

This turned out to be an almost prophetic metaphor for the road the Conservative Party would be on from the extreme turn they were taking.

Benjamin Franklin was perhaps the founding father of a free press, believing it was critical to tempering the acts and policies of government but he also understood that it could, itself, become a tyrant in swinging the moods and movements of the public. Much has been made about MSM's failure to report facts critical of the Conservative Presidents and other political figures, calling it Right-Wing journalism, but when Conservatives do face the music of public exposure, they complain they are unworthy attacks by the liberal press. There is too much tendency to disguise views of political scandals as transparency, after making them become opaque, glossed over, by focusing public attention on the latest sensationalist news.

Afraid to challenge America's leaders or conventional wisdom about the Middle East, a toothless press collapsed.

...perhaps the press's most notable failure was its inability to determine just why this disastrous war was ever launched. Kristina Borjesson, author of "Feet to the Fire," a collection of interviews with 21 journalists about why the press collapsed, summed this up succinctly. "The thing that I found really profound was that there really was no consensus among this nation's top messengers about why we went to war," Borjesson told AlterNet. "[War is the] most extreme activity a nation can engage in, and if they weren't clear about it, that means the public wasn't necessarily clear about the real reasons. And I still don't think the American people are clear about it."[102]

Whether this is compliance of corporate press in political chicanery is not sure, but is certainly suspected by some. Teresa Harrington and Paul Burgarino of the East Bay Times go into more detail:

"It's part of an effort to wake us all up to how much we've lost since the Patriot Act and 9/11," said Mary Alice O'Connor, peace center executive director. "If we don't know what's going on, how do we take appropriate action?"...

...The top story cited by the group is the loss of habeas corpus rights for any person deemed an enemy of the state, as the result of the Military

Commissions Act signed by President Bush in October 2006. Habeas corpus rights allow people to challenge the governmental power of arrest and imprisonment, according to Consortium news stories written by Robert Parry.

"Under the cloak of setting up military tribunals to try al-Qaida suspects and other so-called unlawful enemy combatants," Parry wrote, "Bush and the Republican-controlled Congress effectively created a parallel legal system for "any person" — American citizen or otherwise — who crosses some ill-defined line."

In 2007, the Senate sought to restore those rights.

Charlie Hahn, a 17-year-old senior at Acalanes High School who serves on the peace center board, said he hopes many people — including youths — will come to the presentation to find out about issues they may not hear of through typical news sources.

"Media bias is definitely a big problem in this country, and it needs to be addressed," he said. "There are a lot of the same people running a lot of media outlets, and you get something of a monopoly. A lot of stories that are important aren't covered because media think they're too radical or they just feel that it would be against their best interests and their profit interests to publish them."[103]

One lay writer had this to say about the media coverage of the Bush and Cheney administration, on Dec. 28, 2007:

MSM Still MIA or Confirmed POW?

Where is the press that so covered the breadth, keeping us abreast of every breath, of the Clinton-Lewinsky interlude? Is the press really just a right-wing tool? Is that legal? That is definitely not what our founding fathers envisioned when they imagined the system of checks and balances to protect our system from corruption. There are scoff-laws,

U. S. Constitution violators, war profiteers, criminals—running the U. S. Government. Into the ground, I might add. The press, one of the greatest tools of our supposed free society, has been scared, at best, and compliant, at worst, to speak out about this Executive Administrations' atrocities. There have been dozens of them, rarely publicized, especially on the front page where they should be.

Give us the news, honestly and objectively, or get out of here; our press has become as reliable as Cuba's and China's. I am so ashamed, and so scared, that there are no remaining checks and balances of our government, the "free" press was our last vestige of hope. In our time of greatest need, where is it? There is, and has been, great national outcry and continuing attempts to begin impeachment proceedings for Dick Cheney. Your function in the foundation and maintenance of this great country was to report the good and bad of our national interests, especially the worst of the worst. When are we going to hear about this?

The dependability of the polling devices has come under as great of suspicion as the press. What can we believe? Clive Thompson of the New York Times also figures about the math of our current election process:

In the last three election cycles, touch-screen machines have become one of the most mysterious and divisive elements in modern electoral politics. In hundreds of instances ... they [have failed] unpredictably, and in extremely strange ways; voters report that their choices "flip" from one candidate to another before their eyes; machines crash or begin to count backward; votes simply vanish. Most famously, in the November 2006 Congressional election in Sarasota, Fla., touch-screen machines recorded an 18,000-person "undervote" for a race decided by fewer than 400 votes. The earliest critiques of digital voting booths came from the fringe – disgruntled citizens and ... computer geeks – but the fears have now risen to the highest levels of government. One by one, states are renouncing the use of touch-screen voting machines. California and Florida decided to get rid of their electronic voting machines. Colorado decertified about half of its touch-screen devices. Michael Shamos, a computer scientist at Carnegie Mellon University who has examined voting-machine systems for more than 25 years, estimates that about 10 percent of the touch-screen machines "fail" in each election.[104]

One man's fears of a Constitutionally bereft country have plagued him since the Conservative-heavy SCOTUS interpreted the U.S. Constitution in a unique way in favor of the Conservative candidate in the year 2000. Those fears have since been exacerbated causing him to get others to see the problem on Jan. 8, 2008:

Election Integrity a Democratic Must

Our government is seriously injured, perhaps critically. If we do not apply compression or a tourniquet soon it may be too late. We must ensure, surely and swiftly, that the flickering light of our democracy is not extinguished by any more tainted elections. We must rekindle the faith, hope, and respect of our own citizens' as well as that of the world. The best way to do this is to prove that we mean business when it comes to the integrity of our election process. A "paper trail" verifiable voting system must be allowed and provided to prevent stolen elections.

Progressive leaders knew what was up and not enough stood up and spoke out about the wayward Right Wing. Because of complacency or cowardice, the Right has shifted even farther to the Right, putting them on the border of fascism. Past presidential candidate George McGovern saw the problem more than a decade ago, as a piece he wrote was published in the *Washington Post*:

As we enter the eighth year of the Bush-Cheney administration, I have belatedly and painfully concluded that the only honorable course for me is to urge the impeachment of the president and the vice president.

After the 1972 presidential election, I stood clear of calls to impeach President Richard M. Nixon for his misconduct during the campaign. I thought that my joining the impeachment effort would be seen as an expression of personal vengeance toward the president who had defeated me.

Today I have made a different choice.

Of course, there seems to be little bipartisan support for impeachment. The political scene is marked by narrow and sometimes superficial partisanship, especially among Republicans, and a lack of courage and statesmanship on the part of too many Democratic politicians. So the chances of a bipartisan impeachment and conviction are not promising.

But what are the facts?

Bush and Cheney are clearly guilty of numerous impeachable offenses. They have repeatedly violated the Constitution. They have transgressed national and international law. They have lied to the American people time after time. Their conduct and their barbaric policies have reduced our beloved country to a historic low in the eyes of people around the world. These are truly "high crimes and misdemeanors," to use the constitutional standard.[105]

Established Democratic leaders' words fell on deaf ears and encountered closed minds of too many Conservative zealots. How can one common man hope to enlighten the masses? Regardless, this one continued his barrage of warnings on social media at this time, Jan. 30, 2008:

Which History Will We Choose, or Lose?

I don't know if you have given this much thought, or not, but it is critically important that you do. History is going to record George W. Bush's administrations as either the start of the darkest time in U. S. history or the catalyst of a great democratic renaissance. You are already part of that recorded period. For better or worse is the only question. That is your decision to make.

If we can't take control of this runaway Budweiser wagon and teach the Clydesdales to behave better, we are going to be doing a lot more crying than over spilled beer. Already we are shedding tears over spilled blood, depleted treasury, unemployment, economic upheaval, lack of medical care, and many other negatives created by a thousand or more untruths by the unquestionably worst of American presidencies.

There is only one way to turn this to a positive in the history books and in the global perspective. Make our system work the way it was designed to. Else, it has failed. Impeach Bush and Cheney.

Religious Right Still Burning Women

All the human rights progress made from the 1960's flew out the window with the new extreme Right Wing. Sure, their racism and misogyny were only stored out of sight in the linen closet, but with a Black man and a white woman both running for the Democratic presidential nomination, the doors were flung open and their sheets and pillowcases exposed and there has been no looking back. At least there is an element of honesty in the new Conservative Party, they are no longer hiding their hateful opinions and coating their rhetoric. Thanks to "egalia" for this:

Not that anyone who has been paying one iota of attention needs it, but as "proof" that "there's an ugly strain of misogyny running through

Hillary Clinton's media coverage," Rachel Sklar offers "an unbelievable statement" from Keith Olbermann:

"Olbermann was discussing the election with Newsweek's Howard Fineman, a frequent guest. The topic was, how can a winner finally be determined in this never-ending Democratic race for the nomination? Of course, the assumption was that it was Clinton that should be shown the door (despite clearly still earning her spot in the race thanks to, um, voters). Fineman said that, all the delegate math aside, ultimately it was going to take "some adults somewhere in the Democratic party to step in and stop this thing, like a referee in a fight that could go on for thirty rounds. Those are the super, super, super delegates who are going to have to decide this.""

Said Olbermann: "Right. Somebody who can take her into a room and only he comes out."

What does that mean? Really, it can only mean one thing: Beating the crap out of Hillary Clinton, to the point where she is physically incapable of getting up and walking out. Do I really think Olbermann thinks Hillary Clinton should really be violently beaten to the point of physical incapacitation, or worse? No. But it is an unmistakably violent image. If David Shuster can be suspended for likening Chelsea Clinton to a prostitute, then what happens when Keith Olbermann implies that the only way to stop Hillary Clinton is to inflict some sort of physical harm on her?

This latest swipe at Hillary Rodham Clinton by the towel-slapping, anti-woman frat boy at MSNBC is viewed somewhat differently by Delilah:

Olbermann: How to Snuff Out Hillary Clinton

"Metaphor, my ass. If 2 white guys suggested that "somebody" take Obama into a room and Obama doesn't come out, how would that

sound to you? If it sounds more...um, outrageous to say such a thing about Obama than it is to say it about Clinton, then you need to take a long look at your personal beliefs about human rights."

The misogyny at MSNBC is driving me crazy. When the MSNBC men aren't being misogynistic creeps, they're bashing the Clintons with charges of racism. Most every day the boys at MSNBC like to talk about racism. That's the only ism MSNBC can handle. Because if any of mainly male pundits on any of the networks had to talk about the misogyny directed at Hillary Rodham Clinton, the story would be about them!

Keith Olbermann, Chris Matthews, David Shuster, and everyone on the Misogyny Network who doesn't speak out against it, YOU are the perps.[106]

Keeping silent about evil see has always been part of the problem. Was this one going to quietly stew about the dark acts of the patriarchy? Hell, no. On Apr. 27, 2008, the author had this to say about that:

Women Are Tired of Getting the Shaft and Zero Respect

The media would have us believe that Hillary Clinton has been mathematically eliminated from the Democratic nomination. Well, even if the disenfranchisement of millions of voters, in Florida and Michigan, is not overturned, 600-700 delegates are still available. And don't forget the Republican wives eager to throw off their "Stepford" shackles. Don't worry, Elizabeth Hasselbeck, we will save you.

Women have been subdued, misused, abused, much longer than peoples of color and >99.99% (in my estimation) of the horrible events in the history of mankind were caused by decisions of men. Women's turn to shine is past due in this country and most of the world.

The "liberal" press can be prophetic for those who hear, and remember. More than a decade later, this appears to be coming true, if millions of protestors cannot stop the tanks of Trumpism:

...this administration has a deep, profound and uncompromised contempt for democracy, for the rule of law, and for the US Constitution. When George W. Bush went on the record (twice) as saying he has nothing against dictatorship, as long as he can be dictator, it was a clear and present policy statement.

Who really believes this crew will walk quietly away from power? They have the motivation, the money and the method for doing away with the electoral process altogether. So why wouldn't they?

The groundwork for dismissal of both the legislative and judicial branch has been carefully laid. The litany is well-known, but worth a very partial listing:

The continuation of the drug war, and the Patriot Act, Homeland Security Act and other dictatorial laws prompted by the 9/11/2001 terror attacks, have decimated the Bill of Rights, and shredded the traditional American right to due process of law, freedom from official surveillance, arbitrary violence, and far more...

...Presidential Directive #51, Executive Orders #13303, #13315, #13350, #13364, #13422, #13438, and more, by which Bush has granted himself an immense arsenal of powers for which the term "dictatorial" is a modest understatement...

...All this will be relevant should Team Bush envision a defeat in the 2008 election and decide to call it off. It's well established that Richard

Nixon—-mentor to Karl Rove and Dick Cheney—-commissioned the Huston Plan, which detailed how to cancel the 1972 election.

Today we must ask: who would stop this administration from taking dictatorial power in the instance of a "national emergency" such as a terror attack at a nuclear power plant or something similar?

Nothing in the behavior of this Congress indicates that it is capable of significant resistance. Impeachment seems beyond it. Nor does it seem Congress would actually remove Bush if it did put him on trial.

Short of that, Bush clearly does not view anything Congress might do as a meaningful impediment. After all, how many divisions does the Congress command?

The Supreme Court, as currently constituted, would almost certainly rubber stamp a Bush coup. If not, like Jackson, he could ignore it as easily as he would ignore Congress...

...From the public side, the only conceivable counter-force might be a national strike or an effective long-term campaign of general non-cooperation.

But we can certainly assume the mainstream media will give lock-step support to whatever the regime says and does. It's also a given that those likely to lead the resistance will immediately land in those new prisons being built by Halliburton et. al.[107]

The questions posed and points made in the above article have greater relevance and reality, today, in the middle of the most-deadly pandemic and the pestilence of the Trump Administration. Bush and Cheney seemed to have greatly softened the underbelly of our system so Trump and company's gut punches to the American government and people are having serious effect.

One writer's fears of Constitutional crisis, the most critical crucible in American history, had him on the nearest social media soapbox on July 3, 2008:

Anti-Republican Rant

Yes, too bad that George W. Bush and company are the antithesis of freedom, liberty, hope, responsible government, and what is right with America. People are so ashamed of our government and scared for our democracy that they will vote for anyone offering immediate change. Well, wholesale change, could bring about worse problems, but that is how fearful the country has become for the Constitution and our system of checks and balances.

Don't quote LBJ to me, if you want the real skinny on Johnson read, "Blood, Money, and Power" by Barr McClellan. Lyndon was the "Godfather" of contemporary neocons, Texas politics at its worst has been running our country for too long, now.

My Independence Day wish is that real patriots can restore our democracy, get it back on track, rather than trying to "conquer" the world and have dominion over the oil fields.

A Renaissance, Already?

(or, Dem's Thought Worst Was Over?)

Hints of an oligarchic takeover of the country have been written since at least the Reagan era. Oh, that we wouldn't have paid more attention or felt the fear, then. Alfred E. Neuman had us pegged over half a century ago. Mad men have taken advantage of our apathy, and Conservative sociopathy of Progressive empathy.

With a title like that, you'd expect "How the rich are destroying the earth" to be a marxist polemic. It's not. At least, not entirely. Simply put, the rich are destroying the earth because in the face of environmental catastrophe, "this class opposes the radical changes that we would have to conduct to prevent the aggravation of the situation."

Herve Kempf is a expert journalist committed to fighting France's "environmental illiteracy" through the clear presentation of cold hard facts, and his book is to a plea to get people thinking about the environment in a social context.

The key factor in this, for Kempf, is a wealthy elite: "this predatory oligarchy is the main agent of the global crisis."[108]

Here was this concerned citizen, again, on June 19, 2009, sharing a dark vision and positive request with the few that followed:

Why Can't "Healthy, Comfortable, and Wise" Suffice?

One of Benjamin Franklin's said creations is the idiom:

"Early to bed and early to rise,

makes a man healthy, wealthy, and wise."

It is hugely ironic that the blood, bone, and flesh from the last mass-extinction of the planet is mostly responsible for the fueling of this one. Now fear is furthering the demise of the planet. Human fear of inconvenience and corporate fear of lost profits. Imagine, we would rather sacrifice future eons than give up even a day of our present way of live. How foolish is that? Either we learn to accept Mother Earth's eternal gifts rather than ripping from her that which is residually ruining her, and destroying us, or die. This will not be a Biblically ordained "end of times," it will be a lazy, wasteful, wanton human caused choking, gasping, "Whyyyyy!?!?"

We are why.

We need to all get off of our collective asses and do something. Inconvenient? Well, so is dying. Will humankinds' epitaph read "Killed by Convenience," in this millenium, or will future history books praise us for finding the way to survive and thrive by healthier living as a sustaining part of the whole planet rather than as the self-serving, self-gratifying parasites that we had become. Please opt for healthier, not wealthier, living.

Healthcare costs are the worst in America compared to any other Democratic country. It is a crisis for too many.

A public option, as most Americans want, would have put us nearer to par with the more progressive countries. The Affordable Care Act was as close as we got. Big medicine and probably Big Pharma had their Conservative dogs snarling and snapping at the end of their chains over this:

Now, one year later, the week President Barack Obama addresses a joint session of Congress, support for a robust public option is still sticking. In fact, four out of five Americans support the creation of a new federal health insurance plan that individuals could purchase if they cannot afford private plans offered them (2009 Poll by Penn, Schoen and Berland Associates). Even 61 percent of Republicans support this idea.

This is also unsurprising. The public option presented in America's Affordable Health Choices Act, H.R. 3200, has broad public appeal. It encourages free market competition by driving down costs, incentivizing more effective and efficient service across the industry, and ensuring that the customer is provided with quality, competitive options.

What is surprising, and disheartening, is the level of misinformation. It is pervasive and pernicious. For example, the cry of socialism is not only erroneous but neglects the fact taxpayers are already burdened with covering the costs of 46 million uninsured Americans, through increased use of emergency and social services, decreased worker productivity and weaker economic output. The public option, in contrast, works to save taxpayer dollars by promoting preventive health so that emergency and social services are not so heavily burdened and worker productivity and economic output increase. The savings realized through this prevention-oriented approach will be substantial.[109]

We have to be content with ObamaCare since then, though Trump will take that as soon as he can get his MAGA minions in Congress to kowtow even lower. One word warrior followed up with his own Sept. 30, 2009 review of this disregard of most of the American electorate:

Favored Public Option Finds Disfavor From Health Industry Profiteers

Why do the most of the democratic countries in the world have public medical care but we aren't even allowed an option? Why is the American working class being held down not only by the stranglehold credit requirements and interest costs and penalties of the banking industry, but the artificially inflated cost, and deflated care, of medical insurance? We cannot allow Congressmen to represent corporate America any longer, the majority of Americans are demanding freedom from financial shackles and our representatives are protecting those determined to keep us bound to them. Why?!??!?

Pressure Harry Reid to disclose the names of the democrats working against the majorities' desire for a public option. Please do not give in to those who would continue to prey on the little guys. The more money the average American has to spend, save, or invest, the stronger our economy will ultimately be. Do your utmost to cut our costs. A public health option is step one. We cannot afford to lose this battle.

The issues were, and are, many, perhaps this ever-changing focus is half of our problem. If we could but put the magnifying lens on just one problem for long enough, we could find the objective and concentrate the light on it so intensely, it must be burned out of existence. Now we were back to the fault of the press for their lack of light on important news. George S. Kazolias, reported on the "silence of the press," in KAZODAILY:

The silence of the western press on the situation in Libya is deafening. This is no surprise as the pessimistic predictions of the critics of NATO's war to oust Qaddafi become reality...

...Turkey's decision to abandon Iran for Libya as the source of its oil demonstrates why Ankara sided with the West. Turkey's "moderate" Islamic ruling party is backing the Sunnis in Syria against the Alawites backed by Shia Iran. Turkey's other neighbor, Iraq, is also ruled by Shias who back Assad. This is again the result of a botched imperialist intervention. Thank you George W. Bush! What we are seeing is more and more a Sunni – Shia civil war taking shape and a Salafist take over in those Sunni countries where the West intervenes. We know there are strong Salafist forces operating in the religious and ethnic patchwork which is Syria. Forces backed, financed and armed by Saudi Arabia and Qatar while our obedient press speak of aspirations for Democracy.

The role of the western press in misinforming the public by not informing them is criminal. It will allow western leaders to continue to intervene and destroy people's lives for short-sighted imperial interests. Oil, uranium and gold... that is why regimes are being overturned and people killed. The silence of the press is no accident.[110]

This solitary voice followed the news and gave his own review on Sept. 28, 2012:

Where is the Press? II

During the Bush W. Administration, where was the press that so covered the breadth, keeping us abreast of every breath, of the Clinton-Lewinsky interlude? Is the press really just a right-wing tool? Is that legal? That is definitely not what our founding fathers envisioned when they imagined the system of checks and balances to protect our system from corruption.

There were scoff-laws, U. S. Constitution violators, war profiteers, criminals—running the U. S. Government. Into the ground, I might add. The press, one of the greatest tools of our supposed free society, was scared, at best, and compliant, at worst, to speak out about the last Executive Administrations' atrocities. There were dozens of them, rarely publicized, that should have been on the front page.

Give us the news, honestly and objectively, or get the hell out of here; our press has become as reliable as Cuba's and China's. I was so ashamed, and so scared, that there were no remaining checks and balances of our government, the "free" press was our last vestige of hope. In our time of greatest need, where was it?

There was great national outcry and attempts to begin impeachment proceedings for Dick Cheney. There should have been for George W. Bush, also. The press's function in the foundation and maintenance of this great country is to report both the good and the bad of our national interests, especially when the worst of the worst our country ever saw was happening. Why was the U.S. press so silent when we needed them most?

This symptom of the extreme changes made in response to 9-11, such as the establishment of Homeland Security needs to be cured. This may be comparable to when Truman signed away some of our freedoms when he created the Central Intelligence Group (Agency). How can we get out from under these threats to our privacy and freedoms? Spencer Ackerman describes one related instance:

The head of the U.S. government's vast spying apparatus has conceded that recent surveillance efforts on at least one occasion violated the Constitutional prohibitions on unlawful search and seizure.

The admission comes in a letter from the Office of the Director of National Intelligence declassifying statements that a top U.S. Senator wished to make public in order to call attention to the government's 2008 expansion of its key surveillance law.

"On at least one occasion," the intelligence shop has approved Sen. Ron Wyden (D-Ore.) to say, the Foreign Intelligence Surveillance Court found that "minimization procedures" used by the government while it was collecting intelligence were "unreasonable under the Fourth Amendment." Minimization refers to how long the government may retain the surveillance data it collects. The Fourth Amendment to the Constitution is supposed to guarantee our rights against unreasonable searches...

...Wyden says that the government's use of the expanded surveillance authorities "has sometimes circumvented the spirit of the law" – a conclusion that the Office of the Director of National Intelligence does not endorse. The office does not challenge the statement about the FISA Court on at least one occasion finding the surveillance to conflict with the Fourth Amendment.[111]

A Letter to Congressional Leaders

The following was written by this citizen during the second term of the Dick and Dubya Debacle. With the 2012 election only two months away, it was believed that his complaint was still true and that these men should still suffer the consequences for their actions while heading the Executive Branch of our government. For one reason—to prove that our government is still functional as our founding fathers intended it. This, would also regain the trust of the much of the rest of the world when they comprehend that our form of democracy is more than smoke and mirrors, not propaganda but a working "...government of the people, by the people, and for the people..." that "will not perish from the earth." The letter, December 14, 2007:

Until George W. Bush and his captains are condemned for mutilating our democracy and tens or hundreds of thousands of human beings, our government is in danger, our rights are in danger, and we are not "safe". Everybody has the responsibility, the duty, to condemn the actions of this president and vice president. If you fail to, you are part of the problem. If you try to prevent condemnation of this presidency, you are his abettor. The majority of Americans are crying for action to restore our government, our democracy, our constitution! Too many times this administration has decried, "Let them eat bread!" or "Let them put moldy bread on their festering wounds!" while funneling America's treasury into the pockets of this country's wealthiest. A symbolic guillotine must be erected and the heads of this tainted and treasonous government severed to regain the trust of the American public and our global partners. If Dick Cheney must be the first to answer for his crimes against the United States of America, then so be it.

The best medicine to battle the cancer that has seriously infected our government and the media is in your hands. The health of our government, nay, the existence of our democracy, depends on you to administer the cure. You really have no choice if you value your country, it sorely needs you to act, and act now.

Until we punish violations of the U.S. Constitution, to the full extent of the law, we are fated to the same kind of failure, and will be doomed by it.

This citizen was not only amazed at the Democratic Congress that was briefly held did not hold the previous administration liable for their constitutional transgressions, but when the Justice Department under President Obama gave what can only be taken as final approval to criminal Conservative acts under Republican administrations, his mouth hung agape. Glenn Greenwald wrote of this in the Guardian:

The Obama administration's aggressive, full-scale whitewashing of the "war on terror" crimes committed by Bush officials is now complete. Thursday, Attorney General Eric Holder announced the closing without charges of the only two cases under investigation relating to the US torture program: one that resulted in the 2002 death of an Afghan detainee at a secret CIA prison near Kabul, and the other the 2003 death of an Iraqi citizen while in CIA custody at Abu Ghraib. This decision, says the New York Times Friday, "eliminat[es] the last possibility that any criminal charges will be brought as a result of the brutal interrogations carried out by the CIA".[112]

Baseball, Mom, Apple Pie II

The writer shared his thoughts written during the Bush and Cheney Constitutional Stomp on social media on this date, Sept. 28, 2012. The letter, written five years before, may be even more true during the Trump administration while Congress is again tilted to the right, preventing any potential fixes from getting an honest chance. Held hostage by a Republican obstructed Congress, again, our country's climb out of purgatory is taking even longer. For what? A few measly snipes on the campaign trail, and nothing else.

That politicians would sacrifice our country's gain for election fodder is nothing less than evil. Maybe more important than the Presidential election, those upcoming for Congressional seats are more important than ever. If the Neo-Cons, former S.E. Conservative Democrats, put any more partisan puppets in the

Supreme Court, our system of checks and balances will never recover and our Constitution will be gutted for Right Wing dogma. Dug up from this writer's personal files is this concern in character dated September 25, 2007:

The electorate has been rejected, again, after again and again and again. When will the voter once again be recognized as the voice of America? The media has been editing the truth for too long. Now is the time for all Americans to step up and hit the ball, and our biggest hitters are in Congress. If our Congressmen are content to throw the game then the last of our system of checks and balances is gone and our democracy is a total failure. We must hit every one of these pitches to win the big game. If we strike out... Mom and apple pie are next.

Perhaps the rest of the world is more cognizant of what the political and economic fortunes of the United States of America to every free country. They certainly aren't afraid to call out and convict our corruption, unlike our Conservative politicians and mainstream press. Hurrah for the more social democracies of the world, may we one day unite. Yvonne Ridley courted the trial of George W. Bush:

In what is the first ever conviction of its kind anywhere in the world, the former US President and seven key members of his administration were yesterday (Fri) found guilty of war crimes.

Bush, Dick Cheney, Donald Rumsfeld and their legal advisers Alberto Gonzales, David Addington, William Haynes, Jay Bybee and John Yoo were tried in absentia in Malaysia.[113]

Why does the free world, excluding the American press and most members of both Parties in Congress, see serious problems with the Bush-Cheney Administrations' behavior? It concerns many citizens that, among our system of checks and balances, so many are so willing to ignore, to "look the other way" from, the growing corruption of the Conservative Party?

It appears that the Democrats will always be willing to "turn the other cheek" whereas the Party favored by the Christian Church, the one most often waving the Bible while draped in the American flag, the GOP, turns only to talk out the other side of their mouth.

Looking back on this writer's attempts to sway politicians, this social media communication of Sept. 28, 2012 was recalled, sharing a letter to both of the Democratic leaders of Congress in 2007:

Letter to Reid and Pelosi

Perhaps the last Democrats-held Congress in American history let the entire country down and failed us in our time of greatest need. Frankly, when we had the enemy on the run, a Democratic majority in both Houses of Congress lacked the "killer instinct" that could have ensured our government would remain, or be restored as, a shining light to the rest of the world. Now, the light is flickering and Progressives do not presently have control over that flame. It is not too late to hold these officials up as examples of what happens to those who abuse their office. Letter of Sept. 14, 2007:

"We, the American people, never should have allowed a family so connected to Nazi Germany to reign supreme in U. S. politics. However, the people, in general, do not hold the ultimate blame for these mistakes, our political leaders should have ensured that the voters knew the history of the Bush family and their failures in protecting the American public. Now, we are at a great crossroads in our history. The best that we can hope for is that it will be called our darkest hour. The worst, if we don't restore our government's functionality, recover our system of checks and balances, renew our citizens' and allies' faith in our democracy? Theocracy, oil-garchy, or some mutant variation in

between. If we haven't already, we will have certainly lost our ability to control our leaders. And we, as we already have lost it, will be unable to regain the global respect we once knew.

Please, with all due respect, admit your mistake in disregarding impeachment, and put it back on the table. And pound the hell out of our government with the gavel until it conforms to our founding fathers' design and the current constituency's desire and will not be warped again. Give us our government back!"

Some, including the author, felt that America had descended into a Dark Age after a Republican-appointed majority in the U.S. Supreme Court had awarded the 2000 election to George W. Bush and Dick Cheney, seemingly in opposition to the Constitution. And, then, the Conservatives in power seemed to continue to treat the Constitution like so much toilet paper. Bush and Cheney were reported to have the record when it comes to Constitutional violations. Ivan Eland's article concerning:

George W. Bush's Impeachable Offenses

Several recent presidents could have been impeached for selected unconstitutional or illegal actions during their presidencies. But the sitting president, George W. Bush, may win the prize for committing the most impeachable offenses of any recent president.[114]

GOP Still Medieval, After All

When the Democrats emerged victorious in 2008, it felt like a renaissance. When the Republican Party began its proclaimed obstruction of President Obama's administration of the American executive office, considerably through their attack dog, Mitch

McConnell, violating protocol at least if not the law of the land, the light we temporarily felt was seriously refracted and the monoGraphic Old Party began shining their evil 180 degrees away from themselves, trying to project their sins onto their opposition. Ewen MacAskill, writing for the Guardian, informs of the Obama White House warning to those members of a Conservative blockade in Congress:

Warning goes out to senators who voted to kill off almost the entire program of reforms sought by Obama administration

The Obama administration joined gun control groups on Thursday in vowing to target senators who blocked draft measures that represented the best hope for reform in a generation.

The warning came as the Democratic leader in the Senate, Harry Reid, bowed to the inevitable by announcing he would have to shelve the draft bill. Reid expressed hope that this would leave open the option of further negotiation.[115]

2013? Gun-Control and Giving Everyone a Shot

Some people's claim that the 2nd Amendment to the U. S. Constitution gives us the right to bear firearms of any type, is either self-delusional or crazy. Our founding fathers did not intend citizenry to have cannon or Gatling guns, nor howitzers, tanks, and automatic weapons or their near equivalent.

When the 2nd Amendment to the U.S. Constitution was ratified and adopted, firearms could only be fired once before reloading, approximately a minute of time required, was necessary. Mass murders by sole perpetrators were not technically possible utilizing the firearms of 1791.

The spirit of the law was to intend citizens have firearms for sustenance, and security of home, state, and country, when citizenry were members of the local rapid assembly militias. But this was when the personal weapons used for hunting of game or home and self-defense were, basically, the same as utilized in war.

We definitely have to clamp down on greedy manufacturers and retailers dealing with high-capacity firearms, but that is only half the problem. Given the types and numbers of guns available, probably the foremost fatal flaw in their misuse, today, is the discontinuity of American families.

Past is the time that practically every mother's son learned about firearm uses and dangers from their father. Almost every man's dad trained them to use the family guns in the way they were intended in the safest possible ways; supervising their early target practice and taking them on their first hunting trips, continuing to teach them the proper and responsible use of weapons. Presently, too many young men have never had a father teach them proper use of, and respect for, guns. Even worse, some fathers, who never had the benefit of this paternal training in firearm respect and safety, are proudly teaching their sons their ignorantly acquired beliefs about guns.

The author sees two possible ways of ensuring most young men receive proper gun training most used to receive from their father. One, is to have youth organizations, like scouts, or "Big Brothers Big Sisters," take on this important function, no longer filled by most fathers, of safe gun usage. Two, like Switzerland and other European countries, make some amount of military training mandatory for all. This second option would not only allow all Americans to be fully trained in firearm responsibility, but give them the confidence to find another way to go in life, besides violent fraternities of ill-learned friends and family. This second option will also strengthen our active and reserve military.

Gun proponents' argument that drivers kill people with cars so why don't we take cars away is not valid until high-performance race cars designed to be used solely by trained, professional drivers in tightly controlled circumstances are the main vehicle behind carnage on public roads. The argument that people desiring more stringent controls placed on the manufacture and sale of assault weapons are trying to disarm America is also false, as most of us believe in the right to own hunting rifles, which are also perfectly functional for personal defense. These are just some of the, many, shimmering mirages that too many Americans have been deceived with by greedy, gun-manufacturers' lobby. Whose perceived paradise are we crawling towards, leaving a bloody trail behind?

Business as Usual

The indicator of economic success is different for the wealthy than the average working person. The green, upward-pointing arrow of the stock market is the positive sign the rich demand. Inversely, most people see higher wages, lower cost of living as the best indicator of economic health. Typically, a climb of the index on Wall Street comes at greater cost to the majority of Americans, i.e., greater profits for business usually mean higher costs or lower income (both, it too often seems) for everyone except the corporate moguls and biggest investors. Heather Long, of Gants News, writes of it:

One of the hottest issues in the CNN Democratic debate was Wall Street.

There's a deep rift in the Democratic party over whether America should bring back the Glass-Steagall Act, a bank regulation that was in place from 1933 to 1999.

Bernie Sanders and Martin O'Malley want it reinstated.

Hillary Clinton disagrees.

Then there's flip-flopper Lincoln Chafee. He voted to get rid of Glass-Steagall when he was a senator in 1999. Now he regrets it.

In plain English, big banks had a conflict of interest catering to big-business and everybody else. As mentioned above, corporate American and Americans in general are too often at odds.

The law prevented banks like JPMorgan and Bank of America from dealing with both Main Street and Wall Street. Banks either had to cater to Main Street by taking deposits and doing mortgages and small business type loans or they could cater to Wall Street by buying and selling stocks and bonds or helping big companies merge.

The thinking was that the Wall Street component of banking was too risky and would put regular Americans' savings and loans at risk.

The law came into being after the stock market crash of 1929 and the Depression that followed.

The official name of the law was the Banking Act of 1933, but it became known as Glass-Steagall because it was championed by Senator Carter Glass, a Virginia Democrat, and Congressman Henry Steagall, an Alabama Democrat and former Treasury secretary.[116]

The laws and rules preventing elected politicians from financial interests in opposition to their supposed representation of their electorate seem to be transitory, as well.

We Must Account for Them, All

On Oct. 24, 2015, taking the word to social media, again, this citizen shared what he gathered on the medium traveling through the spacious skies above the amber waves of grain and purple mountains in all of their majesty and perhaps over the deep blue seas:

We have had too much time, and adverse experience, without the surrogate ethics and morals afforded by rules, guidelines, and law that those in power so detest, or, at least, don't believe they can be applied against them. The data is in, and cannot be denied, and neither shall the electorate, the majority want, nay, demand, the economic protection provided by a Glass Steagall Act, or its New Millennium equivalent.

We can never, again, bear the cost of a Republican majority in Congress.

Sometimes the press gets it right about the Radical-Right, Religious-Right, Christian-Conservative, or Nazi majority, whatever label best sticks to them. Here is one of the becoming harder to find instances, by Dana Milbank with *The Washington Post*:

Loaded imagery, violence against dissenters and a racial attack on the president: It's all in a day's work for Trump.

In the preceding days, he had asserted (and later retracted) his confidence that as president the military would obey his orders to do illegal things: torture detainees and target noncombatant kin of terrorists for death. He said House Speaker Paul Ryan, a fellow Republican, would "pay a big price" for defying him, and he said Sen. John McCain, who criticized Trump, needs to "be very careful." Trump explained his initial hesitance to disavow support from the Ku Klux Klan and white supremacists by saying such groups could have included "the Federation of Jewish Philanthropies" — prompting the head of the Anti-Defamation League to call his words "obscene."[117]

And, the Abrahamic religions are a major source of the violence on our planet. And greed, which has ever gone hand-in-hand with the most powerful gods. Rather a little out of the chronology, but ironically, this Catholic official sermonized about fundamentalism:

Pope Francis said, "Fundamentalism is a sickness that is in all religions ... Religious fundamentalism is not religious, because it lacks God. It is idolatry, like idolatry of money ... We Catholics have some — and not some, many — who believe in the absolute truth and go ahead dirtying the other with calumny, with disinformation, and doing evil."[1]

We are seeing something close to a global epidemic of fundamentalism. Pope Francis is right: "Fundamentalism is a sickness that is in all religions." And it strikes at the heart of the common good, because it prevents people from growing as individuals and contributing to the welfare of others.[2]

Fundamentalism is "a religion of rage."[3] Fundamentalists are people who are outraged when they see the world around them disregarding their revered religious values. They respond in dangerously simplistic but militant ways to fears that they will lose their identity. They use words, or recourse to the ballot box, or, in extreme instances, bullets and bombs. Those who dare to question them are intolerantly scapegoated as enemies of the truth.[118]

Fundamental Fascism—Far Too-Far Right

On May 5, 2016, this writer was preaching to the choir ahead of Father Dr. Arbuckle's message, above. The medium with which this may have been shared has faded from memory, but the Word.doc has persevered:

Voices from the past continue to haunt, to this day, reminding those who care to review, of the results of not listening to those who came before. Some might now feel the need to apologize to their parents, though, that may be something to address later. Abraham Lincoln's attempt at alerting us to the potential power of corporations, Arthur Miller's hints of the chasm always threatening to engulf society, and Eisenhower's concerns regarding the burgeoning military-industrial complex—to name but a few of our sage mentors and their concerns.

Our founding fathers' warnings about the ways our democracy could fail and the ways they tried to avert those—all have been ignored by too many who would forego education, i.e., knowledge, for more immediate physical pleasures, or fail to heed brutal honesty for the words that further feed or fuel their ignorance. The multitudes of intellectual crickets, the unreasoning who are too liable to accept as "gospel truth," or knowingly propagate, the poison spat by their partisan politicians and pundits, are creating more legions.

Of utmost importance, knowledge of the ideals that our system of government was founded upon should not be assumed. It is vitally important that every voter study not only American history but each and every candidate's history, political if not personal, and not accept, verbatim, all whom, and what, you are most inclined to listen to, but hear both sides and judge against the context of prior choices and decisions.

Abraham Lincoln was one who foresaw the calamity that must follow the granting of such power to business entities (this is disputed by some who put too much stock in corporations):

I see in the near future a crisis approaching that unnerves me and causes me to tremble for the safety of my country... corporations have been enthroned and an era of corruption in high places will follow, and the money power of the country will endeavor to prolong its reign by working upon the prejudices of the people until all wealth is aggregated in a few hands and the Republic is destroyed.[119]

This was in a time when the Conservatives, predominately in the South, were Democrat. This Conservative Democrat persuasion continued until the 1970's and 1980's. When the influx of Southern Conservatives finally reshaped the Republican party, not the first time in our history that these ideologies have swapped parties, it swept the party dangerously close to the extreme precipice on the far-right. Dwight Eisenhower, when the oil tycoons and many of the growing military-industrial complex had yet to "morph" from Conservative Democrats to Republicans, gave this warning in his closing speech as President of the United States of America in 1961, three days before the inauguration of John F. Kennedy:

Now this conjunction of an immense military establishment and a large arms industry is new in the American experience. The total influence—economic, political, even spiritual—is felt in every city, every Statehouse, every office of the Federal government. We recognize the imperative need for this development. Yet, we must not fail to comprehend its grave implications. Our toil, resources, and livelihood are all involved. So is the very structure of our society.

In the councils of government, we must guard against the acquisition of unwarranted influence, whether sought or unsought, by the military-industrial complex. The potential for the disastrous rise of misplaced power exists and will persist. We must never let the weight of this combination endanger our liberties or democratic processes. We should take nothing for granted. Only an alert and knowledgeable citizenry can compel the proper meshing of the huge industrial and military machinery of defense with our peaceful methods and goals, so that security and liberty may prosper together.[120]

This speech by Eisenhower reminded this writer of the words of one of Hemingway's characters, symbolically fighting fascism in a foreign land:

Ernest Hemingway may have understood more than he wrote in the late 1930's, over eighty years ago, in his novel, For Whom the Bell Tolls,[121] about the fear, of the more enlightened, of the rich depriving the less-fortunate U.S. citizens; a concern, even then. His American protagonist, Robert Jordan, tried to respond to Spaniard Andrés, whom he was fighting and sheltering alongside, when he asked Robert how America would avoid Fascism. Robert explained that taxes should prevent the wealthy from becoming too powerful. He told Andrés that those who are fascists may not realize it until they were made to answer for it, that education must prevent the rise of fascism. Perhaps Reagan and the Bush's weren't all that familiar with Hemingway's writing. Trump?

Understand, now, how our all but elimination of corporate taxes has further endangered our freedom? This increase in corporate power has led to further degradation of our democracy as the "corporate" controlled Supreme Court has dealt two recent defeats (Citizens United v. Federal Election Commission and McCutcheon v. Federal Election Commission) to attempts to prevent the rich from controlling our elections.

The author wrote of his interpretation of Arthur Miller's message concerning the "haves" and "have-nots" in his essay, "Crucibles—Demons or Demagogues?" and how our political system, our country, depends on the decisions we make, today, to avoid our next costly "Crucible," that the author feels is just around a coming corner. It is, very probably, upon us, now. Please read "Crucibles—Demons or Demagogues?" just ahead.

Our immediate efforts must be to educate our fellow voters, present and future, via the "old school" soapbox, or it's modern replacement, instantaneously radiated information via "smart" devices. Most importantly in this fight for freedom is a much-needed low-cost education and regaining control of elections, make them infallibly incorruptible—where every vote counts and the dollar does not.

In the near future, we need to strive for a self-represented government, where the true majority decides every vote; read my environmental/political thriller, *Dream View Two— The Kamikaze Candidate*, available on the link provided below, for an idea how this concept could work. This ideal will be even more attractive after our youth are given much greater opportunity for furthering their education, thus ensuring a more informed electorate, i.e., a more intelligent voting population. Of course, the fundamentalists will endeavor to keep us in the darkness of ignorance, forever. Let us, then, shine our light whenever and wherever and to whomever we can. The book, *Dream View Two— The Kamikaze Candidate* (e-book) can be found via this link: https://books2read.com/u/bwYGvP.

The fear, and the evidence, that the American Conservatives, or their signature Party, has moved, and is moving, to their most extreme Right position, ever, continues to be witnessed by those paying attention but barely spoken about by MSM:

CLEVELAND — After a week of wrangling, Republican delegates officially voted on Monday to adopt their 2016 platform, a policy blueprint that manages to take ultraconservative positions on same-sex marriage, religion, pornography, and even national parks.

The document, which was adopted at the GOP convention by a voice vote, was the product of vigorous debate among the platform committee last week and marks a stark shift for a party that has already seemed to veer toward extremism.

The platform openly opposes marriages for gay and transgender people, states "that man-made law must be consistent with God-given, natural rights," and calls on the U.S. government to transfer all federally controlled lands to states.

The platform also calls pornography a "public health crisis" while making no such designation for guns, which would allow the Centers for Disease Control and Prevention to study gun violence from a health policy perspective.[122]

One has to be a selective shopper to find the news that reports the reality. The trouble is, too many of those who support the Right don't have to be selective because the words that vibe with them, the virtual-reality media, are readily available on the most accessible MSM networks and sites.

Thanks to the Conservative partisan Supreme Court, unlimited funds from the ultra-rich, corporate and industrial America, and any foreign interests, can be channeled into American politics, putting our government up for sale to the highest bidders, even our enemies have friends (and puppets?) in the American GOP, since. For now, let's just look at what an objective journalists, Suzanne Goldenberg and Helena Bengtsson for the Guardian, have to say about the petroleum and munitions industries:

Fossil fuel barons have invested more than $100m in Republican presidential Super Pacs – raising concerns over special interests if GOP takes White House.

Fossil fuel millionaires collectively pumped more than $100m into Republican presidential contenders' efforts last year – in an *unprecedented investment by the oil and gas industry in the party's future.*

About one in three dollars donated to Republican hopefuls from mega-rich individuals came from people who owe their fortunes to fossil fuels – and who stand to lose the most in the fight against climate change.[123]

Let's not forget the Capitol Hill privateers, those who capitalize on the American taxes spent on munitions, equipment, and other supplies to prosecute the latest maneuvering of the military. Lily Dane's article from The Daily Sheeple is a direct hit:

Despite warnings of its existence and imminent expansion, the military-industrial complex (or military-industrial-congressional complex) remains in operation today. It is an iron triangle that comprises the policy and monetary relationships which exist between legislators, national armed forces, and the arms industry that supports them. These relationships include political contributions, political approval for military spending, lobbying to support bureaucracies, and oversight of the industry. It is a major reason we are stuck in a perpetual war.

****

In their article titled Companies Profiting the Most From War, Thomas C. Frohlich and Mark Lieberman listed the 10 companies profiting the most from war. To identify them, they examined the companies with the most arms sales based on information from the Stockholm International Peace Research Institute (SIPRI).

Arms sales, including advisory, planes, vehicles, and weapons, were defined by sales to military customers as well as contracts to government militaries. Also considered were each company's 2013 total sales and profits, the total number of employees at the company, as well as nation-level military spending, all provided by SIPRI.

From the article:

"U.S. companies still dominate the arms market by a large margin, with six among the top 10 arms sellers. In the top 100 arms-producing companies, 39 are based in the United States, and U.S. companies accounted for more than 58% of total arms sales among the top 100. U.S. company arms sales in the top 10 alone made up 35% of total arms sales among the top 100. By contrast, Western European companies, which make up the rest of the top 10 arms producers, accounted for just 28% of the total top 100 arms sales."[124]

Much, if not most, of defense manufacturing and oil production are Red states' biggest moneymakers. The biggest recipients of lobbying money from these industries are the GOP Party and politicians. The publicly, but not congressionally, condemned profiteering chain from the war in Iraq went all the way up to VP Cheney, at least. Was George W. Bush a profiteer in that war, as well?

The author ventured this opinion about on May 29, 2016 about the slippery slide onto a dangerous decline towards the ditch on the right-side of American politics:

The Neo-Pubs—Still Whistling Dixie

George Washington's view of the dangers of "partisan" politics, i.e., the two-party political system, career politicians dividing America, almost immediately achieved fruition and fermentation. This division may not have been territorial, at first, but, definitely, became greatly geographical in our country's first century.

Since the Civil War and its "recovery" both of America's major political parties have continued to move towards the other, like partners in a barn dance, until a half-hearted do-si-do had them exchange places, but stay put, since, with their backs to each other. The Demos, then the "Conservatives," moved to the Left, and the Republicans, having been more "Progressive," have moved to the Right. The final impetus that moved the American Conservative party so dangerously far to the right was when the historically Conservative Democrats of the South jumped parties.

When the Southern Democrats hopped over the fence to the right-wing it was as if the heaviest kid on one side of a see-saw slid onto the other side. The right side ran violently aground, with a solid wallop. Those still on the left side of the see-saw were stuck in the air after feeling the stinging repercussion, futilely kicking and yelling, but effectively powerless. Families traditionally allied with one Party or the other, were often unschooled enough to go about business as usual, voting for the same old side, the Party of their father and grandfather, or so they thought, in the polls to this day.

The South, particularly the wealth-holders of the South, were staunch Democrats, very conservative. Federalists had flip-flopped to join the Liberal splinter-faction of the Democratic-Republican party to become the Liberal Whig party. Those more Conservative Democratic-Republicans then supported the man who inspired the iconic branding of the new Conservative Democratic party with an ass—Andrew Jackson.

The Whigs later became the Liberal Republican party that produced our, yet, greatest leader, Abraham Lincoln (Chapter 3 features theory of possible identity of Lincoln's maternal grandfather, an unknown person that he had shared knowledge of his grand-paternity by, to some).

During the so-called "golden age" of the United States, the 1950's & early 60's, these two parties were much closer in ideology, the Progressive-Democrats (or "moderates') of the North pulling their party towards the left, the "moderate" & extremist (synonym for greediest?) Conservatives—including corporate descendants of so-called "carpetbaggers" who had swept into the South to profit from the poor during "recovery'—pulled the party of Abraham Lincoln ever more to the Right.

These "new" Republicans might have been part of the foundation of the military-industrial complex. This closer proximity to the "fence" (a term for the political boundary between the political right and left) made it easier for them to reach across, to come to agreements, "handshaking," more often. Perhaps this is why America knew its greatest prosperity during this time— this hypothesis would seem to be borne out by the economic performance of the United States during the Clinton and Obama administrations. So-called "lame-duck" Presidents, both Democrats, each managed great economic growth, somehow, in spite of the Republican majorities in Congress—cooperation, not obstruction, perhaps, is key. Though, President Obama has persevered in spite of probably the greatest hatred and obstructionism ever aimed at an incumbent President of the United States.

Post-World War II, the American munitions corporations exploded in economic and political power. Eisenhower, (the last of the great, "pure," Republican Presidents, before the influx of Southern Democrats) warned about the dangers of a liaison between the U.S. government and a war industry. This has, perhaps, for all intents and purposes, resulted in the same political failure as the combination of Church and State (no surprise that arms-manufacturers' greatest allies and defenders are members of the religious right). It is also not surprising that at least three of the top-five world leading manufacturers of munitions are headquartered in what were the bastions of Confederate ideology, in the American Southeast.

This great growth, i.e., profits, of the munitions industries, and, their suppliers, e.g., electronic and mechanical components, automotive needs, etc., made certain Republicans very rich, and powerful. The "oil-rich" Southern Conservative-Democrats were, now, only too eager to "shake hands" across the afore-mentioned political "fence".

Lyndon Johnson, one of the most influential Conservative-Democrats of the South, should be considered the "Godfather" of these combined Conservative elements. He, as the Democrats Senate Majority Leader and, later, Minority leader, worked very closely with Republican President Dwight D. Eisenhower. More and more of these Southerners (the South was strictly Democrats and Conservative-Democrats, Republicans (the party of Lincoln) were reportedly hated for a long time) jumped ship to the Republican Party (horrors) over the next decade or two, into the 1980's.

This new Conservative force, political numbers and wealth, swept Ronald Reagan (Alzheimer's made him the perfect puppet for George H. W. Bush and company) into power. This was the coming out time of the so-called "neo-cons". Dick Cheney (perhaps the greatest puppet-master) moved from Nixon's White House, to Ford's Chief of Staff, Bush, Sr.'s Secretary of Defense (SoD), to become, finally, George W. Bush's Vice President. Donald Rumsfeld (also learning the skills of the puppet-master) utilized positions of power during Nixon and Ford Administrations, various positions for Nixon (whence he hired Dick Cheney, giving Cheney his first foothold in the Executive Branch of the American government) moving up to be Nixon's Chief of Staff and then SoD for Gerald Ford.

Rumsfeld and Bush, Sr. had a falling out that had Rumsfeld moving to industry from politics during the Reagan administration, when

George H.W. Bush stepped above Rumsfield on the political ladder to become Vice President. Bob Woodward's 2002 book Bush at War showed that "Pappy" felt that Rumsfield tried to end his political career when, as SoD, Rumsfield appointed George H.W. Bush to be head of the CIA. Only when old friend Dick Cheney had the power of Vice President, and more(?), under George W. Bush, Rumsfield's long alliance with Dick Cheney brought the two together in their most extreme, and powerful, partnership.

Dick and Rummy's control of George W. Bush (George, Jr. or George III, as some know him) may or may not have been easier than controlling early-stage Alzheimer's sufferer Ronnie, who had über-woman Nancy to fend for him. However, with the two master puppeteers, the string-pullers, "Dubya" did not have a chance to make any "mistakes"; though, one has to wonder how he really got those facial injuries in 2000, 2002, and 2006.

The combination of newer Conservatives, military-industrial afforded wealth, and the older farthest right power-base, once cotton-woven, now oil-fueled, the previous Conservative-Democrats of the South, created, possibly, the original super-funded political base. This was the equivalent of a billiard combination shot where the first ball, with english applied, is projected into the left side of a second ball to send it forcefully to the right, into the targeted pocket; in a Cuban-cigar smoke-filled hall, if you need additional imagery.

The Democrats and Republicans have gradually shifted towards the other side. But the Southern Democrats, always the most fundamental, the most right-wing, of American political Conservatives, rapid switch to the Republican Party, which was still drifting to right, supplied the momentum, the impetus, that sent that party smack over the "fence" to the extreme right, beyond any stretch of political arms to "shake hands" anymore, dangerously close (and getting ever closer) to fascism.

This alliance of the Right-wing, war industry, and oil companies also made warfare very beneficial to all of their bank accounts, particularly when said warfare is used to control Mideastern oil supplies. This, in evil turn, supplies more money to superfunds through whatever "dark" routes are being utilized. These superfunds pay for needed majorities in myriad ways. Now, picture a great whirlpool in Uncle Scrooge McDuck's cash-filled vault and honest taxpayers, symbolized by Donald, Huey, Dewey and Louie Duck, struggling to stay afloat in the hopes of reaching calm economic seas in the trillions of dollars tempest.

You might see, after all of this, how the Republican Party of Abraham Lincoln became the super-slush fund of tomorrow, which is, our, sad and scary, oil-garchy (fueled greatly by Texas politics which are succinctly defined in Barr McClellan's Blood, Money, & Power) of today. To quote Abraham Lincoln, himself, words that seem to particularly apply here, from a speech he made to the Illinois legislature in January, 1838, from Vol. 1, p. 24 of Complete Works of Abraham Lincoln, ed. by Nicolay and Hay (New York: F.D. Tandy Co., 1905) "These capitalists generally act harmoniously and in concert to fleece the people..."

It has been discussed how the Fourth Estate, objective news reports, has become less than the watchdog it originally was imagined and more of a partisan piece press, or subjective bits disregarding the crucial news that could curtail corruption or at least help expose it. To some degree, social media, the internet, has picked up the slack of the selectively silent press, inspiring some to label it the Fifth Estate:

With the advent of information and communication technologies, social networking sites have been growing at an amazing pace, and catalysing civil society movements, and bringing in political changes in various parts of the globe. This has become a challenge to the so-called mainstream media. The social media played a creative role in movements like the Arab Spring, Occupy Wall Street, and India Against Corruption.

The Fourth and fifth Estates

According to Wikipedia, the "Fourth Estate" is a societal or political force or institution... ...Oscar Wilde wrote, "[A]t the present moment it is the only estate. It has eaten up the other three."1 In current use, the term is applied to news media, especially print journalism or the Press.

Today, journalism and media industry are dominated by the media mogul Rupert Murdoch. We live in a world in which both journalism and politics are business. It is the vested interests which determine the agenda of the media, be it newspaper, radio, or television. We had an editors' community which upheld the moral and ethical principles of the profession. But today it is controlled by market-oriented managing directors. Now these newspapers rarely share the interests and anxieties of democratic society or civil society, when they—the "watchdog of democracy"—fill up their front pages and prime time with their own, self-created agenda.

According to Merriam-Webster dictionary, the Fifth Estate is a class or group existing in addition to the traditional four. The definition given by Roy Peter Clark is more suitable: "The Fifth Estate includes the Fourth Estate, the idea and value of a professional press corps as a way of informing and engaging the populace, and holding the powerful accountable. This vision of a Fifth Estate sees the Fourth Estate as necessary but insufficient for democratic life."2

William Dutton has argued that the Fifth Estate is not simply the blogging community, nor an extension of the media, but "networked individuals" enabled by the internet in ways that can hold the other estates accountable.3[125]

On June 25, 2016 it occurred to this one that the World Wide Web and social media were functioning much like the printing press did in the middle-ages. Gutenburg's press brought about near-immediate change in Europe, if not the world. Religious reformation and the so-called Renaissance came about greatly due to this great leap in the ability to share information:

The Neo-Reformation

In the 16th century the printing press spread the news of Martin Luther's and others' radical ideas and concepts of the times, relatively rapidly. Common people suddenly had the tools of reading, and by extension, writing, and many more were soon freed from the shackles of ignorance. Perhaps helping to create a larger Third Estate (middle class, as more had the ability to become learned) or the precursor to the Fourth Estate (as news no longer relied on the ancient "Bardic" system of sharing, e.g., a ditty of the latest dirty deeds by deputies of the king).

Knowledge, however, may have fed people's indignation, resentment, and outrage. Revolts against controlling landowners broke out across Europe. Niklaus Leuenberger (Chapter 5), whose clan, via genealogy supported by genetic testing comparing with other descendants, I appear to be descended from (his father and brother, directly) was one of the leaders of the Swiss Peasant Revolt of 1653 that were beheaded and drawn and quartered. A little overkill, there, methinks.

A freedom from intelligence-deficit, the ability to update our knowledge, continually, and instantly, is what the internet affords us, today. We must, also, break the chains of latter-day knowledge laundering, and air all organizational and institutional "linen," to gain release from financial bondage and regain our independence. Some of this is happening, now, thanks to so-called "social media". The information vacuum that fundamentalism depends on, i.e., ignorance, is being filled with bits of data so fast that we can't keep up.

The darkness of the new conservatism, or neo-con "servatism" as current economic slavery may well be termed, is being illuminated from the light shed by billions of "smart" devices, utilized by increasingly more enlightened potential voters. Many still close their minds to that which they don't want to believe, but the light is shining brighter and brighter; darkness will soon exist only in nooks and crannies, as mere bits and pieces of half-hidden shadows. The author thinks we are now witnessing early stages of the demise of the radical right, because of this phenomenon, this mass revealing. Fascism cannot survive without control of the media. Press be damned, we have to rely on each other, now, more than ever. Everyone sharing the truth via the internet is an extension or member of the Fifth Estate. We have far to go, yet, so Tweet on, fellow "birds of a feather."

Robert Knight of the Washington Times examined the current crucible molding or melting America:

"Public servants" often forget America's fundamental liberties

On a July 4th that fell on a Sunday a few years ago, I made a mistake.

A guest speaker at a suburban Maryland church, I mounted the pulpit after a color guard had gone down the aisle with Old Glory. The congregation applauded those who had served in the armed forces. Then they settled in for what they hoped would be a Christian-themed patriotic message.

I started with humor, but soon fell into a jeremiad about how we were losing America's culture war, turning us into a nation that our Founders wouldn't recognize. It did not go over well. As I shook hands with people filing out, very few looked me in the eye. My wife later told me in a somewhat diplomatic tone, "it was a real downer, Bob."

Well, okay, I won't do the same to you here. Well, maybe a bit. These are weird times. I do want to discuss the Great American Divide, but will resist recapping how our "public servants," especially the new Supreme Court majority, are going postal on our God-given liberties...[126]

The author thinks Mr. Knight's article has a Religious-Right bent message but he believes that Mr. Knight's opening succinctly describes the Left's perception of the contemporary State of the Union. His undoubtedly Conservative audience probably was disgruntled in the same way a scolded dog is. Christians being less Progressive, he definitely wasn't preaching to the choir.

The boundary between the Left and the Right is no longer a matter of a fence between neighbors that could allow civil discourse and mutually beneficial agreements but a yawning chasm that will swallow those trying to breach it. What is it all about? When a Black person or a woman campaigned for the presidency, a seismically-resounding shift in political plates was evidenced and experienced. The Washington Post reported on this after the two terms of Barack Obama and Hillary Clinton had just won the Democratic nomination in the election of 2016:

... This has been a violent and tragic summer, and it follows a period of pronounced divisiveness in American political life. The promoters of national unity may be outgunned, both metaphorically and literally.

...The sense that America is more divided than it used to be is backed by hard data. There's been a sharp spike in the contempt that partisans express for their opponents, according to Pew Research Center polling. More than 4 in 10 Democrats and Republicans say the other party's policies are so misguided that they pose a threat to the nation.

On many racial issues, whites and blacks see different realities. For example, African Americans were far more likely than whites to disapprove of grand jury decisions not to indict police officers in the deaths of Eric Garner and Michael Brown and of George Zimmerman's not-guilty verdict in Trayvon Martin's death.

A separate Pew poll this year showed that 88 percent of blacks think more needs to be done to give blacks equal rights, while 53 percent of whites agreed. A recent CBS News-New York Times survey found that about half of white Americans but three-quarters of African Americans say police are more likely to use deadly force against a black person than a white person....

...Activists with legitimate grievances demand to see changes and social progress before they stand down. Many people feel that their values are under attack and need to be defended vigorously. And some political leaders and media figures prefer to fire up their ideological bases rather than seek harmony or unity. Divisiveness can be a strategy or even a business model.

"They're conflict entrepreneurs. They kind of thrive on the pathologizing of our politics," said Dan Kahan, a Yale professor of law and psychology who studies cultural cognition. "They're a problem. But most people don't have an appetite for this. Most people don't want to ram their values down other people's throats. They just want to put food on the table."[127]

The authors of the above article speak of the American divide growing during the Obama presidency. We noticed that, too, thanks, and attributed it to Mitch McConnell giving the Senate he presided over license to obstruct the first President of color at every turn, to not only attempt to deny success to our President but to hold it out as a top priority, to make, as he openly spoke of, Barack Obama a one-term president. Failing that, McConnell turned even uglier, turning his position into an obvious partisan weapon as no Senate Majority Leader ever has, turning tradition, at least, if not the Constitution, upside-down. Conservatives in Congress seemed to follow suit, en masse.

The Conservative "rebellion" against a Black man as President reopened doors of bigotry and racism that the Civil Rights movement of the 1960's seemed to have merely pushed into a closet. American Christians were, and are, for the most part, fundamentally for all the Republican Party claimed and did. It seems Christian Conservatives got America off on a rocky way from the beginning, punishing individuality via a theocratic court and hearsay, the hunting, hurting and herding of indigenous people, and promoting the enslavement of fellow human-beings.

Leading up to the Presidential election of Nov. 8, 2016, which was eerily coincidental with the author and wife's 13th wedding anniversary, America appeared to many to be on the crumbling precipice of a perilous chasm, symptomatic of our eroding humanity.

Trump's growing ever more obvious ugliness, and his position in relation to Russian leader Vladimir Putin, on the eve of our celebration of our independence, motivated this one to again get the words and ideas swirling like a maelstrom in his head out for some inner peace, and to be recorded for posterity, on July 3, 2016:

Crucibles—Demons or Demagogues?

Reading, anew, the work of Arthur Miller, "The Crucible," I am amazed at how my perspective has changed with age. The continuing slide farther to the right, of nearly half of America, since at least the first

Reagan administration, has again revealed the great dividing gulf that the author explored in "The Crucible".

Utilizing the Salem witch-hunts of the seventeenth century as, perhaps, an analogy of Hitler's "Final Solution" and, or, what was even more immediately concerning to Mr. Miller, Joe McCarthy's "Un-American" threshing machine, the author painted a picture that could have just as well captured the Civil War, the civil rights rebellion of the 1960's, and, now, the fight to save, and restore, a middle class, that has been all but eliminated by the power elite of this country and threatens our very democracy, and liberties.

The apparent shift towards the "middle of road" or "riding the fence" that lasted well into the 1970's was merely a shimmering image, perhaps a hallucination. After what appeared to be political, civil, and human rights' victories of the nineteen-sixties, too many were put off of their guard, relaxed, and did not notice the neo-cons moving their trenches, fundamentally, far to the right, and digging in, during the Reagan years.

Progressive fears, and response, only managed two terms of "lame duck" administrations but, in spite of the Republican Congress, Clinton's economic success restored the left's faith in their view of America. The smoke hazed and funhouse mirrors enhanced image of a recovered middle class was magnified—the mirage of NAFTA attracting attention, much as the TPP "oasis" promotion is, today—until the Persian rug was yanked from under them.

The brown-shirted neo-cons who seized power utilizing vengeance rather than vigilance and a "shock and awe" agenda took quick advantage after allowing the worst attack, ever, on American soil. U.S. strategists made only a token advance in Afghanistan before dropping the Halliburton supplied $4000 hammer on Baghdad.

Americans had been unconstitutionally deprived of a popularly, and electorally (ethically), elected president, for an imposter by a 5-4 vote in the right-wing controlled Supreme Court. Next thing they knew, nearly a trillion war dollars was ripped from their pockets and delivered, for the most part, to the richest Americans. Our privacy was tapped and continues to be infringed on, due to the current Republican congressional majority. Americans' fear of the breakdown of their democracy, their loss of liberty, was much, much greater than that posed by terrorists.

Brought up in a lower middle-class family by parents who, unfailingly, voted Democrat—business and political science college courses in the late 1970's had this one, temporarily, seeing a friendlier, "fence-riding," concept of our partisan form of government. Remember the Republican ideal of less government, stronger business? They now have a fully symbiotic relationship—the right wing cannot survive without mega-business and corporate corruption whose predation cannot survive without right wing politicians and—this is most important—a manufactured majority.

The more the Republicans fear for their survival—the more desperate and despicable their attempts to control our electoral process. And, with the majority of U.S. Supreme Court Justices in their pockets, corporate-America needs not even fear the U.S. Constitution, as they can have anything ultimately decided in their favor. Conservatives only have to maintain control of Congress. Gerrymandering and voter suppression, and the Supreme Court majority treating the U.S. Constitution like so much toilet paper, has worked splendidly to maintain the necessary majorities. Splendidly, that is, if you support an oligarchy—or, oil-garchy as some refer to it.

That's the Catch-22... so far, political corruption is preventing Progressive attempts to restore our democracy, its system of checks and balances has become mere metaphors for the bank funds used to tilt our system to the right. Until we safeguard our election system the Right-wing will violate its sanctity—while they control vital components, we will not see an honest election.

A string of faux cowboys came riding in to D.C., rhetorical guns blazing (though, too often, one misfiring). Reagan took credit for tearing the "wall" of communism down. Though interrupted by two terms of a strong leader, albeit a limping waterfowl running afoul of a snipe hunt, the wild-west show continued, only the scenery was reset. The new, showboating president, "Sheriff Roscoe P. Bush," claimed to have made our "Homeland" safer. Remember the "Mission Accomplished" off-Broadway act? This was after he ignored the warnings and allowed the worst attack on American soil, ever.

Gradually, not so much discreetly as deceptively, during their twenty-plus years in control, the neo-cons burned the bridges that had been built, during the greater Twentieth Century, over the great chasm that has threatened American society in all of our darkest days.

It seems that the Puritans, the earliest American spin-doctors, weren't, and aren't, as pure as they would have had us believe. Empathy-oriented people, less concerned with material growth as inwardly spiritual (the two have been shown to be mutually exclusive), are, ironically on the other side of the great American gulf from self-centered, greed-driven individuals who use the church and their concept of god as a pair of aces showing in a game of stud. Christopher Bigsby hints of both in the introduction to Miller's controversial literal attempt at morally-therapeutic bloodletting, from which, the ricochets and shrapnel wounded him, also.

Bigsby notes of the antagonists in "The Crucible"; prominent pastor, the character most symbolic of the church, and the self-righteous justices, the gargoyle-like figureheads staring down their noses from one side of the chasm; and the protagonist; destined to be sacrificed, standing for those on the other; "It was also a community riven with schisms, which centered on the person of the Reverend Parris, whose materialism and self-concern were more than many could stomach, including a landowner and innkeeper called John Proctor. Proctor and his judges were articulate people, even if they were fluent in different languages: he, in that of a common-sense practicality, they in that of a bureaucratic theocracy."

It is no coincidence that the crucibles that have repeatedly come before us are, more often than not, rooted in the Conservative South. Is the stronghold of the self-styled Puritans in the Deep South, also? Looking at the roots of the religious-right lobby, the answer appears to be, "Yes." The Southern states fought, at the cost of over half a million lives, to deprive humans of freedom for fear of the wealthiest losing some net worth. The strongest bastion of resistance to human rights in this country has been, and still is, the South. Now, they would see most of us financially enslaved, barely able to survive, let alone save and invest. College? Not if they can help it. An educated electorate is the neo-cons second greatest fear—after a tamper-proof election system.

The South is also where the oil money and arms wealth is centered. Several of the largest munition corporations are headquartered in the South. These are the people who profit most from wars in the Mideast. Who wants war? The Conservatives.

Sadly, this is where America appears to be at once again, glaring at each other across this massive rift. On one side, hands reaching out in attempts to assist, are those more concerned with community and what can be done to make it better. On the other side, looking down from an assumed higher bluff, are those with hands extended, palm upward, demanding more; those most concerned with self and social image, their necessary institutions, and what everyone can do—for them. The *question that needs to be asked is, can bridges between the opposing sides of this abyss continually be constructed, only to be ultimately destroyed, again and again, or will the continuing erosion of ethics and empathy wear the chasm ever wider until we can no longer reach across, or even meet in the middle?*

The more community-oriented, which, in its most diminutive sense, intends to include each and every individual, and, in the largest sense means the collective U.S., have failed to hold a political advantage for long. Perhaps progressives don't maintain control because of our very dislike, disdain, or distrust of power-wielding. Empathy apparently has its own intrinsic Catch-22. Power, and authority, usually gained utilizing amassed wealth, that we need to protect our cherished form of government and its systems of checks and balances is, yet, a foreign concept to many progressive-minded people, not necessary in a "perfect" democracy. Part of an, imagined, ideal community, the American constituency failed to realize how great is the need for continual investment in democracy.

The power-elite, neo-cons, religious right, etc., ironically, were much more afraid of the majority, the working class, then we were of them. The cons realized this decades ago and have, since, striven to protect their institutions by seizing control of ours. They were more alert to voters reducing their power then voters were aware of their curtailing of our liberties.

Too many times in the last three decades, the U. S. Constitution has been compromised via a Conservative-controlled Congress and Supreme Court, to a] enable a Conservative Executive Branch, which allowed them to, then, b] load (or "partisanize") the Supreme Court, and lesser appellate courts, with more Conservative Justices to ensure that they could have the final say for a long, long, time, if not permanently. Our founding fathers did not plan for this important tool of our democracy, the U.S. Supreme Court, to be so used, but they did fear it.

The Right-wing takeover of the government was completed when the Republican Party utilized the Conservative controlled Congress and Supreme Court to decide the y2000 Presidential election, effectively turning the U. S. Constitution into so much toilet paper. This placed all three branches of our government, and hence our entire system of checks and balances, under their control. Progressive voters overwhelming ended the Conservatives' control of the Executive Branch with the election of Barack Obama, the Jr. Senator from Illinois, in 2008, but the Republican efforts to circumvent the American majority's wishes have increased.

The ethnicity of President Barack Obama has furthered the Conservatives' march to the edge of the precipice of the Far Right. Obstructionism has never been used to such extremes, ever, in the annals of American politics, to beat a man that they couldn't defeat in the polls. Racism has reared its hidden head, again. Increased numbers of African-Americans are being murdered by police and Black men are finding it even harder, in spite of an elevating economy, to find a job.

The Progressives' indignant realization that our system of government was falling like a cherry tree from a Washingtonian hatchet job briefly fueled them to great achievement. They regained the Legislative and Executive branches of the Federal government. Sadly, they, then, appeared to rest on their laurels, too secure, once again. The neo-cons got right back to their wicked work. They used false claims and mock outrage, mimicking those who had vocalized real concerns and fears during the previous presidency, to power the Republican party to regain the majority in the U.S. House and recapture several states.

Majority Leader Nancy Pelosi should have taken serious actions against the too many to recount broken laws and Constitutional violations by the Bush-Cheney administration. The left-wing majority let those who would have their way with our democracy off of the chopping block, when the most serious of messages should have been sent, to the conservatives, and to the whole world, that our system still works.

The current Democrat "lame duck" presidency, the Progressive repercussion to the perceived rape of America during George III's administrations, may only serve to widen the void beyond our skills to bridge it, again. The right-wing is now the pot calling the kettle black by claiming that the Obama administration is using Orwellian doublespeak. This literary expression was brought painfully back into the collective conscious of the country, as opposed to their unconscious supporters, by the Bush-Cheney Gang. Now, how long will it be before we are, again, faced with the choice of pointing our fingers at innocent others to save ourselves (remember the McCarthy witch hunt)?

Crucibles have been forged maybe a half of a dozen times throughout American history. These times have always been met with the expense, sometimes too great to measure, of human sacrifice. We can no longer assume that the American way will persevere because it is served by Mom, with apple pie on the side. If we don't fight, hard, for every seat, in every house, in every state, the same Justices who condemned John Proctor will decide our fate, forever.

A flawed ballot and electoral system, plus a partisan-controlled U. S. Supreme Court, is our country's Achille's heel. The Right-wing understands that it can get away with almost anything as long as it holds at least five Justices. And, they will always hold that hand, as long as they are dealing. We have seen them use that refuge, a partisan controlled U.S. Supreme Court, too many times since y2000; almost always whittling away at our liberties in one way or another, in spite of the cries of outrage from the American majority.

The Citizens United and McCutcheon v. Federal Election Committee decisions by the Conservative-controlled U.S. Supreme Court has basically given the keys of our democracy to the richest people in the world. Which could, too easily, now, be India, or, China.

Because Justices are appointed by Congress rather than elected by voters, controlling the House of Representatives, and the Senate, is the only way American citizens have to control the political make-up of the judiciary. As stated, our electoral system has proven fallible in its present state, and will be cheated, again, by those with the most monetary power. A verifiable ballot system is necessary to protect the majority of citizens in the United States of America from the power-elite. Gerrymandering and voter suppression are still cheating the American electorate. Only when every American votes and every American's vote is counted will we be able to not only bridge the great American abyss, but effectively eliminate it, entirely.

Honestly, the following article was unknown to this writer when he began searching for documentation to hopefully validate the essay he wrote four years later. He was greatly encouraged about his efforts to enlighten others when he found that they seemed to be mostly in tune with the words of this author, Doug Casey:

In this article, I'm going to argue that the US government, in particular, is being overrun by the wrong kind of person. It's a trend that's been in motion for many years but has now reached a point of no return. In other words, a type of moral rot has become so prevalent that it's institutional in nature. There is not going to be, therefore, any serious change in the direction in which the US is headed until a genuine crisis topples the existing order. Until then, the trend will accelerate.

The reason is that a certain class of people – sociopaths – are now fully in control of major American institutions. Their beliefs and attitudes are insinuated throughout the economic, political, intellectual and psychological/spiritual fabric of the US.[128]

The opinion that both Republican and Democrat politicians bend towards psychopathy is upheld by neither the Dem's platform nor pulpit. The Left, in both Charter and legislative choices, represent the majority of the American people. Sociopathy may drive people from both major Parties to succeed in the upper echelons of politics in the United States, but the author believes empathy and morals lead most Progressives away from the dark-side of psychopathy.

The narcissistic or more selfish and greedy sociopaths, those that seem to deserve a label of psychopath, are, it appears to some, on the Right. It seems a psychopath will stop at nothing to achieve their goals, in the main—serving themselves, despite an electorate's best wishes, ignoring the voices of the voters. It seemed obvious to this writer that only mentally unstable people could place our country in such dire straits as he wrote the following on Sept. 6, 2016:

What Hold Have They?

I'm beginning to believe the only way Right- wingers could be, and act, so immoral and unethical, even criminal, so against the grain and good of our country, and still have the most powerful news organizations in the United States, the so-called mainstream media (MSM), on their side, to the point of fabrications to hurt their opponents, is that, somehow, all are involved in something so bad, so damaging, that not a one is willing to point a finger at another. What the hell evil are these, holding the financial strings of this country, including the aforementioned MSM, hiding? Did it begin with the wealthiest Southern plantation owners? The North's powerful industrialists? Has it continued to our munition manufacturers and oil producers? Greed begetting greed for generations? Or, psychopaths propagating psychopaths perpetually?

Has it come to pass that those most driven to prestige and power, psychopaths, and their genetically similar offspring, are now in too many places of power and control, including the U. S. Congress and Supreme Court (along with the MSM, three of our four supposed government checks and balances), to defeat with our Constitutional power? If so—when George W. Bush's family helped him turn around the obviously failing Presidential attempt with only a phone call from Pappy, a suddenly silent press, help from brother Jeb and the political system of Florida which Jeb governed over, and a stacked U.S. Supreme Court—interpreting the electoral appeal from Florida in a plainly partisan, Constitutionally opposed, way—the heart rending feeling I had, that our most sacred document was no longer valid, was, in effect, so much toilet paper, was correct.

Keep the power of POTUS, people, restore Congress to Blue, then the House and Senate will ensure the far right will no longer use SCOTUS as a Constitution-corrupting partisan tool. If we can do this, People, the mainstream media will have no influence, and social media will have won the right to be the replacement check and balance. We need to vote, everybody, for each and every one of the positions in each and every election, especially now, but, also, endlessly, because, we are still the government of, by, and for—the PEOPLE...

Are Billionaires symptomatic of sociopathic drive or the inherited remains of others? Whichever, some people's desire for accumulated wealth and power seem to be beyond the understanding of most people. Even some in the wealthy-controlled press are concerned about the overreach of the rich to control the picture on our screens:

At first blush, the secret support that the Silicon Valley billionaire Peter Thiel provided for Hulk Hogan's lawsuit against Gawker is a salacious yarn about money, power, gossip and revenge.

But it is also about something more important: an aggressive bid by the very wealthy to control the American news media at a time when it is in a financially weakened state, struggling to maintain its footing on the electronic frontier's unstable terrain.[129]

It is not surprising that mostly one can only read, hear, and learn of criticism of the media moguls from less-mainstream or more progressive ("the liberal") media:

Responsible Behavior Shoved Aside for Biased Reporting

Blog posted by Steven Mintz, aka Ethics Sage, on October 20, 2016. Dr. Mintz is Professor Emeritus from Cal Poly San Luis Obispo. He also blogs at: www.workplaceethicsadvice.com.

The media has been referred to as "The Fourth Estate" with the important function of being the news media – "the press" – and serving as the eyes and ears of the public. The traditional print and media reporting has been viewed over time as the way to insure the American public gets the real scoop on the functioning of government and viewpoints of political candidate. The news media is a societal or political force or institution whose influence is not consistently or officially recognized. A free press serves four essential purposes:

- *Holding government leaders accountable to the people.*

- *Publicizing issues that need attention.*

- *Educating citizens so they can make informed decisions, and*

- *Connecting people with each other in civil society.*

Free media plays an important role in influencing political discourse during elections. When free and balanced, traditional media (print and broadcast) foster transparency and the determination of important electoral information. The rise of new media provides further opportunities for participatory citizenship.

Citizens are increasingly turning to social media platforms to follow election news and developments. Referred to as "The Fifth Estate," this form of "news" media is a socio-cultural reference to groupings of outlier viewpoints in contemporary society, and is most associated with bloggers, journalists publishing in non-mainstream media outlets, and the social media.

The media has immense power within the American democracy because just about all Americans get their news from cable news and social media rather than hard news sources. The problem today is these very people who report the news are biased towards one candidate or the other, as we have learned in the Trump-Clinton campaigns.[130]

The further into the election year of 2016, the more the Conservatives seemed to move to the Right. The Trump campaign and his partisan goons soon stank of Fasces-bearing authoritarians, even more than the Mitch McConnell led Senate of the previous several years or the Dick and Dubya administrations, leading one scared American to write the following on Sept. 10, 2016:

"Fascism Is Just All Right..."

How is the press kept on course for the Right? Are writers recruited from Conservative colleges only, e.g., the University of Truth? Are applicants subjected to custom designed psychological examination, like Rorschach test asking for negative evaluation of "intrusive" black inkblots and positive interpretation of white, background, portions? Perhaps activities, hobbies, volunteer work is clue to quintessential Conservative candidates. Which extracurricular functions would most likely seal the deal to put this guy, or gal, on a national news team? Writer for

Right-wing college rag? Campus Republican club membership? Best Subjective Journalistic Serial award? John Birch Society scholarship recipient? Family connections? Inherited wealth? What is the secret handshake for inclusion in the Fraternal Order of Fascist News Formers/Framers? Is it four fingers... or five? Maybe Orwell aficionados will know.

In addition to the gulf dividing the American voters the obscene income gap between the top 5% who take in over 50% of the income in America, and the rest of us, which adversely affects both sides of the sociopolitical gulf, strangely, or obtusely, effects a widening of the gulf between the common people. The article that Christina Pazzanese wrote for *U.S. News and World Report* rings painfully true:

Inequality leaves many Americans poor and voiceless, Harvard analysts say.

'Christopher "Sandy" Jencks, the Malcolm Wiener Professor of Social Policy at Harvard Kennedy School, believes that the last 30 years of rising American inequality can be attributed to three key factors:

- *The decline in jobs and employment rates for less-skilled workers, which has increased the number of households with children but no male breadwinner.*

- *The demand for college graduates outpacing the pool of job candidates, adding to the gap between the middle class and upper-middle class.*

- *The share of income gains flowing to the top 1 percent of earners doubling as a result of deregulation, globalization, and speculation in the financial-services industry.*

The U.S. government does "considerably less" than comparable democracies to even out disposable family incomes, Jencks says. And current state and local tax policies "actually increase income inequality."

"All the costs and risks of capitalism seem to have been shifted largely to those who work rather than those who invest," he said.

Compounding the economic imbalance is the unlikely prospect that those at the bottom can ever improve their lot.

"We have some of the lowest rates of upward mobility of any developed country in the world," said Nathaniel Hendren, an associate professor of economics at Harvard's Faculty of Arts and Sciences who has studied intergenerational mobility and how inequality transmits across generations.

...For children in parts of the Midwest, the Northeast and the West, upward mobility rates are high. But in the South and portions of the Rust Belt, rates are very low. For example, a child born in Iowa into a household making less than $25,000 a year has an 18 percent chance to move into the upper 20 percent of income strata over a lifetime. But a child born in Atlanta or Charlotte, North Carolina, has only a 4 percent chance of moving up, their study found.

What unites areas of low mobility, Hendren says, are broken family structures, reduced levels of civic and community engagement, lower-quality K-12 education, greater racial and economic segregation, and broader income inequality.

In addition, 90 percent of American workers have seen their wages stall while their costs of living continue to rise.

"When you look at the data, it's sobering. Median household income when last reported in 2013 was at a level first attained in 1989, adjusting for inflation. That's a long time to go without any gains," said Jan Rivkin, the Bruce V. Rauner Professor of Business Administration at Harvard Business School.[131]

Something set this writer off on Sept. 30, 2016, more worry about where contemporary Republicanism will take us, causing him to set his inner voice in silicon, again:

Where We Go From Here

All civilizations have, symbolically, a gold capstone atop a pyramid built by the masses, the populace. Strong economies solidly support a capstone to which one can climb. Others become oppressive and suppose their cups flowing over will bless the rest. This touted trickledown is the grains of sand, gravel, and increasingly larger particles of a crumbling pyramid, the infrastructure; like an economic or societal hourglass running down due to the lack of health, education, and following financial fruition. This is because those who most profit from American infrastructure refuse to pay for its maintenance and upkeep. Why? Because of their paranoid fear of paring a few percentage points of personal profit. Sitting atop the symbolic obelisk built by people in a strong economy, they do not see the correlation and believe their best interest now lies in belittling others. Apparently, they cannot read the writing on the stela.

Where we go from here is up to us. Everyone. Leave it not to a few political leaders, parochial preachers, power moguls, and their pawns. By the way, pawns are always considered the most expendable. However, if the pawns refuse to move, or move en masse, black and white, to block "the game," check, check, check... sooner or later, checkmate will befall the "kings" and it's a new game. "Go Fish," anyone?

We, leaders and electorate, employers and employees, must have faith in human "heart" and abilities, respect it, and refuse to shortchange it. People-powered progress, while not perfect, pushes for positive change, striving for what makes our society the best it can be, for everybody. Progress is definitely not a return to, or stay put in, predatory culture.

Have faith in that point in yourself, call it God, if you must, to appeal to your highest power, to give you strength and guidance—your real cerebral knowledge, confidence, courage, and certainty—to take action, to move the mountains of despair caused by deplorable ignorance, fear, hate, and greed. That means different things to each of us, whether it means merely getting out to register and vote or volunteering to help get others to the polls or promote candidates that you think will best serve the people in their position. Perhaps only peaceful, empathetic, positive discussion will make a difference. But, we should, as difficult as it can be, supposing our knowledge is satisfactory at least, let our heads lead and our hearts follow.

Déjà Vu X-Putintially, Corporate D'état & Cabbage Soup

Trump's Toxic Empire

Pre-Pandemic 2016-2020

I think readers of the following condensed "history" of the American political problems of the 21st century realize, early on, the irony of our prior objections to the behavior of the Republican Party and certain of its members. Compared to the Dick and Dubya debacle, the "Terrors of Trump" is Déjà Vu X-Putintially more concerning—a corporate coup d'état "totalitarianly" blessed and bestowed.

Constitutional attorney John W. Whitehead, president of The Rutherford Institute looks at the effects of sociopathy or psychopathy on politics:

Twenty years ago, a newspaper headline asked the question: "What's the difference between a politician and a psychopath?"

The answer, then and now, remains the same: None.

There are surprisingly few differences between psychopaths and some politicians.

Elected officials lie to their constituents, trade political favors for campaign contributions, turn a blind eye to the wishes of the electorate, cheat taxpayers out of hard-earned dollars, favor the corporate elite, entrench the military industrial complex, and spare little thought for the impact their thoughtless actions and hastily passed legislation might have on defenseless citizens.

Psychopaths and politicians both have a tendency to be selfish, callous, remorseless users of others, irresponsible, pathological liars, glib, con artists, lacking in remorse, and shallow.

Charismatic politicians, like criminal psychopaths, exhibit a failure to accept responsibility for their actions, have a high sense of self-worth, are chronically unstable, have socially deviant lifestyle, need constant stimulation, have parasitic lifestyles and possess unrealistic goals.

It doesn't matter whether you're talking about Democrats or Republicans.

Political psychopaths are all largely cut from the same pathological cloth, brimming with seemingly easy charm and boasting calculating minds. Such leaders eventually create pathocracies—totalitarian societies bent on power, control, and destruction of both freedom in general and those who exercise their freedoms.

Once psychopaths gain power, the result is usually some form of totalitarian government or a pathocracy...

The willingness to prioritize power above all else, including the welfare of their fellow human beings, ruthlessness, callousness and an utter lack of conscience are among the defining traits of the sociopath.[132]

The face of the GOP had changed so in the past half of a century, it boggled the mind on Oct. 4, 2016. Or, did it toggle the mind? Is there a built-in switch to make one altruistic and empathetic versus selfish, unforgiving, unfriendly, unfair, hurtful, unsympathetic, unmerciful, disdainful, spiteful, and/or mean-spirited? We have heard other writers expound about the state and symptoms that sociopathy is having on our country, here is this author's approximately parallel view:

The Effects of Psychopathy on the Face of Our Country

I believe that many Right-wingers act immorally and unethically, even criminally, against the grain and good of our country. This begs the question, why do they still have the most powerful news organizations in the United States, the so-called mainstream media (MSM), on their side, to the point of fabrications to hurt their opponents? It's as if, somehow, all are involved in something so bad, so damaging, that not a one is willing to point a finger at another.

What the hell evil are they hiding, those holding the financial strings of this country, the politicians that seem to be working in their interests, and the aforementioned MSM that, too often, supports the first two? It's as if the Conservatives have developed their own system of illicit checks and balances, designed to support the Right's control of the United States of America. Throw the majority of Supreme Court Justices into the mix, and they have a near unbeatable system.

Did this narcissistic bend begin with the richest colonists, the wealthiest Southern plantation owners, or, the North's powerful industrialists? Has it continued to America's munition manufacturers and oil producers? Greed begetting greed for generations? Or, is it more physiologically driven, psychopaths propagating psychopaths perpetually?

Has it come that those most driven to prestige and power, psychopaths, and their genetically similar offspring, are now in too many places of power and control? Including the U. S. Congress and Supreme Court (along with the MSM) we have been deprived of three of our four supposed government checks and balances. Has this left us too weak to defeat the corporate takeover with our Constitutional power?

Greed, I think, a lust for power, to most rationally thinking people, is a given in the digging of the great gulf dividing our country. How does greed occur, is it learned, or, physiologically woven into one's fabric? Like most behaviors, some people's "design" (nature) allows them to be "better" than others, but this may not be realized without the "training" and "experience" (nurture) that allows those tendencies to thrive. Take a person hardwired for sociopathic or psychopathic behavior and a similarly motivated mentor, be it parent, teacher, boss, etc., that has risen to an extremely provocative position of power, and you create another, perhaps "better," version of "achiever" (or, "overachiever").

———————————————————————————————————

*"According to Wikipedia, the DSM IV-TR gives the prevalence of psychopathy as **3% in males and 1% in females**. http://en.wikipedia.org/wiki/Ant...*

...By contrast, a 2009 study done in the U.K., looking at the combined population of England, Scotland, and Wales, found a prevalence of psychopathy of 0.6%.

http://www.sciencedirect.com/sci...

...Given the above numbers, my best guess is that prevalence in the West is probably roughly 1%. However, I would suspect that an actual study could find anything from 0.5% to 2.5% depending on the methodology used."

(Above, quoted, written by Jim Seidman)

https://www.quora.com/What-percentage-of-people-are-psychopaths-sociopaths

――――――――――――――――――――――――――――――――――――――

For my comparison I will combine U.K. & U.S. studies' low for mean high of 0.5% to 3% range of psychopathy in the U.S. Based on the United States Census Bureau's 2010 Statistical Yearbook, there are a total of 227,431,000 Americans aged 18 and above in 2007. These statistical numbers give us an estimated number of psychopaths in the US anywhere from one million to seven million. Assuming numbers of sociopaths (for lack of a better definition this comparison assumes sociopaths are narcissistic perhaps to a lesser degree and are capable of some empathy) exceed psychopathic people, I think doubling this conservative estimation will give us a number of up to fifteen million voting age people in America with some pathology disabling their ability to relate to other human beings. I admit these are "guesstimates" based on others' statistics, but still give one a feel for how large our inability to relate to others has grown. This is especially concerning considering those driven to gain positions of power over people, and the people who would support them.

Of approximately 55 million registered Republicans, according to the previous numbers, greater than 20% could be severely empathetically challenged. Since we used particularly understated numbers for "sociopathy," our number of American Right-wing voters capable of sociopathic or psychopathic behavior could be anywhere from ten to twenty million.

CEO's, lawyers, media types are the top three most psychopathic careers. Since politician is absurdly missing from this top-ten list, and many politicians have law degrees, or are businessmen, I am lumping them in with the top two. This is, obviously, much greater in Republican ranks where support is typically only for those further enabling one's own success. Media having a high percentile of psychopaths explains why MSM, along with their CEO's seem to be so Conservative biased.

It should be apparent, by now, that psychopathic saturation of positions of power in the United States of America is our reality. This includes the police, who are also among the top ten careers to which psychopaths gravitate, and who are rapidly "militarizing" and becoming more violent. This more than explains the predicament our political system is in, now. CEO's, media, politicians, judges, all supporting each other for the sole purpose of growing their own self and net worth. With a pseudo-military (police) on their side, the "corp. d'état" will be nearly complete.

Career information from— "10 Careers With the Most Psychopaths' By Kali Holloway/Alternet http://www.alternet.org/culture/10-careers-most-psychopaths

The question is, can the approximately 72 million Democratic voters, for the most part empathetic people, and the defectors from the ~55 million strong Republican electorate, eager to avoid the "Deplorables Basket," get to the polls, ensure polling is legitimate, and win America back from the Pit of Depravity?

Near the end of the year 2000, George W. Bush's family helped him turn around the obviously failing Presidential attempt with only a phone call from Pappy, a suddenly silent press, help from brother Jeb and the Florida government he controlled, plus a stacked U.S. Supreme Court interpreting the electoral appeal from Florida in a plainly partisan, constitutionally opposed, way. The heart-rending feeling I had then, that our most sacred document was no longer valid, that it had, in effect, become like so much toilet paper, was akin to losing a loved one. I experienced that pain as a young man, so I had something to compare to.

We, the people, are under the control of, and at the whims of, rich and powerful psychopaths, most driven to climb to the top of the social stratosphere, especially those handed the keys to the Ferrari. Most of these people are genetically spawned and spurred on by the same, nature and nurture of the nastiest type. The majority, almost the entirety of these, often called "entitled," are on the Right side of the political fence and moving ever farther away, from us. They are the majority in the House, the Senate, and, for too many years, the U.S. Supreme Court, where they will be, again, if the Democrats can't seize a congressional majority. For eight long, painful, expensive years, from 2001 to 2009, the White House was theirs, too, and they successfully precluded any means of checking G.O.P.'s unconstitutional actions or balancing their misbehavior. These power-driven and hungry people control the lawmaking, the financial institutions, the police forces, the firearms industry (among many others), and many corporate and governmental positions. They scratch each-others' backs, only to keep their own backs protected, because it is only themselves that they really care about. It is imperative we control the lawmaking as well as the interpretation of the laws to restore the sanctity of our Constitution, our government, our country.

Our job, our imperative, is to keep the power of POTUS, People, and restore Congress to Blue so the House and Senate will ensure the far right will no longer use SCOTUS as a Constitution corrupting partisan tool. If we can do this, People, the mainstream media will have no influence, and social media will have won the fight as the alternative check and balance, the watchdog press envisioned by Benjamin Franklin. We need to vote, everybody, for each and every one of the positions in each and every election, especially now, but, also, endlessly, to continue to be the government of, by, and for—the PEOPLE...

While voting is crucial for a democracy, is it job one? Perhaps as important, especially now, is ensuring the sanctity of election results. Unless each person that desires to vote is allowed to and each vote cast is counted, it is no longer a free country. Ron Rivest and Philip Stark explain why and how:

This should be standard — and it's easy, too.

A Washington Post–ABC News *poll found that 18% of voters — 33% of Clinton supporters and 1% of Trump supporters — think Trump was not the legitimate winner of the election. Sen. Lindsey Graham, R-S.C., has called on Congress to investigate the Russian cyberattack on the Democratic National Committee and the election.*

There are reasons for concern. According to the director of national intelligence, the leaked emails from the DNC were "intended to interfere with the U.S. election process." The director of national intelligence, the Department of Homeland Security, and the National Security Agency concluded that the Russian government is behind the DNC email hack and that Russian hackers attacked U.S. voter registration databases.

We know that the national results could be tipped by manipulating the vote count in a relatively small number of jurisdictions — a few dozen spread across a few key states. We know that the vast majority of local elections officials have limited resources to detect or defend against cyberattacks. And while pre-election polls have large uncertainties, they were consistently off. And various aspects of the preliminary results, such as a high rate of undervotes for president, have aroused suspicion.[133]

The above article evoked this immediate response by yours truly on the same day, Nov. 18, 2016:

Audit Election Results

If the coming from behind to win by 1% in all swing-states isn't suspicious enough, then known Trump-Russian "handshaking," serious debt to China, and Russian and FBI election interference, then Diebold GEMS known percentage manipulation and voter repression has to ring alarm bells in logical and law-abiding peoples' minds.

The United States of America must not be held hostage, nor leveraged like a corporation had by a hostile takeover. Can we ever recover if this is allowed to happen? If ever this country had a chance to instill/ restore/inject (you choose as optimistic or pessimistic a verb as you think appropriate) integrity, it is now. Think about the real gravity of this. Do you want to risk that?

Losing our freedom to Fascist power-grabbers never was a concern growing up. After all, our parents and grandparents had completely scuttled that threat, hadn't they? The fear if not the threat of a Fascist takeover is fast becoming a reality, though MSM won't go so far as to report that. Some lesser big-bucks sponsored outlets are yet unafraid of objectivity if one is willing to search for the truth:

Today's leisure reading is Robert Paxton's essay The Five Stages of Fascism (downloadable PDF). It's a followup to my aprevious post on Umberto Eco's essay on fascism.

According to Paxton (link to biography), even though fascist movements had varying stated goals, the shared elements lay in what they actually did.

He lists the following five steps. The links go to events in 2016 that approximate Paxton's steps.

1. *Intellectual exploration, where disillusionment with popular democracy manifests itself in discussions of lost national vigor;*

1. *Rooting, where a fascist movement, aided by political deadlock and polarization, becomes a player on the national stage;*

1. *Arrival to power, where conservatives seeking to control rising leftist opposition invite the movement to share power;*

1. *Exercise of power, where the movement and its charismatic leader control the state in balance with state institutions such as the police and traditional elites such as the clergy and business magnates; and*

5. Radicalization or entropy, where the state either becomes increasingly radical, as did Nazi Germany, or slips into traditional authoritarian rule, as did Fascist Italy.

He also says that only Nazi Germany and Fascist Italy progressed through all five of these stages.

An argument can be made that in its own way, filtered through its election mechanisms, the U.S. is approximately at stage 3 of this process. Starting decades ago, a radical wing of the Republican Party went through step 2. This wing coalesced in fall 2016, early in the primary season. If you are among those who agree with this, then the next question for you is how to slow or prevent the fourth step....

...As commenter Emigre suggests, "we will know whether a Stage 4 is imminent when the military and police follow the lead of the Border Patrol Agents and align their interests with those of Trump and his allies."[134]

Four years after that was written, it looks like we are firmly entrenched at level four. If the Democrats can't win the elections of 2020, the author expects that the final step will not be denied, not by our former institutions of government, anyway.

A week before the last article was written, this writer Dec. 13, 2016 voiced his latest concerns via social media:

Skewed Election, Screwed Electorate

"If the president-elect is flipping us the finger over the airwaves... WE must become the wind." Gloria Steinem, paraphrased.

WE have to be stronger.

Rich acquire power get richer acquire more power... Rich/power elite have managed to get majority control of Congress, SCOTUS, election laws in their favor, and mainstream media. If Al Gore and company had decided a Constitutional battle was in our country's best interests, put us on the long, painful road that we needed to tread to ensure the sanctity and integrity of our elections, we wouldn't be facing the uphill hike of our and our country's lives. Or, had House Speaker Pelosi and Senate Majority Leader Harry Reid, respective majority leaders of their houses of Congress, taken the Right-wing "bullshittery" by the horns when they had the power, and made an example of Bush-Cheney and company for the assault and rape of our country and Constitution, to keep our country from sliding off of that precipice into the fascism of the far right, we would not be here, today, clinging to the cliff by our fingernails.

Are empathy and fascism inversely related? It certainly seems like empathy and sociopathy are as, respectively, seen in the Democrats and Conservatives:

The Republican Party would do well by spending a few hours on a psychiatrist's couch, as a new psychology study shows that the Party, and America as a whole, has lost empathy towards others, and that's what's driving the rise of fascist leaders like Donald Trump. The Ring of Fire's Farron Cousins discusses this.

According to a new article in Psychology Today, there could be a reason why more and more Americans are actually voting for Republicans. Before we get into their study, it is important to point out that in the 2016 election more people voted for the Democratic nominee than for the Republican nominee, but this specific study was looking more as a whole, at the local level, at the state level, and for the U.S. Congress and Senate. Why are people going towards Republicans?

According to the study, one reason could be because Americans, as a whole, are simply losing their ability to feel empathy towards one another. Essentially, they no longer feel the pain of their neighbors, and they don't care. Americans have become so self-absorbed, again this is what the study tells us, that we don't care what happens to other people. We have not been nurtured by the federal government, the parent figure, and therefore we do not feel the need to nurture others.

...People look to the government as a parent figure, someone who while not intrusive will take care of them when they need it.

In that test, the federal government has failed. There is no denying that, but it failed by design, and that's something the study doesn't mention. The policies of the Republican Party are designed to weaken the federal

government and inhibit its ability to take care of United States citizens.
[135]

The Golden Rule is merely a suggestion rather than a rule when it comes to the Party of Christian-Conservatives:

Opinion:

This isn't the article I wanted to write while watching the Attorney General confirmation hearing for the established racist (his own party found him too racist to be a federal judge in 1986) Republican Senator Jeff Sessions (R-AL). But it has to be said.

Based on the hearing at the time of this writing, Democrats, with the exceptions of Senators Leahy, Durbin and Franken, are wasting air time playing Nice Guys and praising Sessions for things they've worked on together. Typical Senate behavior (on the part of Democrats these days, not Republicans) and typical of Democrats, for whom reaching across the aisle is a value.

But those times are gone, and they are dealing with a dangerous racist...

Did we hear Republicans praising Democrats in the hearing? No. Did they smear President Obama? Yes. Does this seem like an olive branch? No.

Democrats are woefully unprepared for the task at hand, and part of that is due to the very values of the Democratic party. They better find the spine to fight this war at all times, because this is a war and people's lives are at stake.

Republicans already undermined the Senate tradition of decency and civility. They denied President Obama's right to have his SCOTUS nominee heard, and then the first time the shoe is on the other foot, Democrats are using air time to praise Republicans.

...The Democratic need to be nice is a weakness Republicans exploit.[136]

Empathy... Salvation or Damnation?

Events in our country, particularly in the last decade or two, have caused the author to believe that our biggest conflicts, which bring the greatest division of people, are brought about from empathy—and the lack of it. Perhaps for time immemorial this difference has brought pain, suffering, injustice, fear and hatred into human culture.

There are those who at least feel badly about pain, suffering, and injustice suffered by others and are incapable of inflicting those on others. Stronger empathy and resolution may move some to actually take action to try to change circumstances that effect these inequities.

Those without empathy, narcissistic or sociopathic to lesser degrees, may only aspire to wealth or power that doesn't seem to adversely affect others, as their means and abilities allow.

At the far end of this spectrum of empathy, let's call it the right side, are people concerned only with fulfillment of their own wants, desires, and impulses; the effect of these self "achievements" on anyone else never factors into it for these Icons of self, unless punishment and pain for power's sake is the desired goal. Why does it seem that too many who have had not only a silver spoon but a gilded path put before them, so success is available with a mere modicum of effort, are much more likely to be amongst these extremists on the right, those lacking in the ability to know and care for other people?

Is empathy creating a niche for predators? Does our desire to cause no pain embolden those who lust for it or profit from it? The following story from an article about Barn Owls and their seeming empathy at home in the nest makes me wonder if predators are capable of empathy towards fellow predators while joyfully ripping the entrails from those who failed to see the risk or were incapable of doing anything about it?

In comparison, the case of George Cvek's heartless and ruthless use of people's good-nature, their empathy, to rob and rape nearly one-hundred women in 1941 is heart-rendering and enraging, especially when you see this same M.O. being used by political Con's, and not just in America:

Bronx detectives, working with an unprecedented number of city, state and federal authorities from Maine to New Orleans, Louisiana, as well as the surviving victims of Cvek's crimes, traced at least 156 robberies and sexual assaults during a nine-month span from mid–1940 to February 1941 to Cvek. Authorities believed Cvek resorted to a modus operandi of using one of at least one dozen aliases and a false story to win the trust of motorists while hitchhiking. He would tell men he was a drifter from Boys Town, Nebraska, who was searching for work and would collect their addresses under the guise of relocating the men to pay them back for their help, while his actual motive was to break into their houses and bound, rob, or sexually assault their wives.[5][6] He would gain entry to these women's homes by asking for a glass of water and aspirin, which earned him the moniker "The Aspirin Bandit" following the Pappas murder.[137]

However, perhaps more horrifying is how analogous it is to how those striving for power, e.g., economic power, use people's hope and faith in others, particularly their elected officials.

There is no firm agreement on whether it is nature or nurture that makes one narcissistic, too willing to take, and another empathetic, too willing to give. It might be a combination of both. Brain and psyche researchers are still testing to determine if we are hardwired to be one or the other or if there is a toggle-switch in our brain that is flipped one way or the other by our environment and interactions therein.

Our titanic cultural teeter-totter is moving farther and farther away from a point of equilibrium on its fulcrum where empathy and "meopathy" are close to balancing, though the election results say otherwise. Giving corporations status as individuals, albeit the deepest pocketed ones, and allowing unlimited political donations, has put the biggest me's (psychopaths (read, bullies) to a greater degree?) in the controlling position on the societal seesaw, with most of the rest flailing in midair, or falling off. Possibly, empathetic people are concerned about overpopulation while sociopaths and psychopaths are proudly pleased to procreate in plethoric ways, especially where they can avoid responsibility for such. We may have bred, in our inverse ways, to a point of psychopathic saturation, and as the predators share in the plunder, we will be consumed by our inability to.

See previously shared essay, if you missed it, on Psychopathic Saturation—"The Effects of Psychopathy on the Current Face of Our Country."

The following *Daily Kos* article speaks of the long Right-wing tendency towards fascism, mega-materialism, and lack of reasoning (read, religion) supporting it:

Community (This content is not subject to review by Daily Kos staff prior to publication.)

...It would be deeply disingenuous to ascribe Trump's passage to the White House merely as an unexpected conjuring from the heart of the rust belt. His victory was the perfect storm that had been aligning, and ignored, for a generation. How did we get here? At its heart lies the uneasy relationship of the GOP with American conservatism.

On July 30, 1956 a small law was passed that changed the official motto of the United States of America from "Out of Many, One" to "In God We Trust". This heralded a small but significant step towards inculcating religion into the fabric of American governance. More pertinently, it sealed the union of liberalism and traditional conservatism in the Republican Party. Ever since, the GOP has been pushing boundaries of normality towards the extreme- both socially and economically. Coupled with racist elements of southern conservatism, the GOP as a political entity has gradually but irrefutably dragged the country backwards through regressive social politics transforming America into a nation infested by greed, consumerism, and irrationality. The grassroots of the Republican Party is a hotbed of intolerance and irrationality. Trump has been a long time coming.[138]

In spite of their need to be propped up by the cross of their religious iconography, the Party of the Religious Right uses their own" version of the "Golden Rule," or, rather inversion of it... 1/(Golden Rule) = Taketh from others before they taketh from you=f(Do unto others as ye believe they would do unto you). Sadly, their aversion to brotherly love goes far beyond homophobia. Chauncey DeVega questions this in *Salon*:

Paul Ryan has dreamed of slashing Medicaid since his keg-party days— and that blithe hostility is widespread

...Paul Ryan is the speaker of the U.S. House of Representatives. By his own account, in college he used to hang out with his friends and drink beer while sharing his dreams of cutting Medicaid. When Ryan was

15 years old, his father died from an alcoholism related heart attack. Ryan and his family then received his father's Social Security survivor's benefits. Ryan used that money to attend college. This was not the only money that Paul Ryan received from the federal government. His family built its wealth from receiving government contracts.

Like his idol Ayn Rand (who argued against the very idea of government and the commons yet received Social Security and Medicare), Paul Ryan has combined meanness, cruelty and callousness toward the weak and the vulnerable with gross and unapologetic hypocrisy.

...It is normal to feel aghast at and disgusted by the Republican Party's war on the poor. The more challenging and perhaps even more disturbing task is to ask why today's conservatives feel such antipathy, disregard and hostility toward poor and other vulnerable Americans. Certainly greed and a slavish devotion to a revanchist right-wing ideology are part of the answer. But they may not be sufficient.

Conservatives are more likely to exhibit social dominance and bullying behavior. This is a function of their authoritarian tendencies. The election of Donald Trump exemplifies this phenomenon.

American political elites often use language that robs poor and other marginalized people of their individuality, humanity and dignity. This language also creates a type of social distance between "middle class" or "normal" Americans and those with economic disadvantages.

Conservatism is a type of motivated social cognition that by its very nature is hostile to members of groups on the lower rungs of the social hierarchy.

And conservatives are more likely than liberals or progressives to believe in what's known as the "just world fallacy," whereby people who suffer a misfortune are viewed as somehow deserving their fate. Conservatives are also more likely than liberals or progressives to not use systems-level thinking as a way to understand that individuals don't exist separate and apart from society. Conservatives are also more likely to defend social inequality as "fair and legitimate."[139]

Too angry too often about the carelessness of Republican politicians, the social media soapbox served as therapy, on May 9, 2017; this critic of the anti-constitution Christian-Conservatives with their guns in one hand, Bible in the other, and wrapped in Old Glory bathrobes finally spewed his voice into cyberspace, on this topic:

Condemned to Hell by Conservatives

We didn't just get here, we have been moving in this direction for a half century, at least. Being "Bleeding Heart" Liberals has worked against us, to get to this point. I never thought of empathy as a liability, until a decade or two ago. We win political battles and, then, assume everyone will be happy with improved economy, jobs, healthcare, and keep voting our way. It could work that way, if we looked for the "kill," went for the jugular, when we had the power. But, we are too nice, and think that is enough.

After Nixon tried to stop DOJ from doing its job during "Watergate" and, then, Ford pardoned Nixon, next time we had the power we should have amended the hell out of those abilities to circumvent justice. Iran-Contra Scandal we will have to skip over, now, but it is another example of the Right-Wing getting away with crimes and Dems doing nothing to prevent it when they had the chance. You think GOP has seen the error of its ways and will keep their weaker Christian brothers on the straight and narrow. Hah! Suckers!

After the Y2000 debacle, massive voting improprieties became the norm. How? The R-W partisan SCOTUS used the U.S. Constitution like so much toilet paper, albeit in a new and inventive way. This allowed Dick and Dubya and Company to treat our sacred charter in much the same way, lying and cheating their way to over a trillion taxpayer dollars through thousands of Americans' deaths. Then, after we missed our chance to secure them, the Cons, immediately, took our Voting Rights Act away.

What did we do with combined Progressive President and Congress and all that potential gained in 2008? Nancy Pelosi and Harry Reid, House and Senate Majority leaders, respectively, took fast and furious action against the Bush administration, so heavily that those crooks are still paying the penalties. Then, this Super Dem force then amended the U.S. Constitution so gerrymandering, voter repression, and rigged computers could no longer be used to cheat the popular vote, any longer. And we lived happily ever after in our progressive utopia with living wages, universal health care and free colleges, for all. Right? No, that is our fantasy, because we didn't bother to take the initiative to ensure the predators couldn't. Because we are too damn nice.

There are evil, greedy people who have been working for decades to take all we have, and we haven't bothered to protect ourselves, because, who would intentionally do a thing like that? Look at them laughing, now, at the catch-22 we are in. What are we going to do? And, when are we going to do it?

Speaking of the catch-22... side-stream media are the only ones talking about it:

Commentary

The system wasn't supposed to work this way. The Founding Fathers deliberately devised a structure in which someone like Donald Trump — a vain, self-centered, mendacious demagogue — could never become chief executive, and in which the legislature could never be captured by a reckless, ideologically obsessed minority bent on overriding the majority interests of Americans. Those Founders labored to create an independent judiciary that was not captive to any single ideology or party. They carefully crafted a set of checks and balances in which no single branch of government could overpower another, and in which each held its own prerogatives dearly. In doing so, they thought they had provided posterity with a wise, cautious and magnanimous governmental operation that would serve the larger public weal rather than advantage any particular group or party, and that could withstand the gusts of any given historical moment.[140]

Some of the mainstream press were still "telling it like it is" in 2017, the first year of Trump's first term:

One thing is unsurprising, one is heartening, and one is singularly depressing.

The major weakness these six months have revealed in our governing system is almost too obvious to mention, but I'll name it anyway. It is the refusal, so far, by any significant Republican figure in Congress to apply to Donald Trump the standards its members know the country depends on for long-term survival of its government. A system of checks and balances relies on each of its component branches resisting overreach by the others. The judiciary has done its part; Paul Ryan's House and Mitch McConnell's Senate have not. We're seeing the difference that can make.

...There's a reason Donald Trump could joke about shooting someone on Fifth Avenue and not losing any support, and a reason talk-show hosts wonder what, finally, it would take for Republican senators or representatives to stand up to him. So far, many GOP legislators have expressed "concern" or "discomfort" with Trump's words and comments. But they've stood with him when it mattered, in votes on the floor and in committee, to avoid investigations, subpoenas, or hearings into the matters that "concern" them so.

...As a recent assessment of Senator Ben Sasse of Nebraska pointed out, he leads all senators in his thoughtful, scholarly "concern" about the norms Donald Trump is breaking—and then lines up and votes with Trump 95 percent of the time. The architects of the checks-and-balance system were famously concerned not simply about balance in policy but also about limits on the grandiose and power-mad. Sasse and his colleagues know that—if not from the Federalist *papers, then in their bones. But they have so far refused to act on that knowledge. So, we are living through a demonstration of what happens when checks aren't applied.[141]*

...but it's only gotten worse since then. We may survive his first four years but America surviving a second term of Trump is looking very questionable.

A month before the previous article, on June 15, 2017, the present writer noted the self-service of Trump and his enablers, sadly, most of the Republican Party:

*"My Country (supposed to be) **Tis of Thee** (not, Me)"*

This is how our system is supposed to work—the President, no matter which party, should listen to his wise and experienced advisors, Congress-persons, and citizens, all-inclusive of all ethnicities and faiths, to plan our course and then gain the full support of legislators to achieve his goals. As CEO's must be afforded success by support of their officers & organization, so must the President. If he/she fails, in spite of best efforts of those he/she leads, that leader has been unsuccessful. Fire him/her, replace him/her after four years, put whomever seems best fit to replace him/her in office, then, everyone, put your back and shoulder into turning the wheel for him/her.

On the other hand, thankfully, our system also allows us to preclude and prevent the U.S. President from endangering our form of democracy by his/her actions and decisions. For example—some rare exception whereby the election is stolen with the support of and for the benefit of foreign entities and personal gain of a select group. Then, Congress, DOJ, and citizens, united, must come together to, Constitutionally, end this threat, this presidency.

After preempting such a blatant coup d'état, and imprisoning those who would make it happen, the wrenches thrown into the gears of our election system must be removed. "Citizens United," the overturned VRA, gerrymandering, voter exclusions and preventions of all types, and proven failed or "fixed" electronic voting systems must, also, be eliminated.

Why does it seem that, more and more, they who are sociopathic or psychopathic strive for positions to achieve more fame and fortune— greater prestige and power— without qualms or concerns for the constituencies that put them there. Those responsible for the enslavement of the American electorate—too many of whom are obviously too ignorant to realize how they are being used—must be harshly dealt with for their staining, tearing, rending of the very fabric of American freedom and liberty.

Only after we succeed at repair of the damage caused our Republic, by the Uber-Right and super-rich interested in only their own power and glory, will we be able to work together, again, reaching across the "fence" to shake hands and reach agreements for their respective constituencies, in full support (albeit with some grumbling, perhaps) of our leaders (who, also, should have electorate's ideals at heart), for the benefit and betterment of America, and the world.

Will the envisioned "sweet land of liberty" survive the fascist regime being established a full 90 degrees and mega-leagues apart from the political "fence" that used to exist between Parties?

Most of America cannot fathom where we are headed. The more enlightened, or "woke" as Conservatives like to label as one of their supposed denigrations of the Left, such as "Liberal," are greatly concerned and even fear for the existence of our democratic republic. Trump's use of Christianity as an ally and even accomplice, noting the religious affiliations, some radically-leaning, of his first term SCOTUS appointments, the entirety of the six-justice majority picked by Republicans being not only conservative Catholics but members of the Federalist Society, causes fear of America becoming not only fascist but a theocracy, too. Funded to a large degree by great amounts of what is deemed "dark money," the Federalist Society's primary purpose seems to be death to anything Progressive, not even pretending to be open minded and seek or offer "give and take" on issues, in one man's opinion. The organization is part of the force or impetus behind Conservatives' march towards the far Right. Peter Hammond Schwarz offered one of the warnings of a more objective press in an article:

The Heritage Foundation and the Federalist Society are two of the most influential policy institutes to benefit from these infusions. Both organizations internalize and propagate the baseline precepts of Culture War Catholicism, and both have arguably become institutional foundations of Republican Party power no less significant than Fox News, and perhaps more dangerous because gilded with the sheen of academic respectability.[142]

The close comradeship between Trump and American evangelism recalls the alliance of the Judean Temple Sadducees and Roman government of Judea, or, in modern times, theocracies of Iran or Iraq to name but two. Rob Boston describes one sign of Trump-vangelism's seeming dogmatic restructuring of democracy:

For advocates of religious freedom and separation of church and state, Oct. 6, 2017, will be remembered as the day the Donald Trump administration delivered a one-two punch.

In early October, rumors began circulating that administration officials were poised to issue new regulations regarding access to contraceptives. The regulations did indeed come – and they were troubling. But that was just a start. Less than an hour later, the administration also issued a sweeping guidance intended to cover religious freedom issues, a directive critics at Americans United said is really just a cover for discrimination.

AU was quick to respond to both developments. The organization promptly announced it will challenge the birth control regulations in court, and blasted the religious freedom guidance as a reckless move likely to foster discrimination.[143]

Near the end of Trump's first year in the White House, there were a number of signs that indicated that there should be concerned for the constitutional boundary between religion (read, Christianity, to the most part) and American government. Following is the tally sheet of the most noteworthy, by Mr. Boston:

There's no denying that 2017 was a tough year for advocates of religious freedom and church-state separation. Yet despite the barrage of assaults from the Donald Trump-Mike Pence administration, Americans United saw important victories in and out of court.

Top Ten Church-State Stories From 2017

As we look ahead to 2018, here's a list of what are, in our opinion, the top 10 church-state stories from 2017:

GOP attempts to repeal the Johnson Amendment fail: *Earlier this year, President Donald J. Trump vowed to "totally destroy" the Johnson Amendment, a provision in federal law that protects the integrity of houses of worship and other tax-exempt entities by ensuring they don't intervene in electoral politics by endorsing or opposing candidates for public office. This fall, Republicans in the House of Representatives tried to make good on Trump's promise by inserting a provision in the tax bill that would have severely undermined the amendment...*

Trump's Muslim ban struck down by several courts: *Trump made several attempts to bar or restrict Muslim entry into the United States through executive orders. A number of lawsuits were filed against his actions, including two by Americans United and our allies. Several federal courts weighed in on the matter, with most striking down the ban in whole or in part. Legal observers agree that the matter is headed to the U.S. Supreme Court...*

Americans United challenges Trumps birth control regulations: *The Trump administration in October issued regulations that allow employers and universities to cite religious or moral objections in order to deny employees and students health insurance coverage of birth control...*

Supreme Court rules in favor of church in tax-aid case: *The U.S. Supreme Court in June ruled that the state of Missouri could not deny taxpayer aid to a church-owned preschool that sought to take part in a grant program that provides funding for the purchase of recycled tires that are used for playground resurfacing. ...Thus, while the decision is disappointing, its full impact remains to be seen.*

Americans United Executive Director Barry W. Lynn announces retirement...

Houses of worship demand taxpayer aid after hurricanes: *In the wake of a series of devastating hurricanes that battered Texas and Florida, a Religious Right legal group went to court seeking taxpayer assistance to rebuild religious structures under programs administered by the Federal Emergency Management Agency (FEMA). Americans United pointed out that houses of worship can be reimbursed for funds they spend housing and taking care of people post-disaster but that rebuilding aid is usually limited to entities that provide a public service, such as schools, hospitals and libraries. ...the cases are ongoing.*

Supreme Court to decide legality of religion-based discrimination claims: *...The case concerns a Colorado bakery whose owner wants to discriminate against members of the LGBTQ community and possibly others who offend his religious beliefs. If the court rules in his favor, it could open the door for for-profit businesses to deny services not just to LGBTQ Americans but also to non-believers, single moms, cohabitating couples or virtually anyone who is deemed to run afoul of a business owner's theological views.*

Roy Moore loses race for U.S. Senate: *Moore, formerly the chief justice of the Alabama Supreme Court, has twice been removed from that position – once for defying a federal appeals court ruling to remove a Ten Commandments monument from the judicial building in Montgomery and once for ordering state probate judges to ignore the U.S. Supreme Court's ruling on marriage equality...*

President Trump and Education Secretary Betsy DeVos push vouchers...

President Trump appoints Neil Gorsuch to Supreme Court: *Trump named Gorsuch, a judge on the 10th U.S. Circuit Court of Appeals, to an open seat on the high court. (The seat became vacant nearly two years ago when Justice Antonin Scalia died, but Senate Republicans refused to allow a vote on President Barack Obama's nominee, Merrick*

Garland.) Americans United opposed Gorsuch's nomination, noting that his record on church-state cases while he was on the appeals court was poor...[144]

A short history of a long misery, written by this author on Dec. 26, 2017; this is what the prior two articles are concerned with, where such an alliance will take us:

The Conception & Separation of Government & Religion

Religion began as government services of and for the ruler(s). This was first known to be utilized in the Sumerian civilization of approximately 4000 to 6000 years ago. The scribes, monks, priests, or clerks, whatever name they were called by, and their managerial leaders, were responsible for keeping records of laws and transactions, so their kings or queens and their monarchy could best rule, grow, and profit.

These record keepers and administrators were also later tasked with recording history, as long as it met the supreme one's approval. These literal ones schooled others in these scribal, mathematic, and scientific arts to ensure this duty would always have enough personnel. These teachers were also expected to educate the young royals, so they could "wisely" rule.

Generations or ages later, past rulers and their exploits became legendary, mythological, morphing into god-like characters. The rulers, and their scribes, with a monopoly on knowledge, used the illiterate citizens' belief in these past "gods" to better influence and control them. The record-keepers, in their halls of administration, justice, and education, gradually became the hierarchy of the priesthood in the temple.

Over the eons, government, business, and priesthood became more specialized, as a living cell, or conjoined twins, now separated and seemingly autonomous. Though religion and business claim independence of government and all have become more autonomous of each other, or, less obviously connected, these Conservative institutions still rely or use the government to assist in accomplishing their ambitions. A fundamentally paternal rule appears to have always been more useful or controllable than an invisible omnipresent deity.

From early in Trump's first term, and before, self-liberated writers—free from control by Conservative owners—have been warning readers of the danger American democracy is in. Steve Levitsky and Daniel Ziblatt are two such writers. Please take dire messages such as theirs, below, to heart, if you believe in the American ideal and are afraid of demagoguery, which we should always be cognizant of:

Harvard professors Steven Levitsky and Daniel Ziblatt are experts in what makes democracies healthy — and what leads to their collapse. They warn that American democracy is in trouble.

How Democracies Die

By Steve Levitsky and Daniel Ziblatt

Hardcover, 312 pages

In a new book, they argue that Trump has shown authoritarian tendencies and that many players in American politics are discarding long-held norms that have kept our political rivalries in balance and prevented the kind of bitter conflict that can lead to a repressive state...

Well, Stephen Levitsky, Daniel Ziblatt, welcome to FRESH AIR. You know, you write that some democracies die in a hail of gunfire. There's a military coup. The existing leaders are imprisoned or sometimes shot. Not - this is not the kind of death of a democracy that you think is most relevant to our purposes. What's a more typical or meaningful scenario?

STEVEN LEVITSKY: Well, the kind of democratic breakdown that you mentioned was more typical of the Cold War era, of a good part of the 20th century. But military coups, although they occur occasionally today in the world, are much, much less common than they used to be. And, in fact, the primary way in which democracies have died since the end of the Cold War, over the last 30 years or so, is at the hands of elected leaders, at the hands of governments that were often freely or close to freely elected, who then use democratic institutions to weaken or destroy democracy. And we're very hopeful that America's democratic institutions will survive this process. But if we were to fall into some kind of crisis, surely it would take that form.

DAVIES: And it doesn't typically happen the week or month after the elected leader takes power, right? It unfolds gradually.

DANIEL ZIBLATT: Yeah, that's right. I mean, that's one of the things that makes it so difficult, both to study and also as a citizen to recognize what's happening. You know, military coups happen overnight. I mean, they're sudden instances - sudden events. Electoral authoritarians come to power democratically. They often have democratic legitimacy as a result of being elected. And there's a kind of gradual chipping away at democratic institutions, kind of tilting of the playing field to the advantage of the incumbent, so it becomes harder and harder to dislodge the incumbent through democratic means.[145]

Besides the more obvious ways that unworthy power-mongers can upset the system of government, more subtle dangers to existing structure and ability of the institution to function must be watched for and guarded against, as Hal Brands warns, writing for Bloomberg:

The downsides of President Donald Trump's first year in office are legion, but among the most serious has undoubtedly been his effect on American soft power...

Yet, as I argue in my new book, "American Grand Strategy in the Age of Trump," the president's entire first year has represented a veritable assault on American soft power — one that will likely cause damage outlasting Trump's time in office...

...Soft power can easily be overestimated, of course: The country of the Bill of Rights and "all men are created equal" is also the country with a tragic history of slavery and segregation. And the effect of U.S. soft power would be far less if Washington did not possess hard-power dominance. But on the whole, soft power acts as a significant force-multiplier, facilitating cooperation with friends, providing ideological advantages over enemies, and generally enhancing the impact of U.S. policy.

Based on his record so far, however, Trump appears to have little understanding of the benefits soft power can provide. He has repeatedly talked down the power of the American example by arguing that his own country is morally no better than, say, Vladimir Putin's Russia. And during his first year in office, Trump has undermined U.S. soft power in three particular ways.

First, he has sought crippling budget cuts for the institutions that the U.S. government uses to exercise nonmilitary influence overseas... ...it included trims of nearly 30 percent for the State Department and the U.S. Agency for International Development, and therefore entailed drastic reductions in programs focusing on global public health, food security, women's rights, and myriad other issues.

... it would have severely weakened U.S. diplomacy, development aid and humanitarian assistance — all of which the chairman of the Joint Chiefs of Staff, General Joseph Dunford, has deemed critical to achieving a lasting defeat of the Islamic State and other foreign policy objectives. But Trump's disdain for the State Department has still had profound effects: The president of the American Foreign Service Association warned last fall that accomplished diplomats were leaving

the department in droves, taking enormous institutional knowledge with them.

Second, the president has attacked — head-on — the idea that the U.S. should stand for something more than its own self-interest. A year ago, Trump used his inaugural address to frame U.S. foreign policy as a giveaway to an ungrateful world, and to call for a more narrowly nationalistic approach to American statecraft...

...The president has also repeatedly derided America's role as chief promoter of democracy and human rights, thereby undermining the ideological appeal of a nation that stands for universal values. In fact, he has undertaken policies — such as his persistent efforts to restrict immigration and exclude refugees from Muslim-majority nations — that are deemed cruel and discriminatory overseas...

Third, Trump has weakened American soft power through his own behavior. He is hardly the only president to say loathsome things, but he is unique in displaying his unattractive qualities so openly, so unembarrassedly, so repeatedly...

...The real question is how long it will take American soft power to recover once he departs...[146]

The author of this book wrote a message for social media on Jan. 27, 2018 about the how we must fight the greedy elites who through their control of Conservative politics would subdue democratic society and how the threat of the golden temples of power is bringing more progressive-minded people into the fray:

Stormy Yet... Silver-lining Threatens Golden Temples

The days of 2017 have been among the darkest I have known, barring, perhaps, the deaths of some loved ones. Blacker even then when our Constitution and election system were first usurped by the GOP, in

Y2000, for only partisan plans, that was followed soon by the worst terrorist attack on U. S. soil and a duplicitous war. We have weathered anger, anxiety, fear, depression, amongst other blows to our collective psyche, this last year. It might get worse.

That said, I am sure that I am not alone in seeing a silver-lining within the night-tinged, threatening clouds... in that so many of our fellow Americans and—even more spectacular, the radiance—our kindred World Citizens, have come together, are still gathering, in the greatest force of resistance against totalitarians, and would-be authoritarians or oligarchs, ever. Images come to mind of more than four-thousand Allied ships, stuffed like sardine cans with men, munitions, and machinery of war, churning through the choppy waters of the English Channel, to even rougher sailing on the Continent against Hitler's Nazis.

You may scoff at this comparison by one safely attacking only plastic keys at this time. We are headed towards that kind of fascist threat and only now, by peaceful resistance from our super-flotilla of fellow freedom fighters, can we prevent this. Who knows when the secret police will drag us out of our homes for such?

Armed with only hopes, dreams, ideals, vague feelings of what is right and what is wrong, empathy, real knowledge and understanding, and the tempered steel of our wit and words, we write, we march, we sing, we protest, and, we will fight, in whatever way we can, to salvage at least what we have known, for our children, and for even better for theirs. When we have achieved that, true globalization will be that much closer, and a real "world economy," including all of us, will profit.

How long it has taken us, Americans, to see that it is our richest industrialists, corporatists, and market manipulators, and their Conservative cousins abroad, including most recently infected Russia (who is, now, to be feared most due to their recent corporate merger with

American power-mongers) who would defeat world democracy for their preferred oligarchies.

I no longer hope, no, I believe, that the United States of America, with the European Union (including the United Kingdom, I trust) and all looking for and striving for peace, liberty, equality, and justice for all, including health and education, will yet hold that shining beacon of truth and freedom aloft to guide those in the world still adrift, beset by their own storms of oppression and inhumanity. We will, no longer, be enslaved, economically or otherwise, by greedy self-worshippers.

Speaking of the European Union and World Democracy—if that thought pleases you, please read the author's environmental/political thriller, <u>Dream View Two – The Kamikaze Candidate</u>. This story offers dreams of a truly self-governed world of the future, where every vote counts, for every issue, as our archaic representative form of government has been replaced by one of self-representation, thanks to the actions of one of the random reluctant heroes chosen from amongst us. Written in part to protest the fear of a Nazi government aroused by the George W. Bush administration, and his father's, it seems its message is more important, now, with Trump given the keys to the American government.

Please read *Dream View Two – The Kamikaze Candidate*. It can be found at https://books2read.com/u/bwYGvP (e-book).

The wealth elites' hand in America's failure to achieve the idealistic promises of the founders in our charter is nowhere more obvious and damaging than in the South of the Civil War and after. Bad enough that rich landowners so concerned about their profit-margins hoodwinked the commoners of the Southern states to give up everything to protect their wealth. But to continue to wage a not all that clandestine war on the legally freed people of color, after, has effected division to this day, so there is still no peace:

Historians describe white Southerners' varied responses to emancipation and the issue of civil rights, and describe the thinking that gave rise to white supremacist groups like the Ku Klux Klan during Reconstruction.

How did Southern resistance to black freedom play out after the Civil War?

Drew Gilpin Faust: *Mary Lee of Winchester [Virginia] says at the end of the war, "Political reconstruction is inevitable now, but social reconstruction, we have in our hands and we can prevent." And I think that's such an extraordinary insight on her part, and so predictive of much of what happens in the months and years that follow her remark. I think what she means is that Congress is going to do certain things, but there's almost a kind of guerrilla warfare of the domestic, of the local, of people just refusing to let society change in the ways that the architects of freedom in the North might hope for, in the ways that the slaves, the freed slaves, might themselves within the South hope for.*

[Southerners] have all kinds of ways of drawing lines and resisting the egalitarian impulses of freedom, the assumptions of the former slaves, just setting up roadblocks... in every way they can imagine, to change in their society. And in some ways one might say the South succeeded in this, and the women of the South succeeded in this, well into the 20th century, and with inventing new kinds of ways of limiting freedom, and then of course the legal ways that the South itself finds to change the nature of freedom in society, to resist the changes implicit in emancipation.[147]

Risking the threat of being labeled a conspiracy-theorist as a means of discrediting voices interested in pursuing the truth, let us compare violent acts against the democratic functioning of the United States of America. Because he sees wicked people plotting against this country, even beginning to come out from behind the curtains, this writer chose to examine this and originally share on Feb. 16, 2018:

Correlations of U. S. History

There is no question that those who colluded, conspired, or, assisted, in one or more of a number of ways, to cancel regional majorities, i.e., the popular vote, to silence the voice of the American majority in the 2016 Presidential elections, and any others, are guilty of conspiracy against not only the U.S. government, but its citizens. Closest known precedence, in U.S. history, was Confederate actors or agents working together to assassinate Pres. Lincoln.

It is not a stretch to conclude that these two attacks on American government came as a direct result of a lifting up of black persons. The emancipation of slaves and the popular placing of Barack and Michelle Obama in the White House.

Possibly, we can also include conspiracy to assassinate John F. Kennedy and Robert F. Kennedy, in opposition to the civil-rights movement, as other examples of such correlative events.

Brave voices are speaking up against the evils seen being perpetuated by the GOP and their Supreme Leader, but due to the politicizing, even to being an official Party publication, of mainstream media one is not exposed to them except by personal desire. Thanks to Richard A. Arenberg for sounding the alarm in Newsmax:

Children are taken from the arms of their parents at the U.S. border. The Prime Minister of Canada is called "very dishonest and weak," while the brutal North Korean dictator is described as "talented" and "honorable. The American free press is declared "the enemy of the people." The investigation being conducted by a special counsel with the Department of Justice into the interference in the U.S. elections by Russia and culpability of the Trump campaign is repeatedly derided as a "witch hunt" and accused of being an effort to "frame" the president.

264

And a seemingly endless list of unprecedented, chaotic, impulsive, and outrageous acts is carried out by the president and his administration.

And still, the Republican Congress stands silent.

Enough is enough.

Where is the great tradition of the U.S. Senate and its oversight of the executive branch? Where are the voices of conscience?[148]

Late to reading Mr. Arenberg's provocative public service announcement, above, the author of this book was motivated to shout his sentiments, about the danger we are in, to whomever had ears to hear on Aug. 18, 2018:

Hail, Mary

Anybody else notice that the GOP seems to be holding back, waiting, holding their breath, keeping their mouths shut, relatively? They know they should take action against Trump, even if only, in their eyes, it might help them in the polls, if not this year then maybe 2020. They seem to be hoping, as terrible as it seems to most of us, that they can steal this election, a midterm, no matter what it takes, so are ignoring their constituents, the Constitution, their conscience, to go for the "Hail Mary," total corruption of the entire system of checks and balances, so maintaining their illicit control, so they can continue doing whatever they want without repercussions. Stacking the Supreme Court to make it a Fundamental force, perhaps forever, for instance.

The correlation of the Southern insurrection to save slavery to our current political situation was noticed by James DiEugenio and he expertly exposes this long situation that has seriously and adversely hurt American Democracy due to our leaders' and our news agencies' centuries policy of not only remaining silent but too often twisting the truth:

Approximately five years ago, at the fiftieth anniversary of President Kennedy's death, I reviewed Larry Sabato's book, The Kennedy Half Century. In that review, I wrote about something that I had not really noted before in book form. One expects an MSM shill like Sabato not to recognize any of Kennedy's clear alterations to President Eisenhower's foreign policy: e.g., in the Congo, or with the Alliance for Progress. That would be par for the course. But Sabato did something that I had not really observed before. At length, the author tried to revise downward Kennedy's record on civil rights. This was disturbing, since Kennedy's record on that issue was far superior to not just Eisenhower's, but to all the presidents who had preceded him—both during and after Reconstruction. In my review of Sabato, I showed how silly this was by spending a few pages countering the obtuse arguments he had made (see section three of this review).

At the end, I noted that this weird spin indicated once more that it was not enough for the MSM to deny the true facts of Kennedy's murder. There was a concomitant effort to discount his achievements in the White House.[149]

President Kennedy's work towards furthering civil rights was not only above and beyond any previous president, but, in some eyes, in direct opposition to Conservative wishes, which included not only the Republicans of the time but even more so, the Southern Democrats, leftovers from the Party of the slave holders. In later decades these Southern Conservatives became one with the Republican Party, which was no longer the Party of Lincoln:

As the reader can see, no president before Kennedy ever confronted the civil rights issue as he did. No one was even close. It was the preceding century of near inertia that created the immense problem that President Kennedy faced in 1961. But to his credit, Kennedy pressed the issue from the outset. Finally, the pressure from his administration, and the inspiration and support he gave the civil rights movement, provided the opportunity to pass what Clay Risen has called the "bill of the century". What JFK achieved in three years is remarkable, especially when compared to his predecessors. As historian Carl Brauer wrote, what President Kennedy did was to pick up the narrow trail that Truman attempted and widen it into broad avenues. (Brauer, p. 315) And those avenues are still being traversed today. Yesterday (November 2, 2018), Kristen Clarke, the president of the Committee for Civil Rights Under Law, announced a victory for the Democrats in Georgia. Agreeing with Clarke, the court made a ruling weakening the state's attempt to limit voting among the poor and minority groups. Clarke's activist committee was founded in 1963 by President Kennedy for the express purpose of counteracting attempts at discrimination in the Deep South.[150]

Part four of Mr. DiEugenio's cited essay reveals that Lyndon Johnson, as president after JFK's assassination, had planned a "War on Poverty":

In the final part of this essay, Jim turns to the "War on Poverty," showing how the Kennedys, with David Hackett in the lead, were planning that program before JFK's civil rights bill was passed, and how, once Johnson took office, it was altered from its original intent and handed over to local authorities who hijacked it.

As Harrington said of RFK, "As I look back on the sixties, he was the man who actually could have changed the course of American history." (Wofford, p. 420)

Journalist Pete Hammill wrote RFK before the presidential race of 1968:

I wanted to remind you that in Watts, I didn't see pictures of Malcolm X or Ron Karenga on the walls. I saw pictures of JFK. That is your capital in the most cynical sense. It is your obligation in another, the obligation of staying true to whatever it was that put those pictures on those walls. (Schmitt, p. 221)

As Brenda Luckett, one of the young African Americans Bobby Kennedy saw in the impoverished Mississippi delta in 1967, said after his death, "We felt like Kennedy was purged. He should have gotten out. It's like we knew they were going to kill him for helping black people." (Meacham, chapter 12)

Charles Evers, brother of the murdered Medgar, said of him, "Mr. Kennedy did more to help us get our rights as first class citizens than all of the other US attorney generals put together." (Arthur Schlesinger, A Thousand Days, p. 976)

But this sentiment had been previewed several years earlier. During the Freedom Riders' episode, when King arrived in Montgomery, the citizens rallied to him and realized that something new was afoot. One youth said, "President Kennedy is on our side." A woman said, "Bless God! We now have a president who's going to make sure we can go anywhere we want like the white folks in this country." (Brauer, p. 103)
[151]

That Johnson handed that over to the individual states smacks much of Rutherford B. Haye's betrayal of Lincoln's planned "Reconstruction," by pulling Federal power that would have better ensured success.

James DiEugenio's essay, "The Kennedys and Civil Rights How the MSM Continues to Distort History," excerpted above, should be required reading for every primary school student, and, "The History of Race Relations in America," a mandatory course. To a student of American history, the revelation that Charles Houston's role in the birth of the civil rights movement is almost unheard of, is shocking, as well as the whitewashing of America's major "Reconstruction" failure which led to Jim Crow laws and the defeat of former slaves and their families from continuing their initial successes, from prospering and attaining political power.

Conservative state governments preventing factual history from being taught and censoring or banning books is continuing in America. This reminds this writer that even in Switzerland, the Conservatives prevent the truth from being taught about the Swiss Peasant Revolt of 1653 and the unjust executions of many including the popular leader, Niklaus Leuenberger, mentioned in earlier chapters. What Conservatives fear most is "Factism," submitting to a "Factist" state. What the Left fears from them is spelled only slightly differently.

This citizen felt impelled to share his own feelings on this subject, the Civil War having turned into a war on civil rights, on July 16, 2019:

Confederate & Neo-Con Fantasy

The so-called heritage some think that the "Stars and Bars," or Confederate flag, represents is families that have followed, and still follow, the greedy and hateful whims of the Conservative rich. These Southern power moguls got many of their followers' male ancestral relations killed or maimed in a war that would have benefited only these wealthiest few, if successful. Southern wealth wranglers still use every deceit in the books to profit from each and every one of us, either by underpaying, overcharging, lying, stealing, or, probably, all of the above, ensuring that alternatives to a slave-workforce, i.e., schemes for gaining labor at the lowest overhead they can get away with, thanks to political allies, still exists. That includes too many, if not most, Americans, many of my family among them, and, certainly, counting their Southern base, their too long ignorantly willing minions.

By the mid-nineteenth century, the African-slave workforce was a "buffer" that allowed the plantation owners to maintain the illusion that those citizens living in some sort of comfort, even near poverty, were somehow part of a white, superior class. They certainly weren't, then, nor are, now. The middle-class who created a golden age for America a half-century ago, the grapes destined for fine effervescent wines, are, now, withered up into raisins, that, mixed with dry heels of bread, may provide jailhouse hooch. If that is the "heritage" you wish to claim, you are not as smart as the slave work force that was maintained by threat of violence and physical punishment. They knew what to do, which side to throw in with, when the war finally gave them the opportunity, and how to prosper with their newfound freedom, after the war. The premature end to "Reconstruction" allowed the evil men behind Jim Crow laws to take away opportunity and the right to opportunity and force oppression back onto people only too recently removed from it.

That war continues, to this day, because too many still cling to a deception that never provided benefit to them, and never will, because it was never true. If you still want to put the descendant enslavers in power, you, and your children, and grandchildren, should be ready to continue to work long and hard for little gain, and great debt, while the wealthy, and their continuing "entitled" generations, use every dirty trick in the book to utilize their wealth and power to maintain their inherited "grandeur," i.e., semblance of royalty, by keeping the rest of us suffering in serfdom. If your forebears had fought as hard to prevent an oligarchy from taking over a country, to extend their position over those less-fortunate, as they did trying to rescue their fantasy, your "heritage" would not require an iconic instrument of illusion to bolster the belief that the Confederate "cause" was a righteous one.

It appears to this writer that it is predominately Southern Conservative politicians that like to play loose with rules and laws of parliamentarism, even ignoring the Constitution where they have a majority to cover their backsides. Oliver Willis describes Sarah Sanders' ugly baring it all in *THE AMERICAN INDEPENDENT*:

Sarah Sanders bragged on Fox News that when Republicans held the majority in the House of Representatives, they ignored Trump's crimes, unethical behavior, and other misdeeds to boost their own "success."

Sanders appeared on "Fox & Friends" (Trump's favorite Fox show) on Wednesday morning to discuss the recent flurry of document requests issued by the House Judiciary Committee, chaired by Rep. Jerry Nadler (D-CA), to kick off a massive investigation into Trump.

"Jerry Nadler said that the reason they had to do it is for the first two years of the administration, Sarah, there was no oversight," Host Steve Doocy said.

"What Chairman Nadler is missing is, is that the first two years were not about oversight, they were about success," Sanders replied.

It's stunning that Sanders would admit this — that Republicans just didn't care about performing the constitutionally mandated oversight duties of Congress, and that they were more worried about their own "success" as a party than about holding their leader accountable.

For over two years, Republicans in Congress, led by then-Speaker Paul Ryan and Senate Majority Mitch McConnell, refused to follow the Constitution and exercise oversight of the executive branch, instead choosing to focus time and resources on pointless topics like Hillary Clinton's emails.[152]

Progressive congress members tried to hold Trump accountable via impeachment procedures, but his partisan majority save his ass from indictment, both times. Although it seemed our democracy had won a respite by electing Joe Biden, a Progressive candidate to the Presidency, this still-seething citizen wanted action to ensure that our system of checks and balances would be restored when he wrote the following on Feb. 25, 2020:

Partisan Sabotage, Our Failure

A President, as a CEO, depends on their corporate officers (meaning, elected Congress persons), and, to lesser degree(?)—employees in general (read, electorate) to successfully accomplish their plans to lead company (read, country) to prosperity. If corrupt, inadequate CEO (meaning, of course, President) is somehow put in office, especially against the wishes of the majority, putting company in dire straits of bankruptcy or hostile takeover, e.g., then they should be replaced as soon as possible, by whatever corporate rules and laws (read, Constitutional law) apply.

If CEO's (President's) moral/legal plans for moving corporation (country) ahead are stymied or endangered by managers (legislators) hired to, ideally, implement the plans the stockholders (voters) put CEO (President) in office to accomplish, they should be removed/fired (voted out).

This is how successful organizations are supposed to work. If corporate officers', i.e., legislators', only goal is to shoot the Executive in the foot, cause them to fail, the company (country) can never realize the leader's planned successes. This failure needs to be put on them, not the leader whose attempts are willfully stymied.

Of course, again, read above, this assumes a "CEO's (President's) moral/safe/legal plans," if legislators, via their constituency, see things differently, good faith negotiations to iron out the issues should be made.

This is how our country should work, support mentally and ethically balanced Executive for their entire term. If their fully-supported plans don't work, replace them and give another qualified person a chance. If a President's plans are sabotaged by legislators not working in the interests of the electorate through their legitimately-elected Executive, fire them.

Political positioning through postering and punditry is part of the process of gaining popularity, to win at the polls. It's a new world, now. The printing press helped create great changes in Europe, as more and more people became more informed and more voices could be heard. So it is with the world-wide web, the internet, social media, etc.; but now, as then, it can be a double-edged sword without everyone having the ability, or desire, to distinguish facts from fiction, real documents from dogma, is necessary for the enlightenment of each rather than their deception. The positive or negative utility of what should be a reliable resource, depends on user choices. A Kim P., writing for Credit Donkey, has a view on this:

TECHNOLOGY HAS ITS BAD SIDES

What are the side effects of technology?

Technology has its positives, but the negatives must be understood too. In a world of instant gratification and continual distractions, technology has the ability to make users easily distracted, impatient, and continually bored. Technology can also make users forget important information, communicate in shorthand, and be incapable of deep thinking.

NEGATIVE EFFECTS OF TECHNOLOGY ON COMMUNICATION

Does technology affect communication?

Technology makes communication faster and more convenient. However, it can also depersonalize conversations and make bullying a much easier task when you don't have to divulge your real identity. Many people end up replacing face-to-face contact with contact via messengers or texting. This can cause isolation and may lead to other mental health disorders, such as anxiety and depression. Can technology decrease communication and intimacy in a relationship? Technology can even be a problem in committed relationships. In a Pew Research study, 25% of married couples admitted that they text one another while home at the same time. Another 25% of those surveyed admitted that they felt technology distracted their partner from giving them the attention they need.[153]

The Knowledge Review provided an article by Prof. Chetan R. Bhamare describing another way the ideal of the usefulness of internet communications is precluded by its ironic potential to damage our ability to communicate:

Social Media is described as the collection of online communication channels dedicated to community based input, interaction, content sharing and collaboration. Some of the commonly known communication websites are Facebook, Twitter, Instagram, and Pinterest. With the help of this websites people can share memories, reconnect with friends, plan events, and communicate almost instantaneously. The social media has positive as well as negative impacts on communication skills.

Social networks have become the central facilitator for daily communication with peers, family and acquaintances. It is affecting our relationships and decreases the quality of inter-personal communication. Another impairment of communication skills, caused by the extensive use of social media platform is the impoverishment of language. Using messengers' people often use shortened versions of words in order to type and deliver their messages as quickly as possible. Shortened versions like "k", "ttyl", "ur", "der", "gr8","cu","tc" and so on, completely ruins the grammar and syntax. It also develops the use of slang terms and sometimes people tend to forget that they are neglecting the beauty of language when they are online busy with the social media. [154]

Besides the fear of language degradation, there is a question of how the quantity and quality of communication provided by the internet and social media improves our ability to see eye to eye or increases the stepping on of each other's toes. Peter Suciu, writing for *Forbes*, objectively looks at the subjective discourse online:

Social media could be one of the factors that has also contributed to the political rift in our country.

"Social media is a contributing factor to the political divide in our country," explained Dr. Nathaniel Ivers, the department chairman and associate professor in the Department of Counseling at Wake Forest University. "It is hard to know, however, if social media is helping to widen the rift or make salient how deep and broad the divide already is."

One of the factors is that social media companies might not be doing enough to stop the spread of fake news and misinformation.

"With social media, individuals with particular political persuasions seem to "follow" or "friend" individuals on social media who share similar viewpoints," added Ivers. "The difference, however, is that many social media platforms do not appear to filter content based on the

accuracy of the information. Therefore, individuals, groups and even foreign governments can propagate ideas and information; even when such ideas have little to no basis in reality. It seems to me that the goal of those disseminating political information on social media and through some news outlets has devolved into how much they can make the other side seem inconsistent, disingenuous, or absurd, rather than to provide accurate details about events."[155]

Tangential brain-teaser or disgruntled digression ahead.

What role is the degeneration or weaponization of personal communications playing in our apparent slide into democratic oblivion? Please allow this writer, in closing this review of our Conservative Crisis (is it a Constitutional Crisis—if the Conservatives in power would abide by the Constitution, we would not have this problem?), to explore our lost civility or ability for civil discourse.

Politics aside, except for the possible contribution to our political downslide, are our language arts languishing through laziness or impatience? Is the need for speed our Achille's heel? Can we expedite every cerebral endeavor without losing at least the flavor of personal expression and not only the quintessential query, response, or thought, but the very substance of our messages?

Remember when politicians were more prone to leaning on the fence, conversing across it, and, more frequently, reaching over it and shaking hands on an agreement? How can we learn to voice opinions without open hostility, again? Was that ever a reality? Or, can it be? Is this a failure of education, condensed as it has become in the interest of the corporate charter—"better, faster, cheaper"? Is faster and cheaper ever better? This writer does not think so, as he adds his thoughts to the collective community discourse on the ill-effects of cyberspace communications on language skills in his essay of Feb. 29, 2020:

WTF C21 LOL AYOR

Is there a collective, a community, that feels the dearth of descriptive passage is part of a perilous path to an impending doomsday? In the context of current events and turbulence, is the digital age of personal communications, from texting to social media, dispelling language arts? Is the beauty of great word wending and wafting, doomed to Dodo bird extinction except for a few keepers of the literary tradition, e.g., as in Ray Bradbury's 1953 classic, Fahrenheit 451? His "Drifters" strove to stay the demise of written works of art by committing them to memory, in an almost prophetic symbolic vision of the coming digital age, where most works are committed to one type of "memory" or another, too often with the literal life crushed out of them, too abbreviated to be memorable, lol. One perceives a contemporary script entitled "Characters, 280".

Not only are books, and bookstores, disappearing into clouds of ones and zeros, stored in ethereal memory, but our language, also, is becoming so atrophied that there's a sense that it's "morphing" into a limbless entity, simple guttural exchanges and symbols much like those used by paleolithic people. Yes, books are "readily" available to download and read on any one of a diverse choice of electronic viewers, but at what cost, not only to readers and writers, but to the monumental nature of great literature, and, possibly, posterity? A realization that the renaissance is truly past and we are heading into a new dark age will not rest.

A real burning of the literary arts could be fueled by the desire for faster and faster communications, one result, shorter and quicker, or absent, syntax. Hardcopy books becoming bits of light equates to the shrinking to obscurity of the canvas on which literary art has been ever expressed—from symbolic figures on stone walls of caves to the folio of *the Elizabethan wielder of an ink-dipped spear and on and on until the mind piercing publications of the 20th century (C20).*

Abbreviated words and phrases, alphabetic slang and jargon, limited characters, are becoming the mean medium of dialogue, quick and convenient communication, leading to the eradication of the artistic arsenal, symbolic pallet of writing, the virtual paint, chalk, colored pencils, or crayons of creative or well-crafted writing. These elements bring physical, chromatic, and aural vibrancy to the mind from the black and white of written details and descriptions. They are the aesthetic tools of poetry, prose, and song—how long before they disappear from the aged eyes of humanity? A decline of vision not from cataracts, glaucoma, or macular degeneration, but via whims to appease the chronometric craziness of the computer age—reaching climax sans shared approach—mindless orgasm without mindful foreplay—the destination neglecting the joys and jars of the journey. Graphic go-go gratification that requires little to no cerebral effort is the greatest that can be expected, now?

Is digital media to blame for the fading art of written communication or is it due to the earlier electronic revolution where context was reduced to fit a certain time slot for radio, movies, or television? Perhaps the uprooting of words and wordsmithing was preceded by writing becoming redundant in the 19th century (19C) with the newfound ability to replicate sound, giving humans the ability to record and share messages sans the written word.

Fast forward to the 21st century (21C), a new millennium where readers nibble on abbreviated words, MSG FYI IMHO LOL, sip on text of thin alphabetic broth as opposed to nourishing themselves by enjoying a bowl of a wholesome stew of sweet and savory ingredients served with a thick slice of freshly baked, hot, and buttered bread with its aroma rising from the page... diminished characters rather than a *fully seen and felt someone or something, for better or worse... someone rapping hundreds of words per minute to get a rhyming concept across in record time versus a musical note-crafting balladeer evoking crystalline bleeding from needles to the heart. Are the favored modes of thought sharing, today, becoming the scattered skeletal remains of our storied past? Does the disheveled state of human civility and politics have a direct correlation with the disintegration of our language skills? Are they on parallel tracks to oblivion?*

Perhaps the druids, those bards responsible for the teaching and sharing of knowledge via rhyme and rote realized that mnemonic brevity was the only way to immediately influence, persuade, and, ideally, teach and enlighten the early Celtics of varying intelligence and attention spans who, otherwise, had only the education and limited time resources that their harsh life supplied in their struggles to survive, in much more mortal days.

Did the Holy Roman Empire find that their assignment to eradicate "pagan" learning was that much easier because Druidic knowledge was recorded, written, in only very limited fashion and the poor Legionaries were spared the weeding out of hidden libraries and scripted stashes? Killing the teachers was all that was required, though harder than they imagined. Similar to their predecessors, the fraternity of the Dead Sea Scrolls, the Essenes, druids or their protégés entered fraternal orders of monks (perhaps as moles?) and utilized the writing and language skills they learned in this role to record what little Druidic knowledge has survived.

Punish those that dare repeat the verboten ideas until the old knowledge is dead and the only things people can know is that which the State's instructors will teach. Will information saved as digital data in the so-called "cloud" be as easily destroyed as the cerebral and ogham saved knowledge of the Druidic Celts, rather than robust reams and racks of solid story and history telling preserving the word at least as well as Essenes' scrolls in clay jars? Is a new monk-like institution in order, brothers and sisters banded together to preserve the language art "de la plume'?

The sooner the better. May we enlist more empathetic extra-literal people to ensure more XXXOOO, to preclude being— 01000110 01010101 01000011 01001011 01000101 01000100—in the end.

Chapter 6 - Reforging the American Dream

Where is equal opportunity, justice, and liberty for all? Will we be able to sow seeds, reach fruition, and reap the benefits from a myriad of possibilities due to a fair, effective, and caring government? Have we ignored our responsibilities as citizens and allowed democracy to wither and fade and allowed weeds of willful greed and animosity to choke our freedom and take over the paradise our ancestors perceived?

We must find the way to help our society not only survive, but thrive, and produce great things. The author believes we were almost there, once, in the 1950's and 1960's, when the top income tax rate was 91% for those making the most billions of dollars, and we were making strides, albeit painful ones, toward civil rights. We had better schools, better bridges and roads, better postal system, and people could better afford a trip to the doctor without a myriad of payments to a multitude of middlemen.

When the Party of Lincoln became the Party of the Wealthy, the GOP began its slide towards the chasm on the extreme Right. Catering to the rich, the wealthiest began paying less and less in taxes while our infrastructure has slowly crumbled away. People have been getting relatively poorer, children receiving poorer quality education, medical costs have skyrocketed. Underpaid people are suffering from predatory credit and lending practices (it costs a lot more to be poor), more, ever since. Will we ever be able to afford an infrastructure able to build the bridge(s) to span that gulf?

In chapter 5, and his article "Niklaus Leuenberger, Predating Gandhi in 1653?" published in the February 2020 issue of the Swiss American Historical Society Review, Dr. H. Leuenberger presents some of Prigogine and Stengers' ideas from their book, "Order out of Chaos." They show that laws of nature dictate that human constructed inorganic systems will age, become degraded, until entropy is such that chaotic failure ensues, similar to organic entities. Some say governments' eventual failure are an example of this.

Two of the possible reasons behind system failure, seem to be design flaw and operator error. In America's case, we should blame inherent operator error. America's design may have been immaculate, but its exercise was skewed from day one. Others will claim the design was failed, as well, too ambiguous—too many times. Perhaps, then, Shakespeare saw this coming, "Fair is foul, and foul is fair."

Holding up an ideal of equality as your charter while hypocritically forcing subservience on others, via violence and penalty of death, wicked tools still being wielded to this day, has hastened a failure of the American system. No one is free of these risks if any are not. The domination of humans by humans is the greatest threat, today, followed closely by the correlated failure of the global environmental system.

Until "all men, regardless of race, creed, or color, are treated equally, are empowered to achieve their legally ordained rights including life, liberty, and an unencumbered ability to strive for personal happiness[1]," the States will be disabled from "forming a more perfect Union, establish Justice, ensure domestic tranquility, provide for the common defense, promote the general Welfare, and secure the Blessings of Liberty to ourselves and our Posterity..."[2].

[1] from the Declaration of Independence preamble.

[2] as stated in the Preamble to the U. S. Constitution.

The People Will Grow On

The plants are sick but not ready for the mulch heap, yet. Here is how we tend our garden and keep it growing for the future generations.

Citizens' responsibilities

Education.

Ignorance is ally, tool, weapon of those who would oppress us, and has been since there has been knowledge to use to one's advantage or exclude from others to preclude their becoming a threat, to maintain an advantage over them. Too many forego the acquisition of knowledge, cerebral improvement, for more immediate pleasures such as entertainment and physical gratifications at an ever earlier age. The need or desire for acquisition of income and material goods have too often precluded the attainment of education, even though this usually allows one to achieve greater personal financial security. More importantly, probably, those with a superior information base are less likely to let an unqualified or unethical person gain a position of leadership over them, a conman swindle them, or a salesman sell them a "lemon."

Return of higher wealth taxes will allow us to rebuild our educational system. More teachers, resources, and greater curriculum can help us create a better educated citizenry. This, in turn, will not only give us more knowledgeable workers, higher income base to help the economy—helping to create more jobs—but help the electorate make better political choices ('Fool me once...').

Be Informed and Active Participants in Politics

Registering to Vote and Voting

America has a big problem, Apathy, that's right, with a capital "A." It's been a recognized problem for over half a century, at least, demonstrated by the iconic character of counter-culture humor periodical, Mad magazine, the symbolic poster boy of apathy, Alfred E. Neuman, with his signature phrase, "What, me worry?" since the 1950's. With our low voter turnout, is America still a democracy?

Derek Beres points out with an article found in Big Think, that in his book, In Upheaval, Jared Diamond reveal the sad facts of American voter turnout:

Diamond writes that a democracy in which citizens can't or don't vote is not worthy of the name. By those standards, America "is barely half-deserving of being called a democracy." He points to Los Angeles as an example: in 2017, only 20 percent of eligible Angelenos turned out to elect the current mayor. That lack of civic engagement in one of America's largest cities is inexcusable.

Yet the rest of the country isn't much more engaged. Diamond compares America to the rest of the "affluent democracies," using three measures: residents old enough to vote that did vote; the percentage of eligible voters that voted; and the percentage of registered voters that voted. America comes in last every single time.[156]

America hasn't had nearly enough politically-active members of her greatest and most important asset, people, in a long while. This is just one reason why our country is having a Constitutional crisis, now. It is not the only reason, but it is a powerful enough reason that it might just overcome the others, in our election process. Are we lazy? Is it too hard to vote? Is school and work attendance so worrisome that you can't afford to take the time to go to your polling station?

We need to make it less inconvenient to vote, yet certain areas are making it harder to vote, at least for the working class. That these areas are typically Red, conservative, creates suspicion of voter suppression or disenfranchisement. The suggestion to make election days a holiday has some merit, but taking polling stations and voting booths away from certain places has made it next to impossible for everyone in those districts to vote, even so. We do need to make voting more accessible and less apt to cause a loss of pay, reprimand, suspension, or termination of one's job for taking the time, in some location hours of standing in line under whatever conditions. Then, there is the problem of election integrity.

A simple solution, copy the voting practices of states that have been using 100% mail in ballots for many years, successfully. Especially under the current reality of deadly pandemic risks, it should not even be a question, but a, "let's get her done." Can it only happen in dreamland, where every elected official gives their voters' wishes their highest regard? But, on the other hand, it is the voters that put their "non" representatives in office. Read the former section on education, again, if you must. Between ill-informed choices and low voter participation we have arrived where we are today. If we don't care who represents us, they won't care how they represent us.

Finding and Absorbing Objective News

The previous section reminds that the best voter is an informed voter. Life is not all about amusement. If Americans were half as interested in the machinery that is most instrumental in the condition of their life, i.e., the government, rather than on those things that most entertain them, they would pay more attention. "Keep your eyes on the ball".

One of the biggest problems as the ship of state is drawn closer and closer towards the yawning whirlpool on the right is realizing the "factuality" of the news. More and more media are designed to bring the viewer to foredrawn conclusions, dependent thinkers are most susceptible to this. When news programs are broadcasting partisan propaganda, attempting to program the masses, fascism is frightfully near.

More work is necessary for discerning news consumers, which, we must be to stay accurately informed. We must be willing to put in the effort to determine what is real, objective news, i.e., those that offer facts to let independent thinkers come to their own conclusions.

Volunteer in Political Action Groups and Elections

Be involved, politically, know who is running and what is going on. Volunteering will help you learn about and support your candidate, your party, particular issues, and become more knowledgeable in the political arena. Maybe this will entice and enable you to become even more involved.

Please excuse the seeming misogyny in the following article found on the internet site—*Career, Career and Wealth* and add preferred pronouns as necessary to get past those points to learn what should work for every person in becoming involved in politics:

The most direct way to get involved in politics is to run for office yourself, but you don't have to go all-in to make a difference. There are a wide range of opportunities to participate in the democratic process, and along the way you will sharpen your own beliefs, strengthen your connection with your community, and make friendships forged in common values and shared experiences. I've met some of my best friends while working on campaigns, and I hope your journey can be just as rewarding.

If you have never volunteered for a campaign before, gotten involved with a political party, or helped facilitate an election, this is your call to action, and your guide to getting started. If you are already active in politics, you may find a new way to broaden your experiences and take on a larger role in your community.[157]

Communicating with your Governmental Representatives

Representatives can best serve their electorate's needs and desires when they know what those are and how loud (how many) those voices are. Often politicians use polls to determine the general sentiments of voters in their region, but those are too often hit or miss (not necessarily representing reality for lack of a proper sampling or bias of the pollsters).

The best way to get one's representative to represent them is to actively represent yourself, to them. There are a number of ways to do this, e.g., official .gov websites.

For U.S. House Representatives:

https://www.house.gov/representatives/find-your-representative

Your U.S. Senator:

https://www.senate.gov/senators/index.htm

These sites will give you links to email, maybe text, or telephone numbers for your government officials, and even physical addresses for those of us who still appreciate, or have the time, to thoughtfully express oneself on paper. The President's and your state and local politicians' contact information can be found here:

https://www.usa.gov/elected-officials/

The best way to communicate with your elected officials: see your representatives, or the incumbent's opponent for the sake of objectivity, in person, at planned public appearances such as Town Halls. AARP probably offers even better tips in "Six Ways to Check Out a Candidate":

Don't be shy about asking politicians the hard questions.

As the campaign season heats up, voters will be bombarded with information from candidates, from television ads to literature in the mail to social media posts and tweets. Here are six ways you can cut through the clutter and help yourself to become an informed voter:[158]

Pursue quality candidates, or run yourself if the choices don't suit you. Website *Green Party US* offers some good point:

What are your goals for running candidates

• *Winning local office*

• *Running an ideological or educational campaign to build party presence*

• *Ballot access*

• *Challenging an incumbent*

• *Raise important issues, get into the political debate*[159]

However, in the interest of objectivity, here is what the GOP has to say on the subject:

What sort of individuals do you want running for office? Egotistical, self-important politicians or capable humble public servants? You would probably prefer the humble public servant, but these are exactly the sort of people who don't think of themselves as candidates.

If you want better public officials for your local community then you must RECRUIT THEM.[160]

Sociopaths or empaths? Your call. Does the latter even exist among members of the new Conservative Party?

Quality Candidate Looking Back in the Mirror?

Finding too many faults in those attempting to climb the political ladder? Incumbents representing self and corporate interest more than they are the average voters? Are qualified or otherwise desirable candidates scarce or non-committal? Perhaps that person in your steam-clouded morning viewing-monitor is more clear-eyed than first supposed. Put yourself in a position to achieve those things you believe most people think are important for the community, city, county, state, or country. America needs more people like you.

Here's interesting instructions in article "How to Run for Political Office in 2019" on website *Candidate Boot Camp* to help you consider this step, or attempt it:

So, you think you want to run for political office? Congratulations! Our job is to make it easier for you. That's why we've created this comprehensive page to show you how to run for state or local office.

Here are the basic steps we'll cover:

- *Considering a Run for Office?*

- *Political Campaign Structure and Organization*

- *Exploratory Phase*

- *Pre-announcement Steps*

- *Announcement Day*

- *Campaign Strategy, Priorities, and Tactics For Growing Support*

- *The Day After Election*[161]

Good luck to all interested in government by the people, you have the author's vote.

Restore Integrity of Elections

A bought politician is not working for the people nor is a candidate willing to gain office by ulterior methods such as gerrymandering, disenfranchising voters (prohibiting people's vote), misusing digital voting machines, or any other unethical or illegal methods of artificially swinging the vote.

Corporate, mega-billionaires, and foreign interests, including adversarial countries, can put untold amounts of money into American elections to swing results towards their capital interests, gain control over our government by putting a "mole," so to speak, in office, or hide illicitly-gained (launder) money in the "purchase" of a candidate.

A valid take on this is offered by Fred Wertheimer on Legalized Bribery on *Politico*:

Four years on, Citizens United is ruining democracy. Here's how to get it back.

...the U.S. Supreme Court changed the landscape of American politics—and in ways we have yet to understand fully. In its 5-to-4 decision in Citizens United v. FEC, the court struck down the longstanding ban on corporate expenditures in federal elections, a move

that reversed its position on how corporate money enters the political system and created new avenues for corrupting our government.

Today individual Americans are allowed to contribute only $2,600 per election to a federal candidate. Corporations, for their part, are prohibited from giving money directly to office-seekers. The Supreme Court didn't change those facts, but its ruling made them far less relevant. The decision opened the door for anybody—individuals, corporations, interests groups—to give unlimited contributions to groups that then do the spending to influence federal elections. In effect, the donors and candidates are now allowed to circumvent the contribution limits.[162]

America has a critical need to overturn Citizen's United and restore our Voting Rights Act. The Brennan Center for Justice has a simple description in this excerpt from their article:

Citizen's United

January 21, 2020 will mark a decade since the Supreme Court's ruling in Citizens United v. Federal Election Commission, a controversial decision that reversed century-old campaign finance restrictions and enabled corporations and other outside groups to spend unlimited funds on elections.

While wealthy donors, corporations, and special interest groups have long had an outsized influence in elections, that sway has dramatically expanded since the Citizens United decision, with negative repercussions for American democracy and the fight against political corruption.[163]

Voting Rights Act

Voting Rights Act, U.S. legislation (August 6, 1965) that aimed to overcome legal barriers at the state and local levels that prevented African Americans from exercising their right to vote under the Fifteenth Amendment (1870) to the Constitution of the United States. The act significantly widened the franchise and is considered among the most far-reaching pieces of civil rights legislation in U.S. history.

A Right-bending Supreme Court overturned the Voting Rights Act in 2013. The GOP has turned to unheard of dirty tricks to stack the Supreme Court in their partisan favor. This law, enacted in 1965, was considered by many to be the high point of the civil rights movement, then. A Black man in the White House sent Right-wing politics into a conniption fit, and we've seen plenty of those, since, every time the Democrats try to force them to be transparent, to tell the truth. Their tooled SCOTUS overturned the VRA of 1965 by a single vote, on purely partisan lines. This was 1] a slap in the face for putting a Black man in the highest office, and, 2] insurance to make sure it won't happen again. We must restore the Voting Rights Act, as Brennan Center for Justice informs:

The VRA worked. Over the next five decades, it blocked scores of restrictive measures that would have harmed voters and dramatically improved minority voter registration and participation.

Preclearance was critical. Between 1999 and 2005, for example, more than 250 discriminatory voting changes, many at the local level, were withdrawn or altered because of the Voting Rights Act, and the Department of Justice blocked 17 changes to election laws in 2012 alone.

Then, in June 2013, the Supreme Court gutted a core provision of the Act in its 5-4 Shelby County v. Holder *decision.*[164]

Work With Passion, Control Debt, Pay Taxes, Be a Good Sport.

A strong economy is vital for a strong and healthy country. Low debt and high savings and investments will help protect the economy, but the ability to spend money is important, too. The more equitably everyone gets paid, the more purchasing money will, in turn, boost manufacturing and retail sectors. Be sure your representatives are actively working to make sure people are paid fairly and costs are not prohibitive.

Democracy works best with a strong infrastructure. Taxes can provide that and many services that benefit you and your family. It is vitally important to restore wealth taxes to earlier rates. These services include protecting those who are temporarily or permanently unable to work, education, libraries, communications, quality roads and mass transit. And, postal service, among others.

Important for our democracy, a strong infrastructure can also help ensure an election system which sanctity and integrity have not been tampered with, that works for everyone, i.e., the majority always are heard and obeyed and the minority learn to realize this is how the system is supposed to work.

If you are so passionate about the results, work to see that more people feel the same way or to understand why you see things differently. If the losing side of an election always walks away, turns their backs on the system—the country—of course, it will fail, sooner or later. Wars Between the States hurt everyone, except, maybe, war profiteers, mortuaries, and casket sellers.

The good thing about being on the losing side, when what the majority chooses does not work, perhaps they will see things your way in four years. If the majority's choice turns out to be a success, then you should be willing to consider that you may have been championing a lesser choice. If the country is better off, what does it matter rather your guy won, or not, be honest, give credit where credit is due.

We must get off of our sorry feelings that we are entitled to a government that works for the people, not cognizant that the people have to work to make that government. We have to do the work, ourselves, that is necessary to ensure that it is, more importantly, of us—by us—the people—only if the people do their part, including each and every election, it shall not perish from the earth.

...It is rather for us to be here dedicated to the great task remaining before us— that, from these honored dead we take increased devotion to that cause for which they, here, gave the last full measure of devotion— that we here highly resolve these dead shall not have died in vain, that this nation, shall have a new birth of freedom, and that government of the people by the people for the people, shall not perish from the earth. [165]

Forming a More Perfect Union

Say our efforts are successful and it feels like the United States of America is back on a trustworthy and confidence-building track. Or, even, that we are still struggling to achieve integrity in government and the sanctity of our political institutions, including elections. What else can we do to ensure a straight-forward path to an ideal country, and planet?

Living Wages and Universal Healthcare

Ensuring a livable income and affordable housing for every American will surely increase the strength of our economy. Business owners or executives appear to be failing to realize that paying employees more money will have the positive effect of increased sales. People's greater purchasing power will invigorate the retail and manufacturing sectors. Another part of growing disposable income would come from Universal Healthcare. Too many can't afford the expense of American medical care, period. There would definitely be more money in the other, struggling sectors, if medical wasn't draining too many people's monetary resources.

Look at the ever-expanding camps of homeless people. A large number of them would not be living outdoors if wages and costs ratio was closer to what they once were. Many of those people were buckled under by a flood of unexpected expenses while living from paycheck to paycheck. Sure, there are many there because they made really bad choice(s), but a culture should never become this unforgiving. A healthy society can afford to be more benevolent and a benevolent society will become healthier.

When the author was working his way through college on Veteran's Benefits, part-time wages, and his wife's minimum wage job, they were able to rent a residence, buy groceries, pay tuition and textbooks, and pay for her insulin and syringes. In case you are not aware, the price of an education, accommodations, and medical supplies, makes that impossible, now.

Being young, and "reckless," the author got over his head with a vehicle he could barely afford to make payments on, and got behind. He was able to make arrangements with the credit union and got back on track without any damage to his credit. Business and service was less impersonal, then, until the 1980's, at least. Taking a business curriculum in college, then, the standard business model precluded such profit margin as businesses lust for, now. Greed seems to be the increasingly major component of prices, since.

More-Affordable Adult Education

Stated above, a college education was relatively more affordable a generation or two, past. Many civilized countries afford their citizens a post-secondary education. The United States has been moving in the other direction. Not surprisingly, countries more fundamental or authoritative prefer an ignorant populace, they are easier to control and use, as the leader(s) see fit. On the other hand, countries with a better educated populace, profit the people, the industry, and the country, with greater equity. Brent Radcliffe explained in his article for *Investopedia*:

How Education and Training Affect the Economy

Both confer benefits and can help eliminate inequalities

The knowledge and skills of workers available in the labor supply is a key factor in determining both business and economic growth. Economies with a significant supply of skilled labor, brought on through formal education as well as vocational training, are often able to capitalize on this through the development of more value-added industries, such as high-tech manufacturing. Countries need to ensure through legislation and jobs programs that all their citizens have access to the education and training that can lift up workers, companies, and the entire economy. [166]

Stronger United Nations or World Organization

The U.S. and U.K. strong-armed their way into Iraq and Baghdad against United Nations' recommendations and without their supervision, destroying a stable infrastructure and economy in their haste to dispatch the Bush personal enemy, Saddam Hussein, for to suck on the oil teat of Mesopotamia. The situation in the Middle East rapidly fell apart, America could not control the chaos it had helped create.

The Undersecretary of Defense for Policy Douglas Feith supplied bogus intelligence to the White House on Iraqi WMD and links to terrorist organizations to make the case for war, and then "leaked" this intelligence to key journalists such as Judith Miller at The New York Times. Miller had a frontpage article in the Times on September 8, 2002, citing administration officials claiming that Saddam was seeking "specially designed" aluminum tubes to enrich uranium, the so-called "smoking gun." Several days later, President Bush inserted the Times' claim in his speech to the United Nations General Assembly.

The aluminum tube issue was central to Secretary of State Colin Powell's speech to the UN in February 2003, which was based on the phony CIA estimate from October 2002. As Powell's chief of staff, Lawrence Wilkerson wrote in The New York Times in February 2018, the secretary's "gravitas was a significant part of the Bush administration's two-year-long effort to get Americans on the war wagon. It was CIA Deputy Director McLaughlin who lied to Secretary of State Powell about the reliability of the intelligence in Powell's speech. McLaughlin was the central advocate for the phony intelligence on mobile biological laboratories that ended up in that speech.

President Bush would have gone to war with or without intelligence, and once again we are confronted by a president who might consider going to war with or without intelligence. Fifteen years ago, we had a CIA director from Capitol Hill who was loyal to the president and unwilling to tell truth to power. Once again, we have a CIA director, Gina Haspel, who is a White House loyalist and cannot be counted on to tell truth to power.[167]

It is obvious that under some administrations the United States tends to be more of a bully, resembling Russia more and more. Sometimes it seems we just want to throw our weight around to gain control, unilaterally, for the wrong reasons. Why else would the

United Nations neither desire to be, nor desired to be, a part of our government's plans? Perhaps this article by Kishore Mahbubani, past President of the UN Security Council, that was published in the *Globalist* gives a hint:

Why the United Nations Is Kept Weak

Is the West underestimating the value of the trust that the UN enjoys in the hearts and minds of the rest of the world's population?

Even during the Cold War, when Moscow and Washington disagreed on pretty much everything, both nations were united in one regard. They actively conspired to keep the UN weak.

The United States and the Soviet Union did so through a variety of means. They selected all too pliable secretaries-general, such as Kurt Waldheim. They bullied whoever was secretary-general at a given time into dismissing or sidelining competent or conscientious UN civil servants who had shown any backbone.

They squeezed UN budgets endlessly. And, of course, they planted CIA and KGB spies in all corners of the UN system. All this was well known to anyone who worked within the UN system.

As we move into the era of the great convergence, the world clearly needs stronger "global village" councils. The time has come for the West to begin a fundamental rethink of its long-held policy that it serves long-term Western interests to keep institutions of global governance weak.[168]

We have been responsible for turning the United Nations into only a symbolic institution, since at least the Bush-Cheney affair, also known as the Dick and Dubya Debacle. Trump has further damaged the relationship, as well as those with our NATO allies and fellow G8 members. Including our democracy, these organizations are not going to work if the members aren't willing to participate. The majority of American voters think the United Nations is an important institution that we need to work with. Our leaders need to be consistently cognizant of, and obedient to, the will of the people.

If reasonable control of the entire congress can ever be had, again, perhaps an amendment is necessary to ensure that we need to go much farther in making the case to get Congressional approval to go against the United Nations in unilateral military actions.

While Trump or any other American leaders are so willing to cater to the whims of totalitarian figures such as Putin, we need extra safeguards to ensure we will not further enable such despots, particularly against our own best interests.

A stronger agreement, or treaty, with a world organization may work in lieu of a Constitutional amendment. A Virtual World Government suggestion by a friend has sparked this author's interest, along with his concept of using scientific reasoning and methodology to fix political problems, probably by designing better, healthier, systems, read Chapter 5, again. At the very least, a legislative strengthening of our relationship with the United Nations to help preclude an Executive's autonomous allying with authoritarian countries is perhaps what the doctor prescribed.

The End

Epilogue

Trump's Toxic Empire—Pandemic 2020

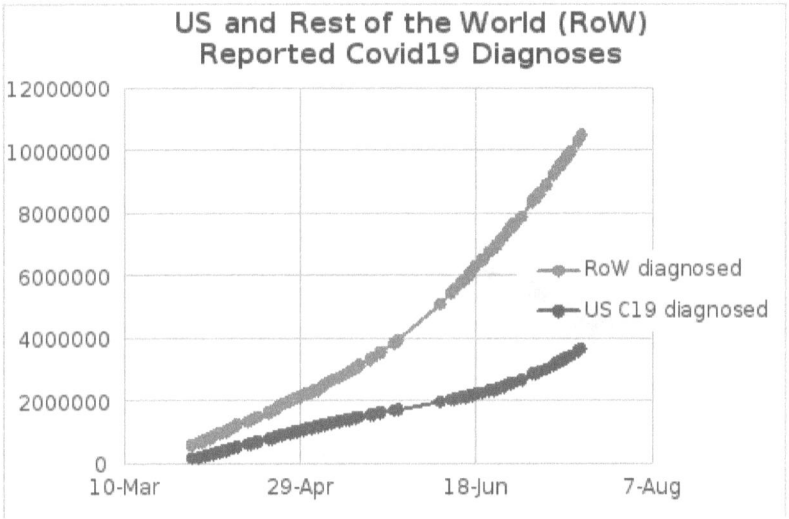

Fig. 24: Chart of reported Covid diagnoses in the US vs the rest of the world. Spreadsheet compiled by the author.

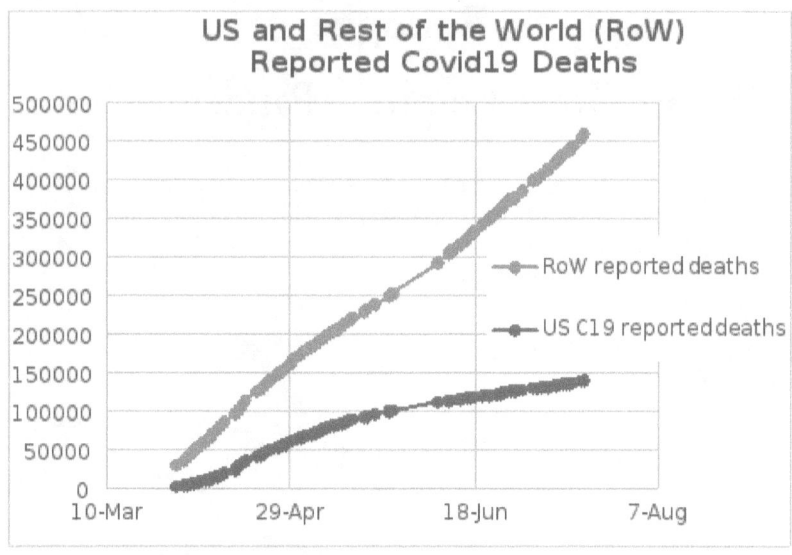

Fig. 25: Chart of reported Covid deaths of the US vs the rest of the world. Spreadsheet compiled by the author.

The Coronavirus, Covid-19 virus, has wrought a world pandemic upon us, now, so the author's "blogging," bitching, or beer-crying, for now, must end here. With luck, it will be continued. The author regrets that his age and family responsibilities have caused him to forego the marches and protests since February, 2020, but, his heart nearly bursts with pride when he see fellow Portland, Oregon people letting their determination to not submit to fascism be shown, night after night after night, for more than 100 days to date, in spite of authoritarian brutality and attempts by opposing forces to put blame and shame on the peaceful protestors for the violence and destruction that certain actors are bringing in. He would, rather, be with them. It reminds him of the previously mentioned ancestral relative, Niklaus Leuenberger, and the Swiss peasants who blockaded

Bern to demand that which they were rightfully due, and the way the authorities betrayed them, as well.

Several previous chapters focused on two men who greatly forwarded the progress towards a world of democracy. These chapters are included for not only the context to humankind's earlier battles, or heroes thereof, towards or for democracy but, perhaps, a relationship between the two. Besides philosophical, a physical link may exist between Niklaus Leuenberger, the leader of the Swiss Peasant War of 1653 and Abraham Lincoln, the man who brought an end to slavery and salvaged the United States of America. These two respected men rose to reluctant leadership in a crisis and suffered resultant ends at the hands of the eternal enemy of equality. Who will next take the reins when they are handed to him, or her—the next hero we hang our hopes on, or our hopes hang?

We are at the crossroads, again, where we are damned, politically, if we do and physically and financially (sorry, unfortunately), if we don't. The author's ancestors include Anabaptists, strong believers in pacifism, he must bow to their ideal, as long as possible, in his attempts to achieve the American Dream, as they did. Pacifist idealists have marched on Bern behind Niklaus Leuenberger, in India behind Gandhi, in Alabama behind Martin Luther King, Jr., WE must also march. We must always be willing to march, putting the immediate danger behind us, to preclude a future full of such. March on, people.

(to be continued?)

Bibliography

"1830 United States Federal Census for Abraham Lionberger." *Ancestry.com*

"1840 United States Federal Census for Abram Lincoln." *Ancestry.com.*

"1840 United States Federal Census for Abram Lionberger." *Ancestry.com.*

"1850 United States Federal Census for John Lionberger." *Ancestry.com.*

"1860 United States Federal Census for John Lionberger." *Ancestry.com.*

"Abraham Lincoln and Family." *Lancaster, Pennsylvania, Mennonite Vital Record 1750- 2014, Pennsylvania Germania, Vol. II.* 316.

"Abraham Lincoln's Father." March 10, 2012. *Little Bits of History along U.S. Roadways - Blogspot.com.*

"Abraham Lionberger in the 1820 United States Federal Census." *Ancestry.com.*

"American Beginnings, 1492- 1690." *National Humanities Center.*

"Anabaptism," *Wikipedia, The Free Encyclopedia,*

"Ancestors of Dwight David Eisenhower" *Ancestral Quest Online.*

Barton, Wm. E. *The Paternity of Abraham Lincoln*, New York: George H. Doran Company, 1920.

Beres, Derek. "Low Voter Turnout." *Big Think.*

Bettinger, Blaine. "DNA Analysis of 5 People Who Helped Create America." (*The Genetic Genealogist*). November 1, 2007.

Burkhimer, Michael. *100 Essential Lincoln Books*, Sourcebooks, Incorporated, 2003.

Cathey, James Harrison. 1899. *The Genesis of Lincoln*.

"Citizens United Explained." *Brennan Center For Justice*.

"Colonial America (1492-1763)." *America's Library*.

Denton, J. William. "The Curious Case of Lincoln's Paternity." *The Historyist, Medium*. Sep 9, 2019.

"Dunmore County (Va.) Levy Book, 1775-1779." (*Local government records collection, Shenandoah County Court Records. The Library of Virginia, Richmond, Virginia 23219*).

"Early Settlers on the Shenandoah River (South Branch), Augusta County, VA." *Werelate.org/Wiki*.

Eland, Ivan. "George W. Bush's Impeachable Offenses." *Independent Institute Newsletter*. December 19, 2005.

Faust, Albert Bernhardt and Gaius Marcus Brumbaugh, *Lists of Swiss Emigrants in the Eighteenth Century to the American Colonies. Vol. 1*, Washington, D.C.: The National Genealogical Society, 1920, *Lists of Swiss emigrants in the eighteenth century to the American colonies*. Internet Archive.

Foner, Eric. "Reconstruction - United States History." *Britannica*.

"Frederick County, Virginia." *Wikipedia, The Free Encyclopedia*.

Goodman, Melvin. "How the Iraq War Destabilized the Entire Middle East." *Counterpunch*. March 15, 2018.

"GRANTEE 1778-1864 (aka Burnt Books)." *Rockingham County, Virginia.*

Guzy, Dan. "Navigation on the Upper Potomac and its Tributaries." *Whilbr (Western Maryland's Historical Library).*

Hallstrom, Suzanne W. and Nancy C. Royce, Stephan A. Whitlock, Richard G. Hileman, M.A., J.D., Gerald M. Haslam, Ph.D, AG, FUGA. "Nancy Hanks Lincoln mtDNA Study, Unlocking the Secrets of Abraham Lincoln's Maternal Ancestry." *Genetic Lincoln.* 2015.

"Herbert Hoover in Oregon." *The Oregon Encyclopedia.*

Herndon, William H. and Jesse W. Weik. *Abraham Lincoln: The True Story of a Great Life Volumes 1 and 2.* New York: D. Appleton, 1916.

"How to Get Involved in Politics." *Art of Manliness.*

"How to Recruit Great Candidates for Public Office." *Talk GOP.*

"How to Run for Political Office in 2019." *Candidate Boot Camp.*

"Illinois State County Map." *Washington State Search Engine & Directory.*

"Jennie Eisenhower." *Ethnicity of Celebs.*

John Leinberger in the Virginia, U.S., Compiled Census and Census Substitutes Index, 1800-1890. *Ancestry.com.*

John Lienberger in the Virginia, U.S., Compiled Census and Census Substitutes Index, 1800-1890. *Ancestry.com.*

John Lyenberger in the Virginia, U.S., Compiled Census and Census Substitutes Index, 1800-1890. *Ancestry.com.*

Joseph Hanks in the Virginia, U.S., Compiled Census and Census Substitutes Index, 1800-1890. *Ancestry.com.*

Kerchner, Charles F. Jr. "YSNP Names and Information Table." *Kercher.com.* 2006.

"Lancaster, Pennsylvania, U.S., Mennonite Vital Records, 1750-2014 for Joseph Rhodes." *Ancestry.com.*

Lazarus, Emma, "The New Colossus." 1883.

Leuenberger, Hans. "Niklaus Leuenberger, Predating Gandhi in 1653?" The Swiss American Historical Society Review. February 2020.

Leuenberger, Hans. *Niklaus Leuenberger, the "Swiss Gandhi" of the 17th century?: The Swiss Peasants' War 1653.* Self-published and available online.

Lincoln, Abraham. 1863. "Gettysburg Address." *Library of Congress.* Nicolay copy.

Lincoln, Bob. "Lincoln-Family.com." *Lincoln-Family.*

Lionberger, Elaine. 1970s. "Children of Mordecai Lincoln." Author's family files.

Lionberger, Glen. *Illinois to Oregon—Lionbergers, Vol. I.* Oregon: Daniel Lionberger, Introduction.

"List of Swiss-Americans." *Wiki.*

Luck, J. Murray. History of Switzerland, *The Society for the Promotion of Science and Scholarship, Inc.*

MacAskill, Ewen. "White House warns senators over gun control reforms in vow to continue fight." *The Guardian.* Apr. 18, 2013.

Mahbubani, Kishore. "Why the United Nations is Kept Weak." *The Globalist*. February 9, 2013.

Minder, Hans. *Hans Minder to Beverly Lionberger Hodgins, Lauperswil, Switzerland*. Leuenberger from Rüderswil. Courtesy of Beverly Lionberger Hodgins.

"Nancy Lincoln." *Wikipedia, The Free Encyclopedia*.

Nicolay and Hay, *Abraham Lincoln, a History*, Cosimo Classics. July 1, 2009.

"Obama's roots traced to Swiss villager." *Swiss Info*.

"One of the First Land Grants From the Crown." *Page News and Courier*. 1950, 1970.

"Papers of Abraham Lincoln." *Abraham Lincoln Presidential Library and Museum*.

Peter Leinberger in the Virginia, U.S., Compiled Census and Census Substitutes Index, 1800-1890. *Ancestry.com*.

Peter Lienberger in the Virginia, U.S., Compiled Census and Census Substitutes Index, 1800-1890. *Ancestry.com*.

"Plymouth Colony," *Wikipedia, The Free Encyclopedia*.

Prigogine,Ilya and Isabelle Stengers. *Order out of Chaos*. Bantam Books, Inc., 666 Fifth Ave., New York, New York 10103.

Radcliffe, Brent. "How Education and Training Affect the Economy." *Investopedia*. Aug 19, 2020.

"Religion and the Founding of the American Republic, America as a Religious Refuge: The Seventeenth Century, Part 1." *Library of Congress*.

"Restore the Voting Rights Act." *Brennan Center For Justice*.

"Rutherford B. Hayes president of United States." *Encyclopaedia Britannica,*

Shakespeare, Wm. *Macbeth*. The Project Gutenberg. November 1, 1998.

"Six Ways to Check Out a Candidate." *AARP*. 2018.

"Slave states and free states," *Wikipedia*.

Spangler, Jewel. "Baptists in Colonial Virginia." *Encyclopedia Virginia*.

"Spanish Florida," *Wikipedia, The Free Encyclopedia*.

Steers, Ed. "Abraham Lincoln's Paternity." *Abraham Lincoln Online*.

Stern, Philip Van Doren. "The Life of Abraham Lincoln." *The Life and Writings of Abraham Lincoln*. Michigan, The Modern Library, New York. 1940. 94-95.

Stern, Phillip Van Doren. "Speech at Kalamazoo." *The Life and Writings of Abraham Lincoln*, Michigan, The Modern Library, New York. 1940. 399, 400, 400.

Stern, Phillip Van Doren. "Campaign biography." *The Life and Writings of Abraham Lincoln*, Michigan, The Modern Library, New York 1940. 599-608.

"Swiss Brethren." *Wikipedia, The Free Encyclopedia*.

"The Paternity of Abraham Lincoln." *Daily Kos*. April 04, 2011.

"The Puritans." *History.com*. July 30, 2019.

"The Thirty Years War (1618-1648)." *Wikipedia*.

Tolles, Frederick B.. "William Penn - English Quaker Leader and Colonist."

"US president grew from Swiss roots." *Swiss Info*.

"Virginia," *Bing.com*.

"Voting Rights Act of 1965," *Wikipedia, The Free Encyclopedia*.

Wertheimer, Fred. "Citizens United Campaign Finance Legalized Bribery." *Politico*. January 19, 2014.

"What are your goals for running candidates?" Candidate Recruiting Manual. *Green Party U.S.*.

Wikipedia contributors, "Page County, Virginia," *Wikipedia, The Free Encyclopedia*.

"Y-DNA Haplogroup R and its Subclades - 2007, Version: 2.08." October 31, 2007. *International Society of Genetic Genealogy*.

Zimkus, John J. "President Lincoln's Warren County Relatives." *Historic Lebanon, Ohio*.

References

[1] Wikipedia contributors, "Spanish Florida," *Wikipedia, The Free Encyclopedia*, https://en.wikipedia.org/w/index.php?title=Spanish_Florida&oldid=1299303100.

[2] "American Beginnings: 1492-1690," Toolbox Library: Primary Resources in U.S. History and Literature, *National Humanities Center*, http://nationalhumanitiescenter.org/pds/amerbegin/settlement/text1/text1read.htm.

[3] History.com editors, 07/30/2019, "The Puritans," *History.com*, https://www.history.com/topics/colonial-america/puritanism.

[4] Wikipedia contributors, "Plymouth Colony," *Wikipedia, The Free Encyclopedia*, *https://en.wikipedia.org/w/index.php?title=Plymouth_Colony&oldid=1289913057.*

[5] Drowning of Protestants, Religion and the Founding of the American Republic, America as a Religious Refuge: The Seventeenth Century, Part 1, https://www.loc.gov/exhibits/religion/rel01.html.

[6] The Expulsion of the Salzburgers - Religion and the Founding of the American Republic, America as a Religious Refuge: The Seventeenth Century, Part 1, https://www.loc.gov/exhibits/religion/rel01.html.

[7] Wikipedia contributors, "Swiss Brethren," *Wikipedia, The Free Encyclopedia*, *https://en.wikipedia.org/w/index.php?title=Swiss_Brethren&oldid=1269974197.*

[8] J. Murray Luck, *History of Switzerland* (The Society for the Promotion of Science and Scholarship, Inc.), 146.

[9] J. Murray Luck, *History of Switzerland*, 147.

[10] Ibid, 183.

[11] Ibid, 260.

[12] Emma Lazarus, 1883, "The New Colossus," *Wikisource*, https://en.wikisource.org/wiki/The_New_Colossus.

[13] Hans Minder to Beverly Lionberger Hodgins, Lauperswil, Switzerland, Aug. 18, 2014.

[14] Hans Minder to Beverly Lionberger Hodgins.

[15] Wikipedia contributors, "The Thirty Years War (1618-1648)," *Wikipedia*, https://enacademic.com/dic.nsf/enwiki/134638.

[16] America's Story, Colonial America (1492-1763), *America's Library*, http://www.americaslibrary.gov/jb/colonial/jb_colonial_penn_1.htmldeceased father.

[17] Frederick B. Tolles, "William Penn - English Quaker leader and colonist," *Britannica*, https://www.britannica.com/biography/William-Penn-English-Quaker-leader-and-colonist/Founding-and-governorship-of-Pennsylvania.

[18] Frederick B. Tolles, "William Penn..."

[19] Wikipedia contributors, "Anabaptism," *Wikipedia, The Free Encyclopedia,* https://en.wikipedia.org/w/index.php?title=Anabaptism&oldid=1296261950.

[20] Albert Bernhardt Faust and Gaius Marcus Brumbaugh, *Lists of Swiss Emigrants in the Eighteenth Century to the American Colonies. Vol. 1,* Washington, D.C.: The National Genealogical Society, 1920, Lists of Swiss emigrants in the eighteenth century to the American colonies (archive.org).

[21] Albert Bernhardt Faust and Gaius Marcus Brumbaugh, *Lists of Swiss Emigrants.*

[22] Dr. H. Leuenberger, "Niklaus Leuenberger, Predating Gandhi in 1653?," the Swiss American Historical Society Review, February 2020.

[23] Dr. H. Leuenberger, *Niklaus Leuenberger, the "Swiss Gandhi" of the 17th century ?: The Swiss Peasants' War 1653,* Self-published and available online.

[24] Lionberger, *Illinois,* 1.

[25] Originally printed March 2, 1950 (author unknown), "One Of The First Land Grants From The Crown," *Page News and Courier,* 1970.

[26] "Early Settlers on the Shenandoah River (South Branch), Augusta County, VA," *Werelate.org/Wiki,* https://www.werelate.org/wiki/Early_Settlers_on_the_Shenandoah_River_%28South_Branch%29%2C_Augusta_County%2C_VA.

[27] "Papers of Abraham Lincoln," *Papersofabrahamlincoln.org*, (Abraham Lincoln Presidential Library and Museum), https://papersofabrahamlincoln.org/persons/LI47499.

[28] Wikipedia contributors, "Frederick County, Virginia," *Wikipedia, The Free Encyclopedia*, https://en.wikipedia.org/w/index.php?title=Frederick_County,_Virginia&oldid=1 209009863.

[29] "Dunmore County (Va.) Levy Book, 1775-1779." Local government records collection, Shenandoah County Court Records. *The Library of Virginia*, Richmond, Virginia 23219, http://ead.lib.virginia.edu/vivaxtf/view?docId=lva/vi04040.xml.

[30] Wikipedia contributors, "Page County, Virginia," *Wikipedia, The Free Encyclopedia*, https://en.wikipedia.org/w/index.php?title=Page_County,_Virginia&oldid=1138339282.

[31] "Virginia," *Bing.com*, https://www.bing.com/maps?q=Virgina&FORM=HDRSC6&cp=38.628471%7E-78.571886&

[32] "Little Bits of History along U.S. Roadways." *Blogspot.com*, http://littlebitsofhistory.blogspot.com/2012/03/abraham-lincoln-father.html.

[33] "1820 United States Federal Census for Abraham Lionberger," *Ancestry.com*, https://www.ancestry.com/sharing/5253309?mark=7b22746f6b656e223a224c6f4f4c516f53775352767159

[34] "1830 United States Federal Census for Abraham Lionberger," *Ancestry.com*, https://www.ancestry.com/imageviewer/collections/8058/images/4411348_00249?_gl=1*8kvoib*_up*MQ.

[35] Lionberger, *Illinois*, 1.

[36] Lionberger, *Illinois*, 1, 2.

[37] "GRANTEE 1778-1864 (aka Burnt Books)," *Rockingham County, Virginia,* https://www.rockinghamcountyva.gov/DocumentCenter/View/15198/Burnt-Book-Index-L?bidId=.

[38] "GRANTEE 1778-1864 (aka Burnt Books)," *Rockingham County, Virginia,* https://www.rockinghamcountyva.gov/DocumentCenter/View/15185/Burnt-Book-Index-Y?bidId=.

[39] "1850 United States Federal Census for John Lionberger," *Ancestry.com,* https://www.ancestry.com/sharing/41850721?mark=7b22746f6b656e223a224c5532784f5870317374776b7C

[40] Elaine Lionberger, 1970s. "Children of Mordecai Lincoln," Author's family files.

[41] "Lancaster, Pennsylvania, U.S., Mennonite Vital Records, 1750-2014 for Joseph Rhodes," *Ancestry.com,* https://www.ancestry.com/imageviewer/collections/60592/images/44308_347527-00572?pId=138766.

[42] Ibid.

[43] Lancaster Co., PA, U.S. Mennonite Vital Records, 1750-2014

[44] Lionberger, <u>Illinois</u>, 1.

[45] Wikipedia contributors, "Abolitionism in the United States," *Wikipedia, The Free Encyclopedia,* https://en.wikipedia.org/w/

index.php?title=Abolitionism_in_the_United_States&o
ldid=1157555009.

[46] Wikipedia contributors, "Slave states and free states," *Wikipedia,* https://simple.wikipedia.org/w/ index.php?title=Slave_states_and_free_states&oldid=10016772.

[47] Jewel Spangler, 2020, "Baptists in Colonial Virginia," *Encyclopedia Virginia,* https://encyclopediavirginia.org/entries/ baptists-in-colonial-virginia/.

[48] "Mt. Carmel Baptist Church - Luray - VA - US." 2014. *Historical Marker Project.* https://historicalmarkerproject.com/markers/ HMO9E_mt-carmel-baptist-church_Luray-VA.html.

[49] Raymond W. Settle, "Abraham Lincoln's Faith," *Christianity Today,* Feb. 3, 1958, https://www.christianitytoday.com/ct/1958/ february-3/abraham-lincolns-faith.html.

[50] Wikipedia contributors, "Nancy Lincoln," *Wikipedia, The Free Encyclopedia,* https://en.wikipedia.org/w/ index.php?title=Nancy_Lincoln&oldid=1208589449.

[51] Allen, Bernard L, "Germans," *e-WV: The West Virginia Encyclopedia,* (wvencyclopedia.org). e-WV | Germans (wvencyclopedia.org).

[52] "German Settlers in the Appalachians," *DigitalHeritage.org.* https://digitalheritage.org/2012/10/german-settlers-in-the- appalachians/.

[53] Wikipedia contributors, "Shenandoah Germans," *Wikipedia, The Free Encyclopedia,* *https://en.wikipedia.org/w/index.php?title=Shenandoah_Germans&oldid=1292737793.*

[54] Wikipedia contributors, "German Americans," (*Wikipedia, The Free Encyclopedia),* *https://en.wikipedia.org/w/index.php?title=German_Americans&oldid=1213 286531.*

[55] Blaine Bettinger, "DNA Analysis of 5 People Who Helped Create America," (*The Genetic Genealogist),* November 1, 2007. https://thegeneticgenealogist.com/2007/11/01/dna-analysis-of-5people-who-helped-create-america/.

[56] Bob Lincoln, "Lincoln-Family.com," Lincoln-Family, http://lincoln-family.com/index2.htm.

[57] Rebecca Fishwick, "Male vs Female DNA Testing – What are the Differences?" dnatestingchoice.com, November 8, 2018, https://dnatestingchoice.com/en-us/news/male-vs-female-dna-testing-what-are-the-differences.

[58] Wikipedia contributors, "Seba Smith," *Wikipedia*, https://en.m.wikipedia.org/wiki/Seba_Smith.

[59] Barton, William, *The Paternity of Abraham Lincoln*, George H. Doran Co., New York, 1920, 61-62.

[60] Joseph Hanks in the Virginia, U.S., Compiled Census and Census Substitutes Index, 1800-1890, *Ancestry.com*, https://www.ancestry.com/search/collections/3578/records/33778120?tid=&pid=&queryId=cb20ae68-95a2-4d92-b2f6-2e14d4c39d6c&_phsrc=hUD23&_phstart=successSourcehttps://www.anc search/collections/3578/records/

33778120?tid=&pid=&queryId=cb20ae68-95a2-4d92-b2f6-2e14d4c39d6c&_phsrc=hUD23&_phstart=successSource.

[61] Joseph Hanks in the Virginia, U.S., Compiled Census and Census Substitutes Index, 1800-1890, *Ancestry.com*. https://www.ancestry.com/search/collections/3578/records/33053174?tid=&pid=&queryId=a1fb6249-5b24-480c-9149-a123bd5cf594&_phsrc=hUD26&_phstart=successSource.

[62] Colin Kidd, "Behold, America by Sarah Churchwell review – the underside of the "American dream,"" *The Guardian,* 07/14/2018, https://www.theguardian.com/books/2018/jul/14/beholdamerica-history-of-american-dream-sarah-churchwell-review.

[63] Lucas Morel, "Lincoln, The Founders, and the Rights of Human Nature," *Lincoln Lore* (Friends of the Lincoln Collection), https://www.friendsofthelincolncollection.org/lincolnlore/lincoln-the-founders-and-the-rights-of-human-nature/.

[64] Lucas Morel, "Lincoln, The Founders.

[65] Hans Leuenberger, "Niklaus Leuenberger: Predating Gandhi in 1653?," *Swiss American Historical Society Review: Vol. 56: No. 1, Article 6,* 2020, 90, https://scholarsarchive.byu.edu/sahs_review/vol56/iss1/6.

[66] Herndon, William H. and Jesse W. Weik, *Abraham Lincoln: The True Story of a Great Life Volumes 1 and 2*, New York: D. Appleton, 1916.

[67] Ibid.

[68] Herndon, *Abraham Lincoln.*

[69] Ibid.

[70] Ibid.

[71] Herndon, *Abraham Lincoln*.

[72] Phillip Van Doren Stern, *The Writings of Abraham Lincoln*, "Speech at Kalamazoo," Michigan, New York:The Modern Library, 1940. 399.

[73] Stern, *The Writings of Abraham Lincoln*, "Speech at Kalamazoo." 400.

[74] Herndon, *Abraham Lincoln*.

[75] Ibid.

[76] Stern, *The Writings of Abraham Lincoln*, "Speech at Kalamazoo," 400.

[77] Stern, *The Writings of Abraham Lincoln*, "The Life of Abraham Lincoln," 94-95.

[78] Herndon, *Abraham Lincoln*.

[79] Eric Foner, "Reconstruction, United States History," *Britannica*, https://www.britannica.com/event/Reconstruction-United-States-history.

[80] "Rutherford B. Hayes president of United States," *Encyclopaedia Britannica*, https://www.britannica.com/biography/Rutherford-B-Hayes.

[81] Herndon, *Abraham Lincoln*.

[82] Wikipedia contributors, "Downing Street memo," *Wikipedia, The Free Encyclopedia*, *https://en.wikipedia.org/w/index.php?title=Downing_Street_memo&oldid=1295002253*.

[83] Fred Kaplan, "What's really in the Downing Street memos?," SLATE, June 15, 2005, https://slate.com/news-and-politics/2005/06/what-s-really-in-the-downing-street-memos.html.

[84] Ed O'Keefe, "Feingold Calls for Bush's Censure," *ABC News*, This Week, 03/12/06, https://abcnews.go.com/ThisWeek/Politics/story?id=1715495.

[85] Gloria Borger, "Bush Vetoes Stem Cell Bill," *CBS News*, (July 21,2006), https://www.cbsnews.com/news/bush-vetoes-stem-cell-bill-21-07-2006/.

[86] Fred Kaplan, "John Bolton's excruciating confirmation hearing," *SLATE* (July 27, 2006), https://slate.com/news-and-politics/2006/07/john-bolton-s-confirmation-hearing.html.

[87] Letter from the Co-Chairs, "The Iraq Study Group Report," *GUARDIAN* (Dec. 12, 2006), http://image.guardian.co.uk/sys-files/Guardian/documents/2006/12/06/iraq_study_group_report.pdf.

[88] Sharon Otterman, "IRAQ: U.N. Sanctions," *Backgrounder* (February 2, 2005), https://www.cfr.org/backgrounder/iraq-un-sanctions.

[89] T. Hamid Al Bayati, "Letter dated 14 November 2006 from the Permanent Representative of Iraq to the United Nations addressed

to the President of the Security Council," *United Nations Security Council,* https://www.globalpolicy.org/images/pdfs/1121maliki.pdf.

[90] T. Christian Miller, "Contractors Outnumber Troops in Iraq," *Los Angeles Times,* (July 4, 2007), https://www.latimes.com/archives/la-xpm-2007-jul-04-na-private4-story.html.

[91] Charles Tiefer, "The Iraq Debacle: The Rise and Fall of Procurement-aided Unilateralism as a Paradigm of Foreign War," *U. of Penn Journals,* https://www.law.upenn.edu/journals/jil/articles/volume29/issue1/Tiefer29U.Pa.J.Int%27lL.1%282007%29.pdf.

[92] Joseph A. Palermo, "Articles of Impeachment Against President George W. Bush," *Huffpost* (06/28/2007), https://www.huffpost.com/entry/articles-of-impeachment-a_b_54243.

[93] Bryan Bender, Globe Staff, "Analysis says war could cost $1 trillion Budget office sees effect on taxpayers for decade," *The Boston Globe* (August 1, 2007), http://archive.boston.com/news/nation/articles/2007/08/01/analysis_says_war_could_cost_1_trillion/.

[94] Melissa Harris, "A Blaring Call for Impeachment," *The Baltimore Sun* (August 06, 2007), https://www.commondreams.org/news/2007/08/06/blaring-call-impeachment.

[95] "Iraq and the Media: A Critical Timeline," *Fair,* Mar. 19, 2007, https://fair.org/take-action/media-advisories/iraq-and-the-media/.

[96] Jane Cutter, "Media complicity and disinformation on the Iraq war," *Liberation - Newspaper of the Party for Socialism and Liberation*

(Apr 03, 2007), https://www.liberationnews.org/07-04-03-media-complicity-disinformation-html/.

[97] Tom Turnipseed, "War Profiteering and Corruption," *COUNTERPUNCH* (August 18, 2007), https://www.counterpunch.org/2007/08/18/war-profiteering-and-corruption/.

[98] "Petraeus Hears Iraq War Criticism- Senior democrat says military "surge" is not providing political breakthrough in Iraq," *Al Jazeera* (12 Sept 2007), https://www.aljazeera.com/news/americas/2007/09/2008525133720873695.html.

[99] Ari Berman, "Why Pelosi Opposes Impeachment," *The Nation* (July 31, 2007), https://www.thenation.com/article/archive/why-pelosi-opposes-impeachment/.

[100] "Halliburton Under Fire Over Rape Charge," *CBS* (December 12, 2007), https://www.cbsnews.com/news/halliburton-under-fire-over-rape-charge/.

[101] Anna Driver, "RPT-KBR, Halliburton hit by ex-worker's rape charges," *REUTERS* (December 20, 2007), https://www.reuters.com/article/kbr-assault-idUSN206868020071220.

[102] Gary Kamiya, "Iraq: Why the media failed," *SALON* (April 10, 2007), https://www.salon.com/2007/04/10/media_failure/.

[103] Theresa Harrington and Paul Burgarino, "Media overlook important news, researchers say," *EAST BAY TIMES* (November 27, 2007), https://www.eastbaytimes.com/2007/11/27/media-overlook-important-news-researchers-say/.

[104] Clive Thompson, "Can You Count on Voting Machines?," *New York Times* (2008-01-06), http://www.nytimes.com/2008/01/06/magazine/06Vote-t.html?ex=1357275600&en=75d.

[105] George McGovern, "Why I Believe Bush Must Go—Nixon Was Bad. These Guys Are Worse," Washington Post (January 6, 2008), https://www.washingtonpost.com/wp-dyn/content/article/2008/01/04/AR2008010404308_pf.html.

[106] Posted by egalia, "Fighting the radical right in Tennessee and the nation—More MSNBC Misogyny from Olbermann: Beat the Bitch Until She Quits," *Tennessee Guerilla Women* (Saturday, April 26, 2008 at 12:15 AM), https://guerillawomentn.blogspot.com/2008/04/more-msnbc-misogyny-from-olbermann-beat.html.

[107] Harvey Wasserman & Bob Fitrakis, "Will Bush & Cheney Cancel the 2008 Election?" *Free Press* (Columbus, Ohio July 30, 2007), https://www.organicconsumers.org/news/will-bush-cheney-cancel-2008-election#gsc.tab=0.

[108] Jeremy Williams, "How the Rich are Destroying the Earth, by Herve Kempf" *THE EARTHBOUND REPORT* (June 2, 2009), https://earthbound.report/2009/06/02/how-the-rich-are-destroying-the-earth-by-herve-kempf/.

[109] Rep. Mike Honda (D-Calif.), "Public Option Enjoys Broad Support Despite Falsehoods Spread by Critics," THE HILL (09/09/09 09:24 PM EDT), https://thehill.com/special-reports/healthcare-september-2009/57961-public-option-enjoys-broad-support-despite-falsehoods-spread-by-critics.

[110] George S. Kazolias, "Blaming Obama for George W. Bush's Policies Libya: the criminal silence of the press," *KAZODAILY* (Apr.

2, 2012), https://kazolias.com/2012/04/02/libya-the-criminal-silence-of-the-press/.

[111] SPENCER ACKERMAN, "U.S. Admits Surveillance Violated Constitution At Least Once," *WIRED* (07.20.12 04:30 PM), https://www.wired.com/2012/07/surveillance-spirit-law/.

[112] Glenn Greenwald, "Obama's justice department grants final immunity to Bush's CIA torturers," *THE GUARDIAN* (Fri 31 Aug 2012), https://www.theguardian.com/commentisfree/2012/aug/31/obama-justice-department-immunity-bush-cia-torturer.

[113] Yvonne Ridley, "Bush Convicted of War Crimes in Absentia," *Foreign Policy Journal* (May 12, 2012), https://www.foreignpolicyjournal.com/2012/05/12/bush-convicted-of-war-crimes-in-absentia/.

[114] Ivan Eland, "George W. Bush's Impeachable Offenses," *Independent Institute Newsletter* (December 19, 2005), https://www.independent.org/article/2005/12/19/george-w-bushs-impeachable-offenses/.

[115] Ewen MacAskill, "White House warns senators over gun control reforms in vow to continue fight," *The Guardian* (Thu 18 Apr 2013), https://www.theguardian.com/world/2013/apr/18/white-house-gun-control-fight.

[116] Heather Long, "What the Heck is the Controversial Glass-Steagall Act?" *GANT News* (October 14, 2015), https://money.cnn.com/2015/10/14/investing/democratic-debate-what-is-glass-steagall-act/index.html.

[117] Dana Milbank, "Trump's flirtation with fascism," *The Washington Post* (March 7, 2016), https://www.washingtonpost.com/opinions/trumps-flirtation-with-fascism/2016/03/07/340cc798-e4ac-11e5-b0fd-073d5930a7b7_story.html

[118] FR. Gerald A. Arbuckle, SM, PhD, "Fundamentalism: An Enemy of the Common Good," *Catholic Health Association of the United States* (November-December 2016), https://www.chausa.org/publications/health-progress/article/november-december-2016/fundamentalism-an-enemy-of-the-common-good.

[119] U.S. President Abraham Lincoln, "letter to Col. William F. Elkins Nov. 21, 1864," in *The Lincoln Encyclopedia: The Spoken and Written Words of A. Lincoln Arranged for Ready Reference*, Archer H. Shaw (NY, NY: Macmillan, 1950).

[120] Wikipedia contributors, "Dwight D. Eisenhower's farewell address," *Wikipedia, The Free Encyclopedia*, https://en.wikipedia.org/w/index.php?title=Dwight_D._Eisenhower%27s_farewell_address&oldid=12 (accessed July 15, 2025).

[121] Ernest Hemingway, "For Whom the Bell Tolls," *Scribner* (January 1, 1995).

[122] Matt Fuller, "Here's The Full Text of the 2016 Republican Platform," *HUFFPOST* (07/18/2016)," https://www.huffpost.com/entry/2016-republican-platform-full-text_n_578bce03e4b03fc3ee513eb9?guccounter=1&guce_referrer=aHR0c HMYxObJBOsDwxJ-cmg4Ab_svXpZhsU61Hq-dZ9XfKKzYMLvEnZ1x0KBSKwQrgUZ7eg0BCJdMMTgmGhwUU.

[123] Suzanne Goldenberg and Helena Bengtsson, "Oil and gas industry has pumped millions into Republican campaigns," *The Guardian* (Mar. 3, 2016), https://www.theguardian.com/us-news/2016/mar/03/oil-and-gas-industry-has-pumped-millions-into-republican-campaigns.

[124] Lily Dane (The Daily Sheeple 24 March 2015), "Blood Money: These Companies and People Make Billions of Dollars from War," *Global Research* (March 25, 2015), https://www.globalresearch.ca/blood-money-these-companies-and-people-make-billions-of-dollars-from-war/5438657.

[125] Sreeja Sasidharan, "Emergence of Social Media as Fifth Estate," *Media* - A Bilingual Monthly Journal of the Kerala Press Academy, http://www.mediamagazine.in/content/emergence-social-media-fifth-estate.

[126] Robert Knight, "The great American divide," *The Washington Times* (Sunday, July 3, 2016), https://www.washingtontimes.com/news/2016/jul/3/the-great-american-divide/.

[127] Joel Achenbach and Scott Clement, "America really is more divided than ever," *THE WASHINGTON POST* (July 16, 2016), https://www.washingtonpost.com/national/america-really-is-more-divided-than-ever/2016/07/17/fbfebee6-49d8-11e6-90a8-fb84201e0645_story.html.

[128] Doug Casey, "The Ascendance of Sociopaths in US Governance," *Casey Research* (March 21, 2012), https://www.caseyresearch.com/daily-dispatch/ascendence-sociopaths-us-governance/.

[129] Jim Rutenberg, "Behind the Scenes, Billionaires' Growing Control of News," The New York Times (May 27, 2016), https://www.nytimes.com/2016/05/28/business/media/behind-the-scenes-billionaires-growing-control-of-news.html.

[130] Dr. Steven Mintz, "The Role of the Media in Politics," ETHICS SAGE (10/20/2016), https://www.ethicssage.com/2016/10/the-role-of-the-media-in-politics.html.

[131] Contributor Christina Pazzanese, "The Rich and the Rest," U.S. News and World Report (Feb. 9, 2016), https://www.usnews.com/news/the-report/articles/2016-02-09/the-costs-of-inequality-the-rich-and-the-rest.

[132] Contributor John W. Whitehead "From Democracy to Pathocracy: The Rise of the Political Psychopath," HUFFPOST (03/31/2016 Updated Apr 01, 2017), https://www.huffpost.com/entry/from-democracy-to-pathocr_b_9566896.

[133] Ron Rivest and Philip Stark, "Still time for an election audit," USA Today, https://www.usatoday.com/story/opinion/2016/11/18/election-audit-paper-machines-column/93803752/.

[134] Sam Wang, "What Actions are Shared to All Fascist Movements?" Princeton Election Consortium (December 21st, 2016), https://election.princeton.edu/2016/12/21/what-actions-are-shared-to-all-fascist-movements/.

[135] Gary Bentley, "Lack Of Empathy From Republicans Is Ruining America," The Ring of Fire (January 1, 2017), https://trofire.com/2017/01/01/lack-empathy-republicans-ruining-america/.

[136] Sarah Jones, "Democrats Are Too Nice When Dealing with Racist Republican Jeff Sessions," *Politicus USA* (Tue, Jan 10th, 2017), https://www.politicususa.com/2017/01/10/democrats-fail-dealing-obstructionist-racist-republicans.html.

[137] Wikipedia contributors, "George Joseph Cvek," *Wikipedia, The Free Encyclopedia*, https://en.wikipedia.org/w/index.php?title=George_Joseph_Cvek&oldid=1293819190.

[138] Progdoctalk (community), "GOP- A Tale of Extremism, Greed, and Irrationality," *DAILY KOS* (Tuesday January 24, 2017 · 11:36 AM PST), https://www.dailykos.com/stories/2017/1/24/1624498/-GOP-A-Tale-of-Extremism-Greed-and-Irrationality.

[139] Chauncey DeVega, "Why are Republicans so cruel to the poor? Paul Ryan's profound hypocrisy stands for a deeper problem" *SALON* (March 23, 2017), https://www.salon.com/2017/03/23/why-are-republicans-so-cruel-to-the-poor-paul-ryans-profound-hypocrisy-stands-for-a-deeper-problem/.

[140] Neal Gabler, Moyers & Company, "America's system of checks and balances has collapsed and can't be fixed — here's who to blame," *Raw Story Investigates* (March 14, 2017), https://www.rawstory.com/2017/03/americas-system-of-checks-and-balances-has-collapsed-and-cant-be-fixed-heres-who-to-blame/.

[141] James Fallows, "What's Broken—and What's Still Working—in American Politics," *The Atlantic* (July 14, 2017), https://www.theatlantic.com/politics/archive/2017/07/checks-balances/533511/.

[142] Peter Hammond Schwartz, September 10, 2019, "Serving God and Mammon: The Rise and Influence of the Heritage Foundation and the Federalist Society," *Patheos - the Creation Project*, Serving God And Mammon: The Rise And Influence Of The Heritage Foundation And The Federalist Society | Peter Hammond Schwartz.

[143] Rob Boston, November 2017, Double Trouble, *CHURCH & STATE MAGAZINE.* https://www.au.org/church-state/november-2017-church-state/cover-story/double-trouble.

[144] Rob Boston, Dec 29, 2017, "Here Are The Top Ten Church-State Stories From 2017," *AMERICANS UNITED FOR THE SEPARATION OF CHURCH AND STATE.* https://www.au.org/blogs/wall-of-separation/here-are-the-top-ten-church-state-stories-from-2017.

[145] Dave Davies, January 22, 2018 1:25 PM ET, "'How Democracies Die' Authors Say Trump Is a Symptom Of "Deeper Problems,"" *NPR OPB.* https://www.npr.org/2018/01/22/579670528/how-democracies-die-authors-say-trump-is-a-symptom-of-deeper-problems.

[146] Hal Brands, January 18, 2018, 7:33 AM, "Not Even Trump Can Obliterate America's Soft Power But the damage may take years to undo," *PSTBLOOMBERG OPINION.* https://www.bloomberg.com/opinion/articles/2018-01-18/not-even-trump-can-obliterate-america-s-soft-power.

[147] Reconstruction: The Second Civil War Article, "White Southern Responses to Black Emancipation," *PBS – AMERICAN EXPERIENCE.* https://www.pbs.org/wgbh/americanexperience/features/reconstruction-white-southern-responses-black-emancipation/.

[148] Richard A. Arenberg, Tuesday, 19 June 2018, "GOP Congress Stands Silent — Where Are the Voices of Conscience?," *NEWSMAX.* https://www.newsmax.com/richardarenberg/republican-party-trump-immigration-oversight/2018/06/19/id/867025/.

[149] James DiEugenio, "The Kennedys and Civil Rights: How the MSM Continues to Distort History (Part 1)," *KENNEDYS and KING (formerly CTKA)* (October 2018), https://kennedysandking.com/reviews/the-kennedys-and-civil-rights-how-the-msm-continues-to-distort-history-part-1.

[150] James DiEugenio, "The Kennedys and Civil Rights: How the MSM Continues to Distort History (Part 3)," *KENNEDYS and KING (formerly CTKA)* (October 2018), https://kennedysandking.com/reviews/the-kennedys-and-civil-rights-how-the-msm-continues-to-distort-history-part-3.

[151] James DiEugenio, "The Kennedys and Civil Rights: How the MSM Continues to Distort History (Part 4)," *KENNEDYS and KING (formerly CTKA)* (October 2018), https://kennedysandking.com/reviews/the-kennedys-and-civil-rights-how-the-msm-continues-to-distort-history-part-4.

[152] Oliver Willis, "Sarah Sanders brags about GOP ignoring Trump's crimes for 2 years," *THE AMERICAN INDEPENDENT* (Mar. 6, 2019), https://americanindependent.com/sarah-sanders-brags-gop-congress-ignore-trump-crimes-oversight-success/.

[153] Kim P, "Negative Effects of Technology," *Credit Donkey* (Oct. 31, 2019), Negative Effects of Technology May Surprise You.

[154] Prof. Chetan R. Bhamare, "Effects of Social Media on Communication Skills," *The Knowledge Review*. https://theknowledgereview.com/effects-social-media-communication-skills/ .

[155] Contributor Peter Suciu, Oct 30, 2019, "Does Social Media Make the Political Divide Worse?," *FORBES*. https://www.forbes.com/sites/petersuciu/2019/10/30/does-social-media-make-the-political-divide-worse/#415ef1b06e3a.

[156] Derek Beres, "Low Voter Turnout," *Big Think*, https://bigthink.com/politics-current-affairs/low-voter-turnout?rebelltitem=1#rebelltitem1.

[157] Guest Contributor, April 13, 2018, "Be the Man in the Arena: How to Get Involved in Politics," *Career, Career & Wealth*. https://www.artofmanliness.com/articles/how-to-get-involved-in-politics/.

[158] Dena Bunis, "Six Ways to Check Out a Candidate," *AARP* (April 30, 2018), https://www.aarp.org/politics-society/government-elections/info-2018/politicians-answer-background-guide.html.

[159] Prepared by the Green Party of the United States Coordinated Campaign Committee, "Green Party Candidate Recruiting Manual First Edition 2004," *Green Party U.S.*, https://www.gp.org/candidate_recruiting_manual.

[160] "How to Recruit Great Candidates for Public Office," *Talk GOP*, https://www.talkgop.com/how-to-recruit-great-candidates-for-public-office/.

[161] "How to Run for Political Office in 2019," *Candidate Boot Camp*, https://candidatebootcamp.com/how-to-run-for-political-office-2019/.

[162] FRED WERTHEIMER, "Legalized Bribery," *Politico* (01/19/2014), https://www.politico.com/magazine/story/2014/01/citizens-united-campaign-finance-legalized-bribery-102366.

[163] "Citizens United Explained," *Brennan Center For Justice*, https://www.brennancenter.org/our-work/research-reports/citizens-united-explained.

[164] "Restore the Voting Rights Act," *Brennan Center For Justice*, https://www.brennancenter.org/our-work/research-reports/restore-voting-rights-act.

[165] Abraham Lincoln, 1863, Nicolay Copy of the Gettysburg Address, Library of Congress, https://www.wdl.org/en/item/9590/view/1/1/.

[166] Brent Radcliffe, "How Education and Training Affect the Economy," *Investopedia* (08/19/2020), https://www.investopedia.com/articles/economics/09/education-training-advantages.asp.

[167] Melvin Goodman, 03/15/2018, "How the Iraq War Destabilized the Entire Middle East," *Counterpunch*, https://www.counterpunch.org/2018/03/15/how-the-iraq-war-destabilized-the-entire-middle-east/.

[168] Kishore Mahbubani, "Why the United Nations is Kept Weak," *The Globalist* (Feb. 9, 2013), https://www.theglobalist.com/why-the-united-nations-is-kept-weak/.

Don't miss out!

Visit the website below and you can sign up to receive emails whenever Daniel Lionberger publishes a new book. There's no charge and no obligation.

https://books2read.com/r/B-A-FCDH-HBYGB

BOOKS 2 READ

Connecting independent readers to independent writers.

Did you love *A World Dream, the American Ideal -- For the Peasants, the People, the Planet*? Then you should read *Dream View Two -- The Kamikaze Candidate*[1] by Daniel Lionberger!

Read more at https://www.instagram.com/dannolion?r=nametag.

1. https://books2read.com/u/bwYGvP

2. https://books2read.com/u/bwYGvP

Also by Daniel Lionberger

Dream View Two -- The Kamikaze Candidate
Fantastic Fiction & Further Fake News
A World Dream, the American Ideal -- For the Peasants, the People,
the Planet

Watch for more at https://www.instagram.com/
dannolion?r=nametag.

About the Author

How many roads must we walk, forks explored, before we find our way? Business, science, it turns out that writing was the forgotten love of my tender youth. So, I never finished writing that mystery. So many distractions from one's inner voice that they may become lost. Don't be that one. I did take typing in high school, so there is that to be thankful for in this aged pursuit.

Read more at https://www.instagram.com/dannolion?r=nametag.